IMAGES AND IDENTITIES

IMAGES AND IDENTITIES

The Puerto Rican in Two World Contexts

Edited by

Asela Rodríguez de Laguna

Transaction Books
New Brunswick (U.S.A.) and Oxford (U.K.)

Library of Congress Catalog Number: 85-9930
ISBN: 0-88738-060-3 (cloth)
Printed in the United States of America

Library of Congress Cataloging in Publication Data
Main entry under title:

Images and identities

Bibliography: p.
1. Puerto Rican literature—Congresses. 2. American literature—Puerto Rican authors—Congresses. 3. Puerto Ricans in literature—Congresses. I. Rodríguez-Seda de Laguna, Asela.
PQ7420.15.I43 1986 860′.9′97295 85-9930
ISBN 0-88738-060-3
ISBN 0-88738-617-2 (pbk.)

This publication was made possible partially by a grant from the New Jersey Committee for the Humanities, a state program of the National Endowment for the Humanities.

To my daughters
Aselita, María Eugenia, and Alexandra María

Contents

Acknowledgments

The first national public conference on *Images and Identities: The Puerto Rican in Literature* was held at Rutgers—The State University of New Jersey, Newark, the Newark Public Library and The Newark Museum, April 7–9, 1983. Although it would be impossible to acknowledge the collaboration of everyone who assisted me with the conference, I would like to express my gratitude to a number of people for their support and advice: Luis Alonso, Judith K. Brodsky, Alan S. Brown, Erma Brown, James Early, Danilo Figueredo, Pat Hynes, David Hosford, Michael C. Jaye, Beatrice Lasker, Miriam Murphy, José R. Olmo- Olmo, Miguel A. Rivera, Marcial Robiou, Alfredo Santiago, Dirk B. Van Zaanen, Francisco Vázquez, Ann C. Watts, and Hildreth York; and the students from Federación de Estudiantes Latinoamericanos, Puerto Rican Organization, Club Cultural Cubano, and Círculo de Español. Special recognition is due for his important participation during opening events to the Honorable Governor of New Jersey, Thomas H. Kean; the president of Rutgers—The State University of New Jersey, Dr. Edward J. Bloustein; the provost of Rutgers-Newark, Dr. Norman Samuels; from the New Jersey Committee for the Humanities, the Honorable Judge John L. Bracken; and the executive director of the Fundación Puertorriqueña de las Humanidades, Dr. Arturo Morales Carrión. I thank my husband, Elpidio Laguna, for his cooperation, understanding, trust, steadiness, and support. And, to Jimmy Luciano, who patiently and critically worked not only during the planning and organization of the conference, but also in the preparation, translation, and revision of the works included here, my most sincere gratitude.

The conference and the publication of this book were possible thanks to the generous contribution of several organizations, institutions, foundations and corporations: The National Endowment for the Humanities, The Ford Foundation, The New Jersey Committee for the Humanities, The Geraldine R. Dodge Foundation, Goya Foods, Inc., New Jersey Bell Telephone Company, The Greater Newark Chamber of Commerce, International Ladies' Garment Workers' Union, New Jersey Region, and The Prudential Foundation. We are greatly indebted to Rutgers—The State University of New Jersey, Newark, the Newark Public Library, and The Newark Museum, for their support.

The author gratefully acknowledges the following publishers and publications for permission to use previously published materials:

Miguel Algarín, ''Nuyorican Aesthetics.'' Reprinted by permission of MELUS, University of Cincinnati: Cincinnati, Ohio, 1981.

Rosario Ferré, ''Cuando las mujeres quieren a los hombres, in *Papeles de Pandora*. Mexico City: Editorial Joaquín Mortiz, S.A., 1976.

Miguel Algarín and Miguel Piñero, editors. *Nuyorican Poetry*. New York: William Morrow and Co., 1975. Special thanks to the poets Miguel Piñero, Archie Martínez, and Américo Casiano.

Introduction

What Is Puerto Rican Literature?

Answering this question might not require too much effort within the geographic context of the island of Puerto Rico. There, people would offer a wide sample of definitions ranging from very simple and general statements to more sophisticated ones, embodying aspects of the history, politics, and cultural and socioeconomic development of the island. For some, Puerto Rican literature could simply be defined as the literary manifestation of Puerto Ricans; for others, it is the literature of Puerto Ricans, written in Spanish by Puerto Ricans; and still others more academically geared would define aspects of its past and present production through different critical approaches. Outside the insular context, Puerto Rican literature is less known, and only during the last two decades has it enjoyed more diffusion, and consequently, more accessiblility among the Spanish-speaking public. In the United States, but only since the late sixties, it has been moderately tolerated and studied, particularly by academics. This boom's *raison d'être* emerged as the result partly of sociopolitical pressures of the sixties, partly of the efforts of newly established Puerto Rican studies. A general enthusiasm for the ethnic literatures of the United States also encouraged the recognition of Puerto Rican literature and the appreciation of the literature written by Puerto Ricans in the continent. In the United States this literature is seen not only as the national expression of a large sector of the Puerto Rican public but also as testimonial literature of a national minority.

This process of recognition and appreciation of Puerto Rican literature within the sociopolitical context of the past two decades is more accurately a perceptual process in the United States rather than what the terms *recognition* and *appreciation* would seem to imply for other ethnic literatures within the social fabric of the country. The Puerto Rican is projected through the literature of the writers who reside in the mainland with a set of images very different from those projected by writers who reside in the island or in other countries. Does the generalized insular conception of its literature as the literary expression of the Puerto Rican, written in Spanish, coincide with that of mainland Puerto Rican writers? Definitely not. One of the aspects that abruptly cancels the equation of identity through literary images in the definitions is the language. By the same token, not only the differences inherent in the use of either English or Spanish, but also the difference in the way writers from the island and the mainland conceive the lexical codes of English and Spanish are appropriate vehicles with which to express their experiences. Besides the language, a careful comparison between the literature of the writers of the island and those of the United States reveals profound differences, despite the existence within themselves of joining bonds that prove a thematic-emotional and cultural continuity. Continuity and disruption, traditionalism and experimentalism, Spanish and English, Puerto Rico and the United States, Catholicism, Protestantism, and religious syncretism, Hispanism and Anglo-Saxonism are now permanent traits of the duality of the Puerto Rican experience. The images projected by literature, whether in Spanish or English, are true methapors of the real, ficticious, or imaginative experiences of the Puerto Rican people that reveal the philosophical, sociopolitical, and cultural conception of life of the Puerto Rican, as well as his personal and collective struggles, sufferings, and goals.

The Puerto Rican experience is frequently one of dualities: between two worlds, mainland and island; between ghetto and mainstream America; between the richness and expressiveness of two languages and cultures, Spanish and English, Puerto Rican and American. Since the island became a territory of the United States as a result of the Spanish/American War (1898), these dualities and their social, political, and economic implications have become major themes in the literature produced in both Puerto Rico and the United States by Puerto Rican writers. Perhaps as a result of the increased migration from the island in the 1950s, Puerto Rican literature now clearly transcends ethnic bounds to influence and be influenced by the pluralistic literary traditions that characterize contemporary American poetry, fiction, and drama.

Puerto Rico's Literary Tradition

Puerto Rican literature is at once old and new. Its roots date back to the sixteenth century. It shares with Latin American literature a similar beginning, one in the form of letters and chronicles written by the Spaniards who captured their experiences during the conquest and colonization of the island. From then on, Puerto Rican writers and thinkers molded their subject matter according to the philosophical and aesthetic theories prevailing in Europe, particularly in Spain and France. The literary historiography of Puerto Rican literature during the nineteenth century gives conspicuous examples of the influence of European *costumbrismo*, romanticism, realism, naturalism, and positivism. It is within these European trends that a different literature begins to emerge: a literature that calls for national distinctiveness from the mother country and which exalts not only the beauty of the island but carefully depicts the culture, customs, traditions, and, above all, the distinctiveness of the jíbaro's speech. The *Aguinaldo Puertorriqueño* (1844), *El Cancionero de Borinquen* (1846), and the most representative book of this trend, *El Gíbaro* (1849) by Manuel Alonso, are the first attempts to create a truly national literature.

During the second half of of the nineteenth century four major figures lead the literary world. Alejandro Tapia y Rivera (1826–82) excelled in his prose—a discourse proper not only for research on colonial history but also for romantic fiction on historical and legendary heroes. He also vividly narrated and accounted for the daily affairs and lifestyles in the San Juan of his epoch in his memoirs. The lyrical and emotive poetry of José Gautier Benítez (1851–80) captured descriptively the beauty of the island, while the essays of the "Apostle of America," Eugenio María de Hostos (1839–1903), summarized his ideals on all areas of knowledge, revealing and noting the most crucial problems affecting the Spanish Caribbean and calling for unity, liberty, and progress. Manuel Zeno Gandía (1855–1930) became the first Puerto Rican novelist. His novels *La Charca* (1894), *Garduña* (1896), *El Negocio* (1922), and *Redentores* (1925), following Zola's *Les Rougon Macquart* (*Histoire naturelle et sociale d'une famille sous le Second Empire, 1871*) were subtitled *Crónicas de una sociedad enferma* ("chronicles of a sick society"), and they depict—in a style and technique of literary naturalism—Puerto Rican society before and after the U.S. invasion of 1898.

Under the new sovereignty Puerto Rican cultural and literary life during the first three decades of the twentieth century was dominated by a climate of confusion, of clash, but also of redefinition and affirmation. Intellectuals—pressed by their perception that the new government had no intention of leaving but wished to impose both its English language and its Anglo-Saxon institutions on the island—began to define in a kind of binary system the distinctiveness of Puerto Ricanness. By opposition, Puerto Ricanness identified more with institutions inherited from Spain, and authors engaged in defending the Spanish language and in exalting the different traits and attributes of Puerto Rican society. The patriotic verse of José de Diego (1867–1918), the *costumbrista* poems of Luis Lloréns Torres (1878–1944) and Virgilio Dávila (1869–1943), and the poetry of negritude by Luis Palés Matos (1898–1959) chanted the heroic deeds of the Puerto Rican jíbaro, Creole and Black, with unparalleled talent. Antonio S. Pedreira's (1899–1939) masterpiece essay, *Insularismo* (1934), became the first truly interpretive essay on Puerto Rico, and more aptly, it stood as the most influential writing on the spiritual and biological essence of the Puerto Rican. Pedreira, together with novelist Enrique A. Laguerre (1906–), dramatist Manuel Méndez Ballester (1909–), and others constituted the so-called Generation of the 1930s—writers intellectually formed under the establishment of the new government, genuinely concerned with the past and the future of the island, and interested in describing the ills of the Puerto Rican man and society. If Pedreira is the leading interpreter of the Puerto Rican man, Enrique A. Laguerre with the publication of *La llamarada* establishes the foundations of the modern insular novel, molding his narrative on the best and most representative of the traditional novels of the preboom Latin American novel—Colombia's *La vorágine*, Argentina's *Don Segundo Sombra*, and Venezuela's *Doña Bárbara*. The Generation of the 1930s shaped future Puerto Rican literature, and since then Puerto Rican intellectuality has continued its search for definition and figuration of the traits of the Puerto Rican. The subject matter of mid- to late-twentieth-century writers has been and continues to be Puerto Rico: its landscape, traditions, people, and the personality of the Puerto Rican. However, since the forties, new themes, styles, and experimental forms have been used to keep expressing Puerto Rican society.

Responding to a changing society immersed in processes of industrialization, the writers began moving away from the rural themes to depict the social changes brought about by the island's modernization. José Luis González (1826–1926) published in 1943 *En la sombra*, followed by *Cinco cuentos de sangre* (1945), *El hombre de la calle* (1948), *En este lado* (1954), and *Paisa: un relato de la inmigración* (1950). Almost twenty years later he resumed his writing career with the successful publication of *Mambrú se fue a la guerra* (1972), *La galería y otros cuentos* (1973), *En Nueva York y otras desgracias, Veinte cuentos y Paisa* (1973), *Balada de otro tiempo* (1976), *La llegada* (1980), and several polemical essays. *El país de cuatro pisos* stands alone among recent publications as the most provocative interpretation of Puerto Rican individuals and society. His style, aimed at the short but precise sentence, meaningful dialogue, chronological flashback, interior monologue, contrasting change from the conscious to the unconscious, and to rapid and surprising endings, accurately and effectively portrays the struggles, miseries, and hopes of the Puerto Rican.

Also during the forties—a period of urban interest—and on moving from country to city, Abelardo Díaz Alfaro published a unique collection of stories, *Terrazo* (1947), a work which epitomizes nostalgically the best of rural life of the *jíbaro* caught in the irrevocable dilemma of prophetically announcing his extinction. The tragicomic and ironic overtones capture the *jibaritos* of the mountainside as well as their teacher trying to cope with an education that demands English and English texts to be used in an environment totally alien to the objectives of the new education. Díaz Alfaro's stories or *retablos* reflect the inner and stoic strength of the *jíbaros*, defending their self, their Puerto Ricanness against modernization and Americanization, and choosing death before any further humiliation.

The 1950s and After

The vitality and complexity displayed in Puerto Rican letters are better embodied in the contribution of the writers of the so-called Generation of the 1950s and the most recent generation of the very contemporary writers of the 1960s and 1970s. Poetry has given form, in the voices of Julia de Burgos (1914–53), Francisco Matos Paoli (1915–), Félix Franco Oppenheimer (1912–), Francisco Lluch Mora (1924–), Laura Gallego (1924–), Violeta López Suria (1926–), E. Rivera Chevremont (1896–1976), and Juan Antonio Corretjer (1908–), to the most suggestive and universal themes affecting insular and international human problems.

José Luis González, René Marqués (1919–79), César Andreu Iglesias (1915–76), Pedro Juan Soto (1928–), and Emilio Díaz Valcárcel (1929–), although representing an ideological continuity with the previous generation, technically revitalized Puerto Rican narrative, particularly the short story. Their literary accomplishments dominated and still dominate the literary scene. Marqués's play *La carreta* (1952), for decades has attracted an audience who has been receptive to the presentation of the flight and tribulations of the Puerto Rican family from the countryside to the San Juan ghetto and eventually to the New York Bronx. Francisco Arriví's (1915–) *Vejigantes* (1958) has captured the trajectory of three generations of a family afflicted by racial problems and by the attitude of denying Blackness in the younger generations.

During the last two decades Puerto Rican literature has experienced an unprecedented renaissance: poets founded many excellent (and some fine short-lived) journals, such as *Ventana*, *Alicia la Roja*, *Zona de Carga y Descarga*, and *Guajana*. Poets came from all levels of society, played a more active role within the existing cultural centers, and massively rejected the traditional lyric poetry for a more politically and socially aggressive one, with an unprecendented openness to deal with topics such as love, sex, war, the alienation of Blacks and workers, militarism, emigration, death, and solidarity with oppression and the Third World. The legacy of Hugo Margenat (1933–57) would be successfully carried out by the new voices of Vicente Rodríguez Nietzche, Andrés Castro Ríos, José M. Torres Santiago, Angela María Dávila, Aurea María Sotomayor, Edwin Reyes, José L. Vega, Juan Saez Burgos, Orlando J. Hernández, Vanessa Droz, Lilliana Ramos, Iván Silén, Sotero Rivera Avilés, Olga Nolla, and Rosario Ferré. Nilita Vientos Gastón's journal, *Sin Nombre* (formerly *Asomante*), among the proliferation of literary journals stood and stands as the most solid and internationally distributed literary publication of Puerto Rico and has helped to promote not only Peninsular and Latin American literature, but the promotion and diffusion of Puerto Rican writers.

The general popularity and influence of the Latin American Boom contributed decisively to the formation of the younger Puerto Rican writers. Borges, Cortázar, Rulfo, Fuentes, Carpentier, Cabrera Infante, Vargas Llosa, Onetti, García Márquez, Lezama Lima, José Donoso have provided insular narrators with models to emulate. Luis Rafael Sánchez—generally considered a link between the Generation of the 1950s and the younger generation of writers—has published a collection of short stories, several important plays, and a best seller, *La guaracha del Macho Camacho* (*Macho Camacho's Beat*, 1976). In *La guaracha*, Sánchez explores Puerto Rican reality through the musical beat of the *guaracha* "Life Is a Phenomenal Thing." Like its Cuban counterpart—Cabrera Infante's *Tres tristes tigres*—*La guaracha* is written from the viewpoint of the Puerto Rican language. Parody, irony, satire, exaggeration, the grotesque, and humor are Sánchez's literary resources to depict contemporary Puerto Rican life, a modus vivendi dominated by clichés, soap operas, popular songs, nightclub and TV show singers such as Iris Chacón, widely disseminated U.S. and Hispanic magazines, and in general images created by radio, television, and the mass media. The names of Rosario Ferré, Magali García Ramis, Manuel Ramos Otero, Juan Antonio Ramos, Carmen Lugo Filippi, Carmelo Rodríguez Torres, Edgardo Rodríguez Juliá, Tomás López Ramírez, Manuel Abreu Adorno, Edgardo Sanabria Santaliz, Angel Encarnación, Roberto Cruz Barreto, and Jaime Carrero have joined González, Soto, Diáz Valcárcel, and Sánchez in keeping alive the rich tradition of Puerto Rican literature, further enriched by the contributions in English of writers of Puerto Rican heritage who—although in another language—deal with the Puerto Rican as the subject matter.

About This Book

The essays and articles here included were first presented at the Conference on *Images and Identities: The Puerto Rican in Literature* at Rutgers—The State University of New Jersey, Newark, on April 7–9, 1983. This conference proposed first to gather representative Puerto Rican writers from the island and the United States as well as renowned critics concerned with the subject of Puerto Rican literature, and second, it recommended addressing many areas of interest, primarily the interrelationship between Puerto Rican literature and the life and culture that literature reflects and creates, to discuss the dualities of the Puerto Rican experience—the constant oscillation between mainland and island, between the insular problems and urban ghetto—and to engage in exploring the richness and expressiveness of the two languages.

The essays collected here correspond to the individual styles, approaches, and subject matter of their authors and critics, and they represent the vitality, diversity, and distinctiveness of contemporary Puerto Rican letters and writers.

Some are informal and others academic; some deal with images generated by non-Puerto Rican writers and researchers; others are autobiographical accounts of experiences in New York (Piri Thomas); some deal with experiences in the apprenticeship of becoming writers, poets; and others address topics such as aesthetics, translation, education, and the contrast and similarities between Puerto Rican literature and other Hispanic-minority manifestations in the United States. All of them, however, provide insights into the content of Puerto Rican literature, of its authors' tribulations in searching for a personal and genuine style, of the writer's function in contemporary Puerto Rico. In general, these essays offer a unique opportunity to the English-speaking reader to examine closely several areas related to Puerto Rican literature and to the processess of reading and writing literature.

Part I
Images and Identities

1
A Puerto Rican Testament

José Luis González

When Dr. Asela Rodríguez de Laguna informed me of her generous wish that I should share with my dear friend, Luis Rafael Sánchez, the honor of being a keynote speaker at this meeting of Puerto Rican writers and distinguished scholars of our literature, my first reaction was to get hold of my best English-Spanish dictionary and look up the meaning of the word *keynote*. I was dumbfounded by the first definition: it refers to music theory and denotes "the tonic note of a key or scale." For an instant I thought: a "key" is, as well, a small instrument used to open doors, including, (why not?) those to fame; and a "scale" is what Calixto used to climb up to Melibea's bedroom. But, of course, the dictionary is not referring to these two meanings but to the first, the one having to do with music theory. Since—wisely enough—I was not being invited to sing or play the piano, I moved on to the second definition in the dictionary, and it was there that my problems began. Because what I stumbled across—and I use the verb in its most literal sense—was *keynote* defined as "fundamental principle, basic idea or keystone." Stones, I said to myself, are what will surely rain all over me if I dare to take on the responsibility that Doña Asela is so keen to put on my poor shoulders. Only God and she know why.

With these reflections I closed the dictionary and wrote my kind prospective hostess a sincere letter, thanking her for doing me the honor of inviting me and regretting that I had to decline. I made in the letter, I confess, no allusion to my apprehension at addressing a demanding and learned audience. I did mention another problem, equally real yet much more imposing. I explained that traveling to the United States always places me in a humiliating and exasperating predicament. It so happens that I am not permitted—for legalistic reasons of which you all possibly are aware—to obtain a visa such as is issued to decent persons who want to visit this country. As is also the case with my old friend Gabriel García Márquez, Julio Cortázar, Mario Benedetti, and many other individuals in a similar situation, I am forced to ask for a "waiver of inelegibility" founded upon reasons valid according to the authorities of the United States Department of Justice. This means, evidently, that I am *persona non grata* unless a respectable institution in the United States is sufficiently courageous to suggest the contrary by inviting me to visit.

I knew, of course, that Rutgers University is a respectable institution. I had known this for a long time, since the time it dedicated one of its public buildings to the memory of a great North American with whose friendship I was honored in my youth. I refer dear friends, to the unforgettable Paul Robeson. And just as General Pershing—the frustrated victimizer of my adopted countryman Pancho Villa—said when he arrived in France, at the head of the expeditionary North American forces in the First World War, before the tomb of a hero of the independence of the thirteen colonies: "Here we are, Lafayette," I feel I have the right to say now, in this illustrious Rutgers University: "Here I am, brother Paul."

However, after receiving the invitiation, my apprehensions of being a bad speaker and my reluctance to ask favors of a foreign government weighed heavily on me and I asked Doña Asela to excuse me from attending in person, but so that I should not be wholly absent, to allow me to mail my "keynote address" and have it read to you by a friend gifted with the eloquence that I lack. Doña Asela, however, would not agree to my proposition. She insisted on my physical presence here, tactfully appealing to my duties as a Puerto Rican writer. In the face of such strong arguments, I decided to present myself at the United States Embassy in Mexico and ask for a "waiver of ineligibility," thinking that if for a certain French king *"París bien valía una misa"* (Paris was worth a Mass), to me the possibility of meeting with you all is well worth a visa.

What I have attempted is entitled "A Puerto Rican Testament." I could not think of anything further from the dictionary definition of *keynote* as a fundamental principle, basic idea, or keystone than the simple testimony of a man who never learned any other craft than that of telling stories—whether true or invented—and who, despite many attempts, has not been able to find the frontier between the true and the invented. This frontier might be very important to other crafts, but not to mine. Someone has said—I do not remember who—that the literature of imagination is nothing but a lie which is useful in order to reach the truth. This should also be the function of any testimony worthy of being believed.

In participating at a conference which happily brings together Puerto Rican writers of three generations, it has seemed justifiable and useful to me, as a member of the intermediate generation, to try— by way of personal testimony and without indulging in a collective representation which no one has either asked from or ascribed to me— to approach certain aspects of what can be considered, somewhat doubtfully or hesitantly, an authentic national literary tradition. I am concerned, because I am a writer and not a professional critic, that there may be some involuntary untruth in what I say. If this is so, please accept it with an indulgence founded upon what I said earlier: that it is a lie of the imagination in the service of truth.

I would like to begin by remembering the kind of country Puerto Rico was when the writers of my generation began to write. I have just said "remembering," and the verb forces me to point out—to you and to myself—something which ordinarily, although it is very obvious, seems not to be recognized with the clarity it deserves: First, one can only remember the past; and second, the past can only be remembered from the present. This may seem a tautology, but from it we can gather an important conclusion: Every retrospective view carries with it the risk that the past will be distorted by the perceptions of the present. It is an inevitable risk and, in my case, a calculated one.

I remember (and I do not believe that in this particular memory there is any distortion) that the Puerto Rico of the early forties was a country where poverty and injustice reigned and, as a consequence, there was noncomformity. Someone may say that none of these three things is really lacking in the Puerto Rico of today. And that someone may be correct, but with one difference. Poverty, injustice, and noncomformity still persist in present-day Puerto Rico, but in disconcerting coexistence with the ideological buffers created by two generations of Puerto Rican and North American reformers in order to disguise and downplay them: poverty with food stamps; injustice with Associated Free State or, more euphemistically, "Commonwealth"; and noncomformity with alienating and institutionalized demagogy.

Forty years ago—this is a precise fact because, according to literary critics, forty years ago the book of short stories with which the work of my generation began was published[1]—poverty and injustice paraded in shameless nakedness in Puerto Rico. Because of this, collective dissent crystallized in a historical movement that enjoyed the hopeful support of the majority of Puerto Ricans for many years. The failure and frustration of that movement in the long run does not invalidate—it seems right and neccessary to point out—what it meant as an expression of the popular will for change and the self- realization of the most conscientious and well-meaning sectors of the Puerto Rican people of those years.

Poverty, injustice, and noncomformity were the great literary themes of my generation. True, they had also been those of the previous generation of Puerto Rican writers: from Alejandro Tapia y Rivera, Salvador Brau, and Manuel Zeno Gandía to Enrique A. Laguerre, Tomás Blanco, and Emilio S. Belaval. But even if the themes were not essentially the same, the reality which generated them was. Within that poverty, injustice, and restlessness, Puerto Rican society had been undergoing transformations. From the archaic colonialism of the Spanish captain-generals it had passed to the then modern colonialism of North American politicos who received as a prize for political favors the government of the only outright colony of the Imperial Republic. What that change entailed, strictly speaking, was the implantation in Puerto Rico of a dependent capitalism which, among other things, displaced and pushed to one side an important sector of the old Creole ruling class. This is most important in the context of my present theme, because that class has produced most of the country's literature. The restlessness with the status quo expressed in the literature of the thirties was not unexpectedly a class restlessness—but not exactly that of a progressive class. The Creole had been a progressive one, at least fundamentally, under the Spanish Colonial regime when it struggled to transform itself from a subordinate class into a ruling one. Within three decades of U.S. colonial rule (dependent yet modernizing capitalism in the Puerto Rican context) that class could not be anything but determined to preserve its lost preeminence. Its writers protested against a situation which objectively deserved such a protest; but their protest, in most cases, was conservative. Thus, for example, the remedy they proposed for the evils of the monopolistic and single-crop sugar economy was an impossible return to an idealized agrarian and patriarchal precapitalism incarnated in the vanishing traditional hacienda. This I have tried to explain in my book *El país de cuatro pisos* and in other texts, and Angel Quintero Rivera has explained it much better in his brilliant studies of Puerto Rican social history. But this is not the time to expand on the subject.

I should like to dwell, however, on the subject of what my generation represented and continues to represent as a reaction to the conservative attitude of the preceding generation. At this point I must warn you that limited space forces me to generalize; and, as we all know, every generalization leads to inexactitude. The ideology of the majority of the writers of the thirties was, indeed, conservative. But majority does not mean totality. The greatest exception—and certainly not the only one—was Tomás Blanco, a singular and admirable example of the Puerto Rican intellectual patrician who surpassed, in intelligence, sensitivity, and talent, the ideological horizons of his own class. The ideology of my generation of writers was—and still is—essentially anticonservative (for reasons I will try to explain later). But, once again, majority is not synonymous with totality. The greatest exception—and certainly not the only one—among us was René Marqués, a very important writer, a great formal innovator in his best works and, at the same time (in a most revealing contradiction—which Arcadio Díaz Quiñones has studied with his customary insight) ideologically committed to an irrecoverable past.

In the works of Pedro Juan Soto, Emilio Díaz Valcárcel, and César Andreu Iglesias, a younger and insufficiently known member of our generation (not because of age, but because of the salient characteristics of his narrative work), as also in my own works, I see the expression of new forms and themes derived from the accelerated transformation of an agrarian society more or less closed within itself, into an urban society, more open to the rest of the world. Moreover, as a consequence of this transformation, the literary expression of a new group of cultural progenitors was also transformed. Just as the literature of preceding generations had been the cultural product of the Puerto Rican patriciate and their ideologically assimilated elements (a most heterogeneous product nonetheless: reactionary in José de Diego, liberal in Lloréns Torres, and fairly progressive in Nemesio Canales and Luis Palés Matos), the most characteristic literature of the generation of 1950 was the cultural product of a new social milieu whose exact definition is still to be determined but which undoubtedly included, in a preponderant way, elements derived from the old proletariat and incipient petite bourgeoisie who only recently had gained access to the cultural world hitherto reserved for the ruling class. Just one illustration will suffice: neither the father of Pedro Juan, nor Emilio's, nor César's, nor mine went to the university. But their children, with different degrees of financial strain, were university students.

We were college students, but not patricians—for a very simple reason: by the 1940s there was no longer a Puerto Rican patriciate capable of absorbing lower-class intellectuals. A university degree could turn the son of a worker or peasant into a petit bourgeois or even a bourgeois, but not into a patrician, because the Puerto Rican patriciate was already a historically closed social class. At first, the writers of my generation confronted the same general reality of poverty, injustice, and dissent which our immediate forerunners had known. But we did not see it in the same way, since various historical events made an identical vision impossible. Among these events were two international wars in which my generation participated directly and under compulsion; a massive exodus of Puerto Ricans to the United States of which at least one of us, Pedro Juan Soto, was a part; the transformation of our peasantry into an improvised and cheap industrial workforce, which, far from being able to continue and strengthen the cultural and political tradition of the Puerto Rican working class, witnessed and suffered the ideological castration and social alienation of that class; the matter, of course, positive in itself, of the betterment of the social status of women; an imposed or sought-after familiarity with a language and culture already the most influential in the world; the repercussions of anticolonialist and anticapitalist struggles on several continents after World War II; and so many other similarly transforming and innovative events. All these events—of which there were many—precluded our longing for the past and forced us to focus our literary sight on the present and our ideological sight on the future.

First we were called the Generation of the 1940s, possibly because one of us published his first books during that decade. I tried to rectify what seemed an unjust and misleading term and claimed instead that of the Generation of the 1950s. Luis Rafael Sánchez—from the perspective of an understanding, committed, and critical successor— rebaptized us the Generation of World War II. I believe now (and this is the first time I say it publicly) that in reality we were the rebellious first-born children of the Associated Free State or Commonwealth. But, since nobody wants to be known as the son of a mother of ill repute, I prefer that we continue to be referred to as the Generation of 1950. It seems proper now to begin to retrospect our completed work without renouncing the idea that the best is still ahead of us.

On my own strictly personal responsibility, I believe I can say that we have tried to regenerate—through words and sometimes through action—our poor and maligned mother, wresting her from the colonial brothel in order to make her a free woman, mistress of her own actions. For this, we have been outspoken supporters of our national independence; we have been in solidarity with the Cuban Revolution and the struggle for the liberation of our Caribbean and Latin American brethren; and we have discovered in socialism—some of us ahead of others—the future of humanity. We have loved, nurtured, and cultivated our language as one loves, nurtures, and cultivates an inalienable patrimony, yet without ignoring or despising other languages. We have felt as if in our own flesh, for it is our own flesh, the vicissitudes, sufferings, and successes of the great Puerto Rican community in this country—and we have tried to express these in some of our writings. We have tried to write much and well, as an act of service to our people and to literature itself, which also deserves it. I sincerely believe that, in general terms, we have fulfilled and continue to fulfill our task. But it will be the task of others to assess our endeavors and cast final judgement.

To close, allow me to express a good wish. In the work sessions following this inaugural ceremony, we will have the opportunity to share ideas, opinions, convictions, and even likes and dislikes. I know we will do so with freedom and firmness. I hope we also do it with cordiality and good spirits, even if it is only to affirm and exalt our identity and condition as true Puerto Ricans. I say no more, *compañeros*, because I did not come here to teach, but to learn. Thank you.

Translated by Elpidio Laguna-Díaz

Note

1. González's first book, *En la sombra*, appeared in 1943.

2
The Flying Bus

Luis Rafael Sánchez

After the terrified scream, silences descend one by one. The stewardess, angelic and innocent like one of Horacio Quiroga's characters, a blonde with the sort of frozen intensity that would enliven the libido of any lovesick King Kong, begins to back away. The anxious faces of the passengers share the most bizarre premonitions as they search for the hand carrrying the gun, the knife or a homemade bomb. For the terrified scream could easily be the hysterical and uncontrollable telltale sign of still one more skyjacker or any menacing madman. An *Our Father* bursts, the catalytic silences one by one. The stewardess proceeds on her retreat, she has seen herself in the mirror of fear, and fear has stamped her with the lividity of a massive, overpowering fainting fit. But the skyjacker or frantic madman is nowhere in sight. Contrite, mumbled, the *Our Fathers* advance at different levels of faith and orality. Suddenly, light comes into being, and halogenous glare violates the retina and illumines the gallop of myriad heartbeats. The flying bus becomes a mammoth, autopsied by indiscreet fluorescences at thirty-one thousand feet above sea level. The Captain, or flying bus driver, and the Flight Engineer or mechanic, show up, and their studied inexpressivity incites an expression of cautiousness; the rest of the crew is alerted, the assault of general hysteria creeps in, grows, threatens, and the bleached stewardess is just half an inch from being consumed by terror. But the skyjacker or the menacing madman is nowhere to be seen.

Suddenly, unparalleled as a scandal or a surprise, a burst of laughter corrodes at once both the silences and the *Our Fathers* that in some lips were about to reach the first *a* of Amen. Pristine in its offensiveness, the clean-cut parentheses of laughter could have been collaged onto any page, were it not on account of its contagiousness which begins to contaminate the hundreds of passengers of the flying bus that ferries every night between the airports of San Juan and New York; an attractive laughter due to its inordinate and ferocious rashness, a disorderly laughter that underlines an almost automatic agreement, a ferocity that translates secret and unforgetable resentments. The timid of heart would immediately think that the flying bus is about to stall on account of the pitching and rolling generated by the mushrooming laughter. And low-flying angels with the curiosity of Peeping-Toms would gladly give away the gold of their curls just to know what the hell is the source of the laughter of that airbound crowd of mestizos who dare to trespass into their own turf. Only the flight crew, uniformly gringo this evening, seems immune to the plague of laughter, seems immune to the general ridicule of the terror that had distorted the innocent and angelic features of the blonde stewardess.

The general laughter now seems at the point of depressurizing the cabin and off-setting the angle-of-attack of the flying bus. No relief is in sight because, now, everyone can see the incredible culprits of their first terror. Down the carpeted aisle of the flying bus, walking defiantly into a "High Noon," bullying, snapping and squirming their way along, indifferent to the scandals and terrors their presence had provoked, a couple of self-conscious, proud and healthy mangrove crabs are making their way.

Paradoxically, the notorious splendor of their health is the omen of their presumable fate-tomorrow, they will become crab gumbo in Prospect, or Alcapurria (Puerto Rican fried meat plantain pie) stuffing in the South Bronx, or marinated crab-in-the-shell in Sunset Park, or crab Asopao (mixture of rice and crabs) in the Lower East Side, or temporary tenants in the cultivated darkness of a basement, away from the surveillance of a super or a landlord. But tonight, their notable splendor and the surprising use of the flying bus as an improvised frontier, as a means of access, are the subject of imaginative commentaries, of loquacious witicisms which precipitate from the absolute anxiety which now reigns over the free expression of attitudes and even over the passengers' recourse to more agitated speech in that anarchical choreography of bodies bending, twisting and curling in the prisons of the planes seats. It is an absolute anxiety spurred on by speeches in favor of independence immediate attached by the prostatehood, by the avalanche of off-colored jokes and the winks of daring Don Juans and temporary floozies, by the detailed confessions- because autobiography seduces us. It was an absolute anxiety born in irate accounts of successive humiliation in crosstown buses, in the elevators and on the fucking job, at the liberal university and the Jew's corner junkshop store, an absolute disquiet that, suddenly, draws an invisible but tangible line between them, the gringos, and us, the Puerto Ricans; frontier of discourse that underlines the unsustainable assertion of the mulatto woman who present her newborn child with a juicy and radiant breast: "the blonder they are, the more of an asshole," A disquiet that disquiets-or seems to disquiet-tonight's uniformly gringo flight crew. The crew, dumbfounded by this sudden collapse of electronic modernity, amazed at the fact that the rigorous security devices were unable to detect the infamous contraband, demands the POSITIVE IDENTIFICATION of the owner of the crabs with imposing gestures resembling a much too-German Expressionist comedy, toned-down by the pleasant and parodical memory of the antics of a Buster Keaton or a Charlie Chaplin. The insistent demands of a vigorous gesticulator and the insistent offering of a would-be crab executioner, are met with theatrical boastfulness by the half-asleep half-annoyed middle-aged man who stumbles his way to the first rows of seats of the flying bus and, with flashy manual dexterity (improperly termed "underdeveloped") grabs the fugitive couple of crabs and rebukes them "either you guys stay put or I'll shove a squirt of Valium up your joyholes, all included in today's shit-pay". Euphoria reigns, becomes collective. The laughter that decongests the reason of all fogged-up horizons, and the lungs of excessive mucosity, congests the thinking canals of the passengers of the flying bus. Someone who brooded over the belly-torn cadavers that illustrate the daily occur-rences of the newspaper *El Vocero* excuses himself: "I choked"; a lady who was praising the Gallito de Manati's last show at Jefferson Theater declares "I almost pissed myself", another remarks that the evening is just cut out for enjoying a jug of something, a remark that elicits the approval of those within ear-range, while another poetic type sings in octosyllables the rationality of having a momentous chicken stew, out of the blue.

The flying bus fizzles, oscilates between a tumultuous atmosphere and the gravity of a chimera, between the agressiveness of a will to succeed and an atavic burden of self-pity or charity, *Ay bendito*. A well poised woman who hides a multitude of hair rollers under a flowery turban informs us that she flies over *the pond* every month and that she has forgotten on which bank of it she really lives; an adolescent lady crisped by cosmetics and on the verge of desperation because Rene's voice changed and he was forced to retire from *Menudo*, listens uninterestedly to the adolescent gentleman, crisped by disorientation, who knows that he is going to Newark but cannot figure out why. A gregarious and outspoken lady stands up and unravels the folds of a kingsized bedspread forming a tent under whose artisanship an improvised quartet bleats the ballad *En mi viejo San Juan*; and a gentleman of educated and sober poise asks the mulatto woman of the juicy and radiant breast if they have not met before, perhaps, in the feast in honor of the Virgin of Monserrate in the town of Hormigueros. The virginal mulatto woman of the juicy and radiant breast tells him that she has never been to Hormigueros. He then asks the young lady stuffed in pumpkin-colored mechanic's jeans if, perhaps, they have not met before, possibly in the feast (in honor) of the Holy Guardian Angels in the city of Yabucoa. The young lady stuffed into the pumpkin-colored mechanic's jeans answers that she has never been to the city of Yabucoa, that she goes into *Bachelor, Bocaccio and Topaz* . . . or any other place as gay. From the make-shift kitchen of the flying bus a purposefully plaintiff Orpheon stridently nags to the chorus of *Si no me dan de beber, lloro*, (popular Christmas song which repeats "If they don't give me something to drink, I'll cry."), another man obsessed with indignation narrates the imprisonment of a son who refused to testify to the Federal Grand Jury, while another categorizes that to be a nationalist in Puerto Rico carries with it a certain prestige but to be a nationalist in New York is received with public hostility.

And so, a chain of anecdotes is linked to a chain of resounding interjections; anguished and laughable anecdotes, some heart-breaking, other superficial, other dearly heroic in their formulation of resistance against insult, against open or concealed prejudice; an infinity of anecdotes where Puerto Ricans take a center stage in acts of roguishness, of witticism, of impudence, of craftiness: Deligthful anecdotes on account of their intelligent narrative montage; moving anecdotes on account of their unbelievable events, anecdotes narrated with the most surprising circumlocutions of spiced rhetoric, and anecdotes narrated in the most rice-and-beans style. Anecdotes told by a waspish hick who is far from being docile and who speaks with a sharp tongue, and who speaks good English whenever need demands, a hick who speaks with smashing common sense; anecdotes of Puerto Ricans who have been guests of the same unemployment lines; who have been hosts to the same hunger and its allied hopes of a straight meal; pathetic anecdotes of the submissive who deny and excuse themselves for the involuntary error of being Puerto Ricans, and anecdotes of Puerto Ricans who raise hell and curse if anyone questions their being so; anecdotes of atrocious or shiftless lives, of life dealt with in the most willful and straight terms; anecdotes of tough-skinned survivors and debt-free hearts, anecdotes (sparkling) with a Puerto Rican Spanish, exact in its mumblings and in its brokenness, with a Puerto Rican Spanish stupendously vast and coarse, with a Puerto Rican Spanish vivificantly corrupt, just like Argentinian Spanish, just like Mexican Spanish, just like Venezuelan Spanish, and just like Spanish Spanish. A thousand anecdotes of travelers who come and go between the precarious and discredited paradise of New York and the eroded and uninhabitable paradise of Puerto Rico . . . .

The timid of heart—just like a Walter without Zodiac, without universal temple, without mystically-spangled gowns, like an underclass Walter Mercado—would now prophesize that tonight the flying bus will certainly explode because the sedicious laughter and the load of human energy it carries is a very dangerous kind of fuel. And low-flying angels with the curosity of Peeping-Toms would gladly sacrifice the gold trimmings of one of their eucharistic and brief wings just to know about what the hell that crowd of airbound mestizos flying through their own turf, is yapping about. Only the uniformly gringo flight crew tonight seems to be immune to the laughter and is determined to stamp it out with a barrage of insipid turkey sandwiches, peanut shrapnel and Coke dispensed in hydrant-strong doses, with playing cards and the celluloid meditations of the Captain who risks himself to the pacification of the growing jokeful atmosphere with a few little jokes of his own, little jokes which do not catch on, do not cling, do not threaten anyone—*Ladies and Gentlemen, this is the Captain speaking, now that the dangerous skyjackers are back in their bags, now that we won't be taken to an unexpected meeting with that poco simpático (not so likable) señor Fidel Castro, I invite you all to look through the windows and catch the splash of the Milky Way. In a few minutes we will be showing, without charge tonight, a funny movie starring that funny man Richard Pryor.*

The lady sitting next to me asks me *"What did the man say?"* But the guy sitting in the front row, the one who boasts about travelling without luggage and who repeats over and over *"I live with one leg in New York and the other in Puerto Rico"* and who repeats over and again *"I make my dough in Manhattan but I spend it in Puerto Rico"* and who repeats every now and then *"I'm everybody's brother and nobody's friend. The only friends I have are my balls; they are always hanging around when I need them,"* takes a headstart on me in answering the lady and forces me to agree with his monotonous, serialized, sarcastic answer *"the Captain wants to kill us because he's high, he wants to spoil it for us so we let go and he can take over."* And he lowers and tones down his voice to a murmuring, orgasmic dialect with the most acid inferences about the Captain and the blonde stewardess which, if written, would be published immediately by *Penthouse* or *Playboy*. My lady neighbor does not catch-on to the inferences for she has developed simultaneous converstations about the strike at an asylum for the insane in Puerto Rico where the patients are *"threatening to get sane if their demands are not met"* and about President Reagan's staunch stubborness *"they say, that butcher is massacring El Salvador."*

The initial outburst which opened the door to the sedicious laughter, almost unanimously fertilizes the noisy cordiality that overwhelms the coach cabin of the flying bus; noisy cordiality which expresses itself in the noisy tolerance with which biting opinions are denied or agreed to, and in the noisy gratitude with which a compliment to the paper flowers someone brings as a present for an aunt who moved to a housing project in New Jersey is received; and in the noisy sharing typical of those who have suffered together and love the same things, a box of *guava* pastelillos (guava-filled pastries), a bag of *polvorones* (sugar cookies), a dozen *piononos* (baked sweet plantains), a string of *pirulies* (fruit-shaped candy bars), some slices of salami, a barrel of moonshine, rum cured with raisins . . . the one you can drink without any qualms of conscience . . . ; a noisy cordiality, passionate and indifferent to the sneers that their racket and indiscreet handlings, their coarse gastronomic delights and their proclivity to being friendly with just anyone because simply they are cut out that way, provokes in those who take refuge in the first class cabin and who, between sips of California champagne, establish a *tit-à-tête* with a stewardess of well-proportioned nose and subtle manners, venture a rationalized "*they are my people but* . . . ." Or a resentful "*I wish they'd learn how to behave soon*" or an unexpected "*They'll never make it because they are trash;*" noisy and passionate cordiality that rises, fizzles and overruns when the fibrous middle-aged man recites his self-justifying postdata of "*I cannot live in Puerto Rico because there's no life for me there, then I'll bring it with me bit by bit; in this trip, four crabs from Vacía Talega, in the trip before, a fighting cock, in my next, all of Cortijo's records.*" And he presses on with the inventory, defending it with the serial editing of amplified smiles, governing the relished memories of other cherished salvages, of other pretexts that efface any sense of distance, of other dear belongings that if seen with malice or judged by a myopic heart would amount to no more than folkloric junk, mediocre local color, light folk-lore . . . the *leolai* syndrome.

But junk that, trasncended from its not too impotent appearances or straightened-out from its crooked prestige as spendable triflings, become reiterated, useful, and necessary revelations of a temperament that, day after day gauges its diversity and underscores its permanence in spite of, even though and even if, although of course, perhaps or perchance, and other like dialectical stammerings or resources of enunciative discourse sprung from a catastrophic grammar which persists in conjugating into Spanish our inexorable and devastating *yankeezation*; a unique temperament, different, permanent, ours; a temperament which binds together our holiest dependence on the militant love of family and community . . . if you go to New York, you are seen off by four, if two return from New York, they are welcomed by eight; a temperament that keeps our reserves of humor from drying up . . . for we like the kind of laughter which shakes and scandalizes, and the spicy jokes; temperament which upholds our affective empire, for we suffer and cry out, operatically, Mexican-cinema-like; this laughter of ours, this crying of ours, so indiscernible one from the other, just like the ones that now dispute among themselves the pressurized confines of the air bus. Because now, boasting of being outgoing and a helluva someone, unaware of the Chinese shadow that his body projects on the movie screen that a flight attendant is rolling out, the fibrous middle-aged man displays his gossip with one Cayo from Cayey who is travelling in order to hug his two grandsons whom he has not seen since September and with a Soledad Romero who jets down to Puerto Rico every time the energy cells of her soul run low, and with a certain Isidro from Juncos who had gone down to sell some land in order to get bail money for a son who fell in *trobol* and he does not want the boy to be ruined by jail, and with a Laura Serrano who cannot stand the winters but cannot miss her prefigured rendezvous with destiny in New York; and with a certain Yacoco Calderón from Loíza who moves for a few months to El Barrio so he can *"stuff himself with money,"* and with a certain Gloria Fragoso who is going to New York to prevent her dying son Vitín from dying, and with a certain Bob Márquez who greets him with a daring *"I'm Black and Puerto Rican, and to hell with it,"* and one other someone who mumbles his name and affirms that *"In New York, I'm strictly 'on loan' "*; all of them suddenly catapulted into the heated chatter in the aisles, sharing recently dusted hopes, repeating to each other *where are you from?* with the passion of a census taker, or meddling *if you are from Río Grande you should know Mr. Pagán, who teaches Industrial Arts or if you are from Aguadilla, you must know for sure Tata Barradas. . . .* In the flying bus Puerto Ricans reconsider the adversity and the joy of the provincial fragrances of a country that became a huge town or the town that became a small country. Puerto Ricans who ritualize the difficult illusion of believing that they come to New York strictly "on loan", Puerto Ricans who swear by the revered memory of their dead that they will only remain temporarily in New York, just long enough to make ends meet or only while things get better for Puerto Rico, or just so long as it takes them to raise enough money for a down payment on a house in the seventh section of Levittown; Puerto Ricans who any night of the week jump into the flying bus making sure they have the open return trip ticket which guarantees they will someday return, the open return trip ticket that, at any moment, takes care of the urgent need to return because grandmother is in agony or dad died suddenly, the open return trip ticket that, in short notice, can cancel out the hunger to go back to that island, treasured in the limelight of a gentle and distorted memory, the island *"of the Palm trees and the swaying Sugar Cane flowers"* the island whose *"sandy waistline is gilded with foaming reefs"*; the open return trip ticket, the possession of which sooths the sudden urge to back-track your life over tropical mountains and beaches of the island, and waste your precious time strolling around the town plaza, and on morning, noon and night to level out those streets—so beautiful because their so ugly town streets of an unique yesteryear, or to become an ineffable worker in some ineffable Idler's Company, and to recover your long lost friendships in a three-day talk-a-thon or in collective drunken frenzy with those who really know how to start it but ignore when to end it. And yes . . . return once again, momentarily, to what is left, to what remains, to what survives unaltered due to its constant erosion, its failure, or because of a fascinating inertia and which possesses not the glamour of any magical realism nor the lyricism of nostalgic repercussions; the open return trip ticket that certifies that in New York you are insured against the growth of roots that can only grow in your island, against the risk of being buried in an icy land unlike yours.

Puerto Ricans who cannot breathe in Puerto Rico but catch a lung-full in New York can achieve a ballpark average of four hundred; Puerto Ricans who are uneasy with the island's easy-going struggle and at home with the metropolitan sink-or-swim alternative; Puerto Ricans who wrest and tumble with their not being able to live in Puerto Rico and find themselves unnecessarily pissed and embarassed when they have to verbalize their realities—*Listen, man, in the island the only thing you can do is drink and joke around, man, in Puerto Rico everything is a screwed-up complication, man, in Puerto Rico I feel amused and spaced-out by the verbal apotheosis and lack of discipline, man, in Puerto Rico people fail you and they keep their peace as if they would be eating yams, well, you know buddy, I've already cast my luck here, and there I feel lost, though maybe I'll give it a try there for a while and if things don't add up I'll scurry back to New York.* Puerto Ricans who want to be there but must remain here; Puerto Ricans who want to be there but cannot remain there; Puerto Ricans who live there and dream about being here; Puerto Ricans with their lives hanging from the hooks of the question marks *allá? acá?*, Hamletian disjunctives that ooze their lifeblood through both adverbs. Puerto Ricans installed in permanent errancy between "being there" and "being here" and who, because of it, deflate all the adventurous formality of the voyage until it becomes a mere "ride in a bus" . . . however aerial, so it may lift them filled with assurances over the blue pond . . . the *blue pond*, the Puerto Rican metaphor for the Atlantic Ocean.

A chauffered flight over the Atlantic and the plain fact of an arrival accomplished in order to be able to-go-out-again-and-come-back-again, a fact consecrated with the general applause that will follow the imminent touchdown of the flying bus.

The lady sitting next to me recollects now over the incident of the crabs which had unchained the three-hour long accidents, and she hurls at me the unavoidable *"where are you from?"* at the very moment that the PA system says *"in a few minutes we will be landing at John F. Kennedy airport"*. And I answer: *"from Puerto Rico"*, in order that she should be able to retort, as a sort of medium in a rehearsed séance, *"one can tell THAT from your looks"*, adding immediately, *"I mean, from what town?" "From Humacao"* I answer. And anyone can tell that she is pleased because pleasantly, smilingly, she adds *"Oh, I was to Humacao once"*, while she looks at me as if I owed her. As if I were rudely avoiding the unavoidable ritual of asking her *"and you, where are you from?"*, as if, stupidly, I would be unaware that in the flying bus one must abide by the rules of the remnants of the tribal community and the unclogged flow of dialogue and the openness to everyone just for the asking, and to acknowledge the consciousness of an apparent yet pressumed equality in risks and fate which binds together all the solidarity of the islanders who, after all, are "all aflame". *"Where are you from?"* I ask her although

I do not even have to guess at the answer. Her playful, teasing glance and the shameless, divined blush under her bronze-skinned face underlines her answer; *"from Puerto Rico . . ."* forcing me to say, as a reasonable medium in a rehearsed séance *"even a blind man can see THAT,"* and, still, I add *"from what town, I mean."* And she clearly specifies, *"from New York."*

It all may seem, of course, either a smoothed-out commonplace or a pitiful geographical blunder, or a sarcastic joke out of a resounding box or a new category of the frontier or, perhaps, the sweet and swift revenge of the invaded who succeeded in invading the invader's domain. It is, of course, all that and a bit more. It is the other face of the political coin, the counter-flow of political rhetoric politicians fail to sound. It is the unstoried story not historicized in history books. It is the unre- corded datum of statistics. It is the transparent assertion that confirms the pragmatism of poetry. It is the belated justice that avenges the sorrows of those who once saw their beloved island blurred forever from the observation decks of the *USSS Borinquen* and the *USSS Coamo*; it is the vindication of those who crept, dazed, pioneering, into the fourteen hours of droned-in flight of the narrow, shaking, uncomfortable and silvered flying clippers of Pan American. It is the imposing flow of reality with its hallucinating proposal of newer, furiously conquered spaces. It is the relentless flow of a people who float between two ports, licensed for the smuggling of human hopes.

Translated by Elpidio Laguna-Díaz

3

The Islander

Pedro Juan Soto

In the islands of the Caribbean one frequently hears the cries of those who feel that they have been punished by geographic circumstances. Until a short while ago the sea was for the islander a great wall of water separating him from all that he envied. That sea still changes into a winged monster which devours the cautious traveler as well as the brave pilgrim, and which penetrates into the territory of the Antilles to level off everything. Surrounded by water, accosted by hurricane-force winds, submitted to constant floods, tormented by prolonged droughts, the West Indian is resigned to suffer a precarious existence.

The sea continues there (careful if it draws back when hurricane winds change direction!), but it no longer represents the imposing wall of water which formerly held it captive. Air transportation gives to the West Indian a means of escaping from, as well as returning to, that island territory which he loves as much as he hates. One West Indian says:

> But if this island were populated by you the French, or the English, Scandinavians, Dutch, or Germans from the north . . . , with high productive efficiency, I assure you that we would not be what we are now; there would not be as much hunger, ignorance, or crime here.[1]

The statement is that of a character from *El tiempo jugó conmigo*, a novel by the Puerto Rican J.I. de Diego Padró. He blames the racial element for the rate of hunger, ignorance, and crime on the island of Caoyara (a name which the author gives to Puerto Rico).

Does this merely represent the erroneous opinion of a character, refuted later in the novel? No. It represents the opinion of the author himself, since nowhere in this, or in any other novel by de Diego Padró, is the racial determinism voiced by the character Jerónimo Ruiz denied.[2] As a matter of fact, the French physician Fausto Legrand, with whom the writer, Ruiz, is talking demonstrates:

> That which builds physical and psychological characteristics in the painful and biting *caoyareño* is, above all, his weak, languid sickly constitution (probably due to hereditary, climatological and dietary factors), and, in addition, a capricious tendency toward perpetual inconsistency, a condition which he drags along with him, surreptitiously, deep inside, a vicious sense of dependency and inferiority.[3]

To the racial element which Ruiz points to as a determinant of the islander's psychology, Fausto Legrand adds the geographic element (climatological factor, as he calls it).

The presence of such geographic-racial determinism in a Puerto Rican novel of 1960 represents nothing original on the part of its author, de Diego Padró. The novelist is echoing what was exposed in 1934 by the Puerto Rican essayist Antonio S. Pedreira, who argues the following:

> At the base of our population we will find without too much difficulty a biological struggle of disjointed and contrary forces which have slowed down the definitive formation of our ways of being. . . . The strength and will of the European retain on their side the doubt and resentment of the African . . . . I do not assert that everything comes from that diversity of family origins and racial mixtures, but that a starting point for interpreting our character "so mixed and mixed-up," is the variety of reactions which respond to secret biological stimulus. . . . The Climate melts our will and causes a rapid deterioration of our psychology. The Heat matures us before our time and before our time decomposes us. From its unnerving pressure on men comes that national characteristic which we call *aplatanamiento* (disregard or cowering). This, in our country, is a kind of inhibition, a mental slumber and absence of combativeness.[4]

Genes and geography condition our island being, according to some theorists. According to others, social struggle creates ambivalence, contradictory attitudes, and constant doubt in the islander. The Barbadian Edward Brathwaite, for example, calls attention to the dichotomy in the behavior of the English-speaking inhabitant of the Antilles:

> The dichotomy . . . is a permanent part of our heritage. It comes, in a way, as an almost physical inheritance from Africa where in nature, drought and lushness, the flower and the desert, lie side by side. It is a spiritual inheritance from slavery and the long story before that of the migrant moving from the lower side across the desert to the Western ocean only to meet the Portuguese and a history that was to mean the middle passage, America, a rootless sojourn in the Caribbean Sea.
>
> This dichotomy expresses itself in the West Indian through a certain psychic tension, an excitability, a definite feeling of having no past, of not really belonging . . .; and finds relief in the laughter and [more seriously] in movement—dance, cricket, carnival, emigration.[5]

Brathwaite's comments emphasize the phenomenon of slavery as a cause of the atavistic uprooting suffered by the islander. This social factor perhaps explains, also in a dichotomous sense, the collective cowering which Pedreira laments in the Puerto Rican and the psychological tension which forces him to move constantly (emigration, sports, dance), something which Brathwaite also seems to regret.

In sports a much more important element than who wins the game is perceived. The Trinidadian writer V.S. Naipaul writes:

> Cricket has always been more than a game in Trinidad. In a society which demanded no skills and offered no rewards to merit, cricket was the only activity which permitted a man to grow to his full stature and to be measured against international standards. Alone on a field, beyond obscuring intrigue, the cricketer's true worth could be seen by all. His race, education, wealth did not matter. We had no scientists, engineers, explorers, soldiers or poets. The cricketer was our only hero-figure. And that is why cricket is played with such panache; that is why, for a long time to come, the West Indians will not be able to play as a team. The individual performance was what mattered. That was what we went to applaud; and unless the cricketer has heroic qualities we did not want to see him, however valuable he might be. And that was why, of those stories of failure, that of the ruined cricketer was the most terrible.[6]

That which Naipaul describes of the game of cricket in the English-speaking islands of the Caribbean also goes for soccer players in French-speaking West Indian societies (Martinique, Guadeloupe, Haiti), as well as for others initially motivated as individuals—baseball players or basketball players—in Spanish-speaking Caribbean societies (Cuba, Puerto Rico, and the Dominican Republic).

Sports represent for the islander the search for international prominence. The West Indian usually takes on a social struggle through the particular recourse of sports because he desires fame and fortune while still alive, in the same way that he longs for prestige abroad and after he is dead.

The same may be said of the musician of this area: he sings to the island nation and hopes for the nation's approval. It is easy to recognize the reciprocity which exists between the individual and the masses, since the nation has discovered a resonant note of the masses' desire to praise themselves through that individual.

Cuban musicologist and novelist Alejo Carpentier argues:

> The name of "sonorous islands," which the great classic of the French Renaissance Rabelais gave to some islands, could also be applied to the islands of the West Indies. Everything rings in the West Indies, everything is sound. The West Indies have . . . music as a common denominator. It may be the extraordinary Cuban music in its long evolution . . .; it may be Dominican *plena*, so similar and yet so different to Cuban music; it may be the extraor-

> dinary, devilish calypso from Barbados and Trinidad; it may be the steel and orchestras for which musicians from the island of Trinidad and Barbados have created such an instrument of a richness of notes, possibilities, and expression from the tops of gasoline and petroleum drums molded to a certain extent by hammer blows, that they can perform with these genuinely West Indian instruments, even the music of Bach.[7]

It all deals, then, with the individual who stands out, who seems to act on his own behalf and who responds effectively—in a logical, paradoxical, or dichotomous way—to the desires of the tribe. The masses for their part see him as an individual who is representative of themselves. He will be able to obtain all kinds of individual triumphs in his solo or group performances (the work of his musical colleagues), but he will never be able to forget that he acts, for good or for bad, as a representative of the masses which gave birth to him.

The academic education of the baseball player and the basketball player—as well as that of the boxer and other athletes—is similar to that of the popular musician. Few of them have been able to go beyond high school. The temptation of a good contract and the desire to stand out as an individual motivate different kinds of bravery in a society lacking in collective and individual advantages. (In Cuba it is a different story for the musician and the athlete: the financial gain of the individual is less, while the fame he acquires by representing a socialist society is that much greater.)

We have dealt with the cases of the musician and the athlete in relation to an island society. Some may object to my raising certain points about the West Indian police as well. I find in their occupation, nevertheless, great affinity with what I said earlier.

The athlete, the musician, and the policeman are victims of the subculture of poverty, which makes them suffer the same poverty, thereby forcing them to emerge from nothingness. With respect to the subculture or culture of poverty, anthropologist Oscar Lewis—who uses both terms indiscriminately—explains the following:

> The economic traits which are most characteristic of the culture of poverty include the constant struggle for survival, unemployment and under-employment, low wages, a miscellany of unskilled occupations . . . , the absence of food reserves in the home . . . , the pawning of personal goods, borrowing from local moneylenders at usurious rates of interest . . . , and the use of second-hand clothing and furniture.[8]

In the same way that misery produces individuals lacking in initiative, who regret that they are not fortunate enough to succeed, that same miserable atmosphere also stimulates others to stand up and march triumphantly.

Probably with only one parent, lacking academic skills, surrounded by numerous relatives, in an extremely gregarious neighborhood, the creature of misery longs to obtain, before anything else, his own home—a house where he can be sheltered under a safe roof, together with a minimal family—and later, to make himself a collective home where he can be lord and master: the home of the island society to which he will respond without fail and from which he expects warm recognition.

The athlete and the musician will surrender perhaps prematurely to competitors in their respective fields. Their desire for gradual prominence—communal, national, island, and international progressively—is curtailed for different reasons: poor health, hopes and ability are not in harmony, muscles lose agility, voice goes, hearing becomes distorted.

What can the frustrated athlete or musician do? He will have to give up his international ambitions—resign himself to belonging to a smaller home than the one he desired and to competing in an initially small town circle. He will become a policeman.

The nonprofessionally inclined individual (contributing to this is individual motivation as well as the lack of advantages for the masses themselves) will decide to continue in competition—whether this be the next musical gig or a new game—playing not professionally, but rather semiprofessionally. The ex-athlete or ex-musician will study some texts so that he can join the police department after passing the necessary examinations, he will rely on his developed physical resistance and a little mental agility, he will face risks alone or with the support of others. There, in the police station, he will make his home away from home.

Rarely will the policeman feel alone. In him will rest the sense of esprit de corps (which ties him to a kind of collective responsibility) and working in his favor is that same esprit de corps (which brings the sweat of others to his aid).

The future policeman joins a monastic hierarchical organism. The novice's conduct is puritanical—he must never set a bad example to society, according to that which is specified—he will finish his police internship by becoming a model being. By obeying necessary cautions—obedience to that which is imposed and to rules and regulations—he will earn systematic promotions in the police hierarchy, which represents the origin of a greater hierarchy: the National Guard in the case of colonial Puerto Rico, the national army in the case of independent West Indian societies.

The financial stimulus is minimal for the novice policeman in West Indian society. It is nothing like that of the starting athlete or musician. Nevertheless, his prestige increases day by day after he completes six months of training in our Puerto Rican Police Academy. It is laughable to point out that the policeman is hailed as a public servant, that he is photographed detaining motor vehicles so as to allow children, women, and elderly persons, to pass. It also seems rather insignificant to point out that the starting policeman is not charged for his refreshments and does not require a ticket to attend any public event. But be careful not to disdain such apparently small matters! The policeman is made from the total of trivial matters, from a handful of acknowledgments which give him communal, island and national notoriety.

The uniform, the badge, the firearm, and the billy club are the obvious distinguishing characteristics of the policeman. His face is as anonymous as that of any other West Indian. If he does not wish to show himself anonymously beardless, he will grow an anonymous moustache. His face can be that of a physician, as well as that of a construction worker. (He should not wear a beard, unless he is assigned the task of secret agent among clandestine groups.) As far as height is concerned, he must not measure less than one meter and seventy-four centimeters (five feet, eight inches).

In his official interventions, as he was repeatedly told in the academy, human life is always in danger, his own as well as that of others. And it has also been drilled into him that his firearm is to be treated as a luxury object, while at the same time, paradoxically, he is made to practice continually his target shooting skills. (His weapon is an overused luxury object.)

The policeman can always count on the support of his colleagues and other officials involved in maintaining public order (district attorneys, judges). His repeated defense against any accusation of doubtful weapon handling will be: "It was in self defense."

The ex-athlete become policeman now participates in a more dangerous game than he could ever have imagined on any field, dance floor, or boxing ring. The ex-musician become policeman sounds off quietly or shuts up so that he can hear clearly the chorus of his superiors.

The policeman represents, after all, the same individual and collective authority as any musician or athlete. His refrain is the same as their's: "This is my/our field, this is my/our team, this is my/our turf. Or isn't it like that?"

I have said already that the policeman's face is not in any way different from that of any other West Indian. I have looked for descriptions from newspaper writers of the faces of police agents involved in one or another case. Not even in special reports, where those details can be manipulated with delay, have I found the physical description of a policeman.

As far as the facial description of a policeman is concerned, I must say that even in the literary works of our islands I have come up with nothing. In a few documentary works—in the style of *Puerto Rico*: *grito y mordaza*[9] or *Huelga y sociedad*[10]—I have found countless fleeting photographs of policemen who emphasize, above all, the way they handle themselves during a confrontation: a policeman at attention, a policeman to one side, a policeman crouching down, a policeman with his elbows against the ground, a policeman running aggressively, a policeman with his knee on the ground.

The policeman, after all, has no face. Violence, I should add, also has no face. It is perhaps that synonymy which places best the policeman in our Caribbean islands. The policeman, the musician and the athlete are heroes on our islands. Individual accomplishment imposes itself on the collective accomplishment (even when personal initiative would like to be of a gregarious nature).

This brings us back to certain questions raised by Pedreira in 1934 and by Naipaul in 1962. Pedreira tells us:

> Puerto Rico is a deprived nation; but it loves life and will never give up. The native is an individual, resistant and brave. He does not give in to hunger; he is not nullified by natural disasters; individually he is not concerned with losing his life, which he would jeopardize for any personal foolishness; collectively, it is the opposite: he demonstrates a great inability to die in a group. Just the opposite of other West Indian nations, ours feels a great fondness for life. From Quisqueya is the *areyto* which says: "Ijí, ayǎ bombé" (death before slavery). A hatred of life characterizes the Dominican and the Cuban nations, which to the astonishment of everyone, gamble it away every moment. Our population, on the other hand, is docile and peaceful: it is characterized by resignation. It defends its right to live with great caution, and demonstrates an instinctive prudence which some identify with fear![11]

What does Naipaul add to this (without meaning to, because I doubt that he has read the Puerto Rican Pedreira)? Naipaul has said (and I emphasize):

> In a society which demanded no skills and offered no rewards to merit, cricket was the only activity which permitted a man to grow to his full stature . . . and to be measured against international standards. Alone on a field, beyond obscuring intrigue, the cricketer's true worth could be seen by all. His race, education, wealth did not matter. We had no scientists, engineers, explorers, soldiers, or poets. The cricketer was our only hero figure. And that is why cricket is played with such panache; that is why, for a long time to come, the West Indies will not be able to play as a team. The individual performance was what mattered.[12]

One argument after another points to the individualism of the islander and only in passing do they mention the islander's inclination toward the masses (the ill-named "hatred of life" which Pedreira points to in the Dominican and Cuban nations, the popular acknowledgment which, according to Naipaul, the cricketer obtains).

In the same way that the West Indian seeks to stand out in popular music, sports, and in lesser government dealings which grant him maximum authority (the case of the policeman), he also desires to convert that individualistic anguish into a respected symbol of the society to which he belongs. Once the individual is triumphant, what can we hope for? The cacique (Indian chief), or to put it in other than modern terms, the *caudillo* or supreme leader, will undoubtedly be born.

The *caudillo* is the maximum ambition of a being like the athlete, the musician, and the policeman. The politician says, while struggling to become a *caudillo*, the same thing as the musician, the same thing as the athlete, and the same thing as the policeman: My life is dedicated to render services which will make my nation proud.

Let us go back then to the attitudes which, according to my outline above, characterize the West Indian: (1) The islander is a resigned being, and at the same time a rebellious being, due to his geographic isolation and racial condition (Pedreira, de Diego Padró); (2) the islander is never sure whether *to be* or *not to be* in the territory which he inhabits, which responds to his atavistic feeling of uprootedness (Brathwaite); (3) the islander is thouroughly individualistic (Pedreira, Naipaul). As for the idea that the islander is a radical individual, following Pedreira's and Naipaul's opinion, I believe I have already expressed my doubts by utilizing the cases of the musician, athlete, policeman, and politician.

If we accept that the islander wishes to make his "I" out to be something worthwhile before the "Is" present in his particular society (an obvious conflict of egos not at all integrated into the collective means), we will run into disturbing contradictions and illuminating conflicts. The "I" of the islander wants to stand out alone and, at the same time, wants to figure as a representative of other "Is" who are less aggressive or more complacent, because he does not want to isolate himself from the society which, for good or for bad, has created him. His individualism seems punished at first with a turbulent panorama of egos showing him his own nation. Multiple egos recognize in the long run, after many tribulations, that they make up a needed collective ego of a symbolic I. That collectivity, therefore, will respect the *apparent* supremacy of a particular "I," which it must convert into an important groove of the machinery of the island society. The accomplishment of that particular "I" must always be superior to that of any other disputed egos which await the other person's demise or mutual deceit.

Let us look at the case of the Haitian writer and politician Jacques Stéphen Alexis (1922-61) as an example of the West Indian ego conflict. After traveling to Moscow and Peking from his European exile, Alexis returned to Cuba, his country of birth, on 22 April 1961—his thirty-ninth birthday. He anchored in Saint Cristobal, together with four companions, aiming to penetrate the same rural area which he had defended in four literary works.[13]

I cite from a review of Alexis's case:

> The invaders, bound with sisal cords and thrown into a cell at the Mole, drew a select contingent of Tonton Macoutes and military officers from Port-au-Prince to handle the situation. The Alexis band was dragged to a grassy field in front of the old British port, Saint George. There peasants and urchins, under the effective urging of the Tonton Macoutes, stoned them in true Middle Ages style. Alexis' right eye was torn out of its socket and the stoning left all five dead or very close to it.[14]

I allude to cannibalism in this case, with some reservations, but I bear the example in mind to demonstrate the evident conflict of egos. This ''I'' of Alexis proclaims itself defender, spokesman, of a West Indian society. The other ''Is,'' obviously incited by the ego of a policeman aware of his own survival, end by tearing to shreds the ''I'' that wanted to impose itself, without employing the collaboration of those who, yes, felt oppressed, and who, yes, wanted to be freed, but who feared more the vengeance of an obviously greater force which was in power. Risk oneself for what, in the name of what, and with what guarantees?

I deduce that the islander loves his individualism—his isolated being, his particular being, his being a product of himself—at the same time that he loves the masses to which he feel he belongs. The masses, for their part, respect the individual if that ''I'' is able to stand out indisputably among the different ''Is'' of his society. If the individual and presumptively collective ''I'' is able to stand out, the island society will convert him into a self-elevating element. If that ''I,'' on the other hand, does not show sufficient wisdom or strength, it will end up between the teeth of the collective ego. In such a conflict of ''Is''—each one of which wants to count for the rest—the individual tries to isolate himself from West Indian society, even though later on he may dedicate himself to fight within it and on its behalf.

I am halfway consoled and halfway irritated by the so-called dichotomy of the islander exposed by Edward Brathwaite: To be or not to be? Should I love or hate my West Indian society? Who am I within my island, and who am I outside of it? I find myself between contradictions which I suffer and hate, I find myself—for good or for bad—trying to prevail.

Notes

1. J. I. de Diego Padró, *El tiempo jugó conmigo* (Barcelona: Rumbos, 1960), p. 255.
2. Jerónimo Ruiz is the protagonist of three other novels by de Diego Padró (1896–1974). Those novels are *En babia* (1940), *El minotauro se devora a sí mismo* (1965), and *Un cencerro de dos badajos* (1969).
3. *El tiempo jugó conmigo*, p. 256.
4. Antonio S. Pedreira, *Insularismo* (Río Piedras, P.R.: Edil, 1975), pp. 32, 39; 1st ed. 1934.

5. Edward Brathwaite, "Roots," *Bim* (Bridgetown, Barbados, July-December 1963): 10–11.
6. V. S. Naipaul, *The Middle Passage* (Middlesex, England: Penguin, 1975), pp. 44–45; 1st ed. 1962.
7. Alejo Carpentier, "La cultura de los pueblos que habitan en las tierras del mar Caribe," *Casa de las Américas* (Havana, January-February): 3–4.
8. Oscar Lewis, *The Children of Sánchez* (New York: Random House, 1961), p. xxvi.
9. Luis Nieves Falcón, et al. *Puerto Rico: grito y mordaza* (Río Piedras, P.R.: Librería Internacional, 1971).
10. Luis Nieves Falcón, et al. *Huelga y sociedad* (Río Piedras, P.R.: Edil, 1982).
11. *Insularismo*, pp. 35–36.
12. *The Middle Passage*.
13. His bibliography consists of the novel *Compère Général Soleil*, 1955; the poetry collection *Les Arbres musiciens*, 1957; the novel *L'Espace d'un cillement*, 1959; and the collection of short stories *Romancéro aux étoiles*, 1960.
14. Bernard Diederich and Burt, et al. *Papa Doc (The Truth about Haiti Today)* (New York: Avon, 1970), p. 155.

4
Images in Contemporary Puerto Rican Literature

Gerald Guinness

I shall examine three dominant images in contemporary Puerto Rican literature and offer some personal comments—the comments of an "outsider" who yet prides himself on having more than a trace of the proverbial *mancha del plátano* in his upbringing and literary sympathies—on each of them. In particular, I wish to comment on the degree to which these images help us to understand current Puerto Rican reality. But before I begin I should like to put in a good word for "images" in general.

Images have had a bad press in recent years, evoking as they do something that can be packed and sold to a gullible public. For example, a would-be presidential candidate complained recently that he would never be elected president because he did not have enough hair. Obviously images at this level are harmful and frivolous. But images in the hands of a literary artist can also be creative and liberating, particularly if they help define an identity that is struggling to become aware of itself, or, in negative terms, if they help define or demythologize one's enemy. In England the combined image of Lucky Jim and the "angry young man" in the mid-1950s helped to bring about a class breakthrough in the arts hitherto dominated by the gentry; the spate of working- or lower-middle-class actors, men like Peter O'Toole and Albert Finney and women like Rita Tushingham, was a secondary but delightful result of this new image. And, if I may be allowed a moment's personal testimony, it was the image of a sympathetic liberal Englishman who "travels light," Fielding in E. M. Forster's *A Passage to India*, that took me on my own passage to India at the end of that decade, where I acted Fielding to an audience of Azizs until I realized what a fool I was making of myself. This too is part of the usefulness of images. They can be assumed, revised, and discarded—and the process of learning and growth this affords the reader has always been one of the ways in which literature sets a mark upon the moral climate of its time.

As I have just mentioned, negative images can help define and demythologize the enemy. This must be the rationale for the first of my three images, that of the colonial overlord or gringo. Here is a personage who seems to be feared and despised by our literati to the degree that he exercises an uneasy, perhaps even reluctant, fascination over the rest of the population. Perhaps, in response to this threat, most writers cast North Americans in the role of "ugly" Americans. In fact, I can hardly think of a recent work, with the exception of *La llegada* by José Luis González, where gringos can be found who are both efficient *and* humane. If a gringo is efficient, then he uses his efficiency to exploit the "natives," run down the local culture, and make it with every local girl in sight; if he is humane, as with Simpson in Pedro Juan Soto's recent novel *Un oscuro pueblo sonriente*, then he is so inept that after thirty years on the island he still "doesn't know more than two dozen words of Spanish." In this combination of incapacity and antipathy I am reminded of those one-dimensional Englishmen in Indian novels of the 1930s, for example those of Mulk Raj Anand, and of the overbearing British bullies, like the school inspector in Chinua Achebe's *Things Fall Apart* who knocks down any teacher he does not like. If a writer cannot defeat his oppressor with his fists, then at least he can give him a good jap in the ribs with his pen.

North Americans are for a start sexually rapacious and hopelessly promiscuous. A flagrant example comes from *La mirada* by René Marqués, a writer no one could accuse of pro-Americanism. The hero goes to Washington, D.C., to visit his *piti-yanqui* brother (of whom more in a moment). At a party he meets an unattached young lady who vamps him in less time than it takes to say "tramp." This is how their conversation goes, as written in English:

— My name is Millie. What's yours?
— Whatever you want it to be.
— Bill then.
— All right.
— Are you here to make sex?
— Are you?
— Could be. Are you a homo?
— Would you like to find out?
— What are you drinking?
— Scotch.
— Get me one.
— Go get it yourself.[1]

At this point most Millies I know would have disappeared into the red sunset, but not this Millie. Instead, she lures her innocent young Puerto Rican friend into the garden, pulls her mu-mu over her head, and plunges naked into the swimming pool. A few minutes later they are tucked in bed together in the spare room, smoking pot like two chimneys. Obviously there's no vice like North American vice.

Here is another example, this time of gringo bad manners. The appalling Yunito from Emilio Díaz Valcárcel's *Mi mamá me ama* is describing a scene at a dance where a friend sees his mother coming across the dance floor toward him. When mommy asks the boy how he is enjoying himself, Ted (and this time I quote in translation) "had a critical reaction: he dropped his jeans and showed his back side. Mrs. Morrison fainted in the middle of the dance floor and someone had to call the ambulance."

These are but two instances, but I could find many more. In short, North Americans are congenitally vulgar, shamefully oversexed, they drink too much, they cannot pronounce one word in Spanish correctly, they treat their women like dishcloths, and they have an unmitigated disgust for all those not born White, capitalist, and in love with Ronald Reagan. Such, North American ladies and gentlemen, is the image of you presented by such works as *La mirada, Un oscuro pueblo sonriente, Harlem todos los días, Los amos benévolos, Un decir de la violencia*, and *Mi mamá me ama*. Go crawl into a corner and be ashamed of yourselves.

Well, there are excellent reasons why a patriotic writer might feel less than amiable toward a people who have occupied his country by force for more than eighty years and whose culture, allied to the power of the dollar, threatens his own. Nonetheless the disparity between the monsters I've described and the people one meets in a place like, say, Newark, New Jersey, is rather striking, and it might be argued (though I have no time to argue it now) that there is little point in destroying one myth about one's enemy only to put another one in its place. My second image, however, is no myth, as this is a reality Puerto Rican writers know only too well and with the immediacy of daily experience. I refer of course to the native-born Puerto Rican who imitates, admires, flatters, and sometimes fawns over his North American neighbor, a type known in Puerto Rico (and I believe in other parts of Latin America) as the *piti-yanqui*. The type exists in many varieties, from the loudmouth in bermuda shorts and yachting cap who brings his powerboat up to the quiet lake where I live every Sunday, to the *tipo bien criollo* (nationalist type) who nevertheless has a sneaking feeling that "they" after all really do everything a little better "over there." I can supply a real-life example of this second variety from a letter that came into my hands, written by an executive vice-president of a company I shall call, for discretion's sake, Exotic Exterminators, Inc. I shall read you the first paragraph of this letter, changing only the names:

> I live at 772 Saint James Street in the urban development of the Sacred Heart. This indicates that I am your neighbor and I wish to inform you that I have been appointed Vice President of Exotic Exterminators, Inc. This is the first time that this company appoints a Puerto Rican to such a position and I wish to succeed in order to prove our ability to hold these positions and higher ones.

There are equivalents for this at all levels of Puerto Rican society, and even university administrators have been known to quake in their shoes when a visit from the Middle States Association looms imminent. For the colonial, "our ability to hold these positions" is always a matter for soul-searching and doubt.

I mentioned earlier that the protagonist of René Marqués's *La mirada* has a *piti-yanqui* brother who lives in Washington, D.C. Not only does this Humberto fail to recognize the lamb on the crest of San Juan Bautista, mispronounce Bac*a*rdi, keep his fireplace alight even though it is almost summer, and bawl out his wife Manuela (alias Molly) in English, but he is so ashamed of being Puerto Rican that he has told the neighbors that he and his wife are really Argentine. That detail of the blazing hearth in hot weather recurs in another ferocious satire of the *piti-yanqui*, Díaz Valcárcel's *Mi mamá me ama* from which I have already quoted. Yunito's father is so proud of his fireplace that he turns up the air conditioning whenever there is an important visitor so that he can warm his hands in front of the glowing coals, for all the world like a bank president in Maine. Here are a few lines from this scene in my own translation:

> With his scarf hanging down over his chest, my godfather rubs his frozen hands in front of the flames, puffing on his pipe and commenting in English on the severity of the weather, the drop in the temperature, and the delicious feeling of drinking a glass of brandy next to the fireplace. And Dad says that the temperature, the fireplace, the pipe, in fact our whole lifestyle help us to be more and more like fellow-citizens up North.[2]

I confess I find this amusing, although it is perhaps rather broad—like taking a machete to a *coquí* (a small Puerto Rican frog), perhaps. What is more, I wonder whether Díaz Valcárcel is on the right track when he focuses on the *piti-yanqui* as characteristic of the Condado and the *blanquito* (White) caste. In my limited experience, upper-class Puerto Ricans are very conscious of their ancestry, their descent from Ferdinand and Isabella and their European manners, and as a consequence often tend to be subtly superior about North Americans whom they consider vulgarians and lacking in lineage. Another complicating factor about the *piti-yanqui* phenomenon is that pro-Americanism in Puerto Rico is particularly rife among the poorer classes, as José Luis

González pointed out in *El país de cuatro pisos*. Not all satirical onslaughts on the *piti-yanqui* always take these ironies and contradictions into account.

There is however one aspect of *piti-yanqui* satire that seems dead on target, and that is where it focuses on the effects of the love affair with North America on spoken and written Spanish. "The language problem in Puerto Rico is fundamentally a political problem,"[3] says José Luis González in his *Conversación* with Arcadio Díaz Quiñones, and he goes on to point out that this is a particularly severe problem at the level of the speech of our "educated" classes. Benny, from Luis Rafael Sánchez's novel *Macho Camacho's Beat*, is a good specimen of this class. He is exhorted to dance with "little Betty and dance with little Kate and dance with little Mary Anne and dance with little Elizabeth"[4] but never "con la nena de María Cristina," "la nena de Juanita," or "la nena de Carmencita." Benny is so greasily gringo that he has earned the nickname "Benny Kool-Aid." When José Luis González says in *Conversación* that "here [in Puerto Rico], the educated classes have been and continue to be the ones most affected by foreign linguistic interference,"[5] it is obviously a linguistic mishmash like this one of Benny's that he has in mind:

> Papito Papitín decía: celebrar en fecha a convenir un get together de maestros en el molto bello jardino de tu Mamá: get together con mozos uniformados, cold cuts, a *La Rotisserie*, toneles de Beaujolais y Lambrusco espumoso: get together que carga a mis gastos de representación senatorial [p. 129].[6]

For this unholy alliance of English, Spanish, French, and Italian we need some derisive new term along the lines of "Spanglish." How about *Italofrangspañol*?—a word as ugly as the Babylonian dialect it describes.

La guaracha del Macho Camacho is probably the most prolongued assault on the *piti-yanqui* misuses of languages written to date. But there are a growing number of works on the same theme and of these I particularly like the transcultural confections of Ana Lydia Vega in stories like "Pollito Chicken" and "Puerto Rican Syndrome," the later from a book only just published, *Encancaranublado*. In "Pollito Chicken," from *Vírgenes y mártires*, Suzie Bermudez returns to the island after many years in New York and achieves orgasm in the arms of a local bartender: "Brother, the gal from 306 doesn't know whether she is North American or Puerto Rican," says the bartender; "She orders room service in English but when I make love to her she opens her mouth to cry in Puerto Rican."[7] And what Suzie cries in sexual *extremis* is perhaps proof that, when confronted by primal experience, even the alienated *piti-yanqui* will revert to the uncontaminated language of her ancestors: "Long Live Puerto Rico Freeeeeeeeeeeee!"[8]

What I miss in elaborations of this second image are attemps to treat the human plight of people like the vice-president of Exotic Exterminators, Inc.

in a way both sympathetic and unaggressive. For in fact the man who has to come to terms with North American culture because he works for a North American firm shades off into the man who has to come to terms with North America because he lives there. I am referring, of course, to the Nuyorican; here is someone who *has* been described in literature with sympathy and without aggression, as in the admirable stories by José Luis González, Emilio Díaz Valcárcel, and Pedro Juan Soto. In particular I admire the latter's *Ardiente suelo, fría estación*, which is, as far as I know, the only full-length book to explore the dilemma of the Puerto Rican exile who attempts to reestablish links with the homeland. In *Ardiente suelo, fría estación* the true *piti-yanqui* is Jorge Vélez "The Linnet" who changes his name to Jorge Guabina "The American" to further his career, thereby forfeiting the good opinion of his contrymen in Caramillo. But Eduardo, hero of the novel, is no *piti-yanqui*, determined as he is to come to terms with "este sentimiento de extraño en tierra propia" (this feeling of being a stranger in my own land). I shall transcribe a short paragraph illustrating the pain and perplexity of this attempt to bridge the gap between two cultures, where this mixture of English and Spanish is not without its own dignity:

> I didn't go up there because I wanted to!. . . They put me on a plane and dragged me up there and . . . and then they said: "Live, boy, live!" And I wanted to come back, I swear I did! But not to this. Not to a bunch of people as prejudiced as the ones I found over there![9]

Here is an image that, because of its painful actuality, cannot be held at arm's length with satire and I wish that more of the sympathy and understanding it enlists would occassionally, in our novels, spill over onto *piti-yanquis* of the Exotic Exterminators stripe. God knows they need our sympathy quite as much as Eduardo and his friends.

I now come to my third and final image, and here I must be more tentative and circumspect than with my previous two. For this third image is that of the Puerto Rican standing four-square on his native turf, uncorrupted by North American influence, secure in his natural identity, and offering a positive example—as did E. M. Forster's Fielding for a young Englishman almost a quarter of a century ago—for self-definition and emulation. Does such a Puerto Rican exist? We must assume so, if only for the sake of our collective morale. For the moment let us assume that he does, and for purposes of graphic presentation let us call him the "Handsome Puerto Rican," on the analogy of the Handsome Sailor of Melville's story "Billy Budd" and in opposition to the Ugly American mentioned earlier.

Since I have borrowed from *La mirada* by René Marqués for both my previous images, let me follow suit and ask how the protagonist of the novel supplies material for our image of the "Handsome Puerto Rican." Now this figure has many excellent qualities. He is patriotic, brave, loyal to family and friends, and determined not to be shaped in the *piti-yanqui* mold. A positive figure, in fact, and one from whom much might be expected for the redemption of the motherland. Imagine our dismay, then, when we reach the penultimate page of the novel and watch this figure preparing to leave home for the last time:

> Then, his own room, larger, the walls loaded with banners and flags, with symbols of victory (What victory?) and peace (Peace, where?) and with satirical caricatures, political cartoons, engravings and a small oil painting, all by various Puerto Rican artists. And clippings from the revolutionary weeklies *Claridad* and *La Hora*. So what? And pictures of Mao and Fidel and Guevara and the recently assassinated Allende. So what? Pure shit! Puerto Rico was still a colony and no one in that whole world gave a damn. He would not take anything from there. Not even the flag of Lares, which symbolized the first cry for independence and which was the one closest to his heart. Nothing. None of that shit which he dearly loved but which led nowhere! Nowhere![10]

This must be one of the saddest moments in contemporary Puerto Rican literature when the illusions of a lifetime turn to dust, just as they seem to have turned to dust for René Marqués himself in his declining years.

A little earlier in the novel is a discussion between the hero and his father, who wants to know his future plans. To each question the young man answers "I dunno," until the father shouts out: "Then what the devil do you know?" to which the answer is, "Just that. That I don't know."[11] Reading this reminded me of the comment in José Juan Beauchamp's *Imagen del puertorriqueño en la novela*, that the most typical hero in contemporary Puerto Rican fiction "does not know himself in spite of his inner struggle to achieve this. He does not know exactly what he wants."[12] That tentativeness and circumspection I mentioned earlier as characterizing our description of this third image comes from precisely this difficulty in knowing exactly "what people want." And even some of our most positive and polemic writers seem to leave us stranded in this particular limbo.

A convenient example comes from a novel I have reviewed recently for *The San Juan Star*,[13] and I speak about it now in partial retribution for what I said about it then. For I had one particular complaint about Pedro Juan Soto's *Un oscuro pueblo sonriente* that I should now like to retract. In this novel the gang of particularly umpleasant North Americans who populate its pages are set against a pair of natives, Carolina and Anselmo Brunet, who spoil their plot to start a political party for the benefit of the North American community on the island ("Naughty Outsiders foiled by Virtuous Locals" is how I expressed it in the review). Pedro Juan Soto's comment, in an accompaning interview, was as follows: "No, no. I don't think so. You can find that even there Carolina isn't a good character in that she's ambiguous, she's ambivalent. . . . She plays with [George Fowler] constantly and he plays with her—and that's the whole game we are having." Carolina plays the game because, like the protagonist of *La mirada*, "she does not know exactly what she wants."

There is a passage illustrating her perplexity that I must quote in full:

> She had never taken anyone seriously since Henry abandoned her. Have fun, sometimes. She would listen to what was said here and there, without letting words stimulate her, at least, to utter an opinion. Her position then? Neutral. Neutral in everything, even more so when it came to politics. She came across people of all factions and no creed had any effect on her. Neutral. She was a woman. She was ignorant. She was a small vacuum acting within an enormous vacuum.[14]

Here is a state of mind that anyone who lives in Puerto Rico can understand and sympathize with, even when it takes the form of a student who, when asked how he or she liked a certain book, answers with an expressive wave of the hand and the word "Okay." "Neutral," "Okay," and "I don't know"—all legitimate responses to the perplexities and incongruities of modern Puerto Rican life, although in the context of our present investigation they hardly add up to the image of the Handsome Puerto Rican that we are searching for.

Such an image does exist, although it is only to be found in partial and particular circumstances. For example, I find it in certain collective instances, as in José Luis González's splendid story "La noche que volvimos a ser gente," where the Handsome Puerto Rican is a group of people organizing an impromptu party in the middle of an electrical blackout. In Ana Lydia Vega's story "Letra para salsa y tres sones por encargo" the Handsome Puerto Rican is a feminist showing a *macho* who it is that really wears the pants. And in Emilio Díaz Valcárcel's *Mi mamá me ama* it is a delightful nurse whose simplicity and good sense shows up the *piti-yanqui* pretensions of Yunito. And yet with this nurse as with the heroic *jíbaro* of a previous literary generation there is something not quite commensurate with the complexity of the problems involved. They affect us perhaps as the slogan "Todos pal Capitolio" (all to the Capitol) affects José Luis González in *Conversación*, as a sign of condescension. (It reminds me of the cheerful Cockney soldiers and sailors in the war movies of my youth: A torpedo has hit the ship, the life boats are welded fast to the derricks, but the Cockney sailors still go on cracking jokes.) It is the element of patronage in the portrayal of these figures, permitting the innocence of the "common people" to redress the corrupt sophistication of the "cultured classes," that makes such figures as Díaz

Valcárcel's nurse inappropriate for the image of the Handsome Puerto Rican I am looking for.

Where then (if anywhere) is one to find this image? A partial answer is to be found in the ending to that fine novel by César Andreu Iglesias, *Los derrotados*. The hero, Marcos, is in prison, himself a *derrotado* (defeated). His friend Paco explains that the trouble with the nationalist cause he has served is that it turns its back on the workers; only collective action will solve Puerto Rico's problems as indeed it secures his own release from jail. Here at least is some sort of answer to the *nada* (nothingness) of René Marqués and the *vacío enorme* (enormous vacuum) of Pedro Juan Soto's Carolina. The fast-flowing waters of the class struggle are channelled into the stagnant pools of cultural schizophrenia, and as a result there is an access of new life and optimism.

I am as willing to settle for an extension of subject matter as for a solution along the lines suggested by César Andreu Iglesias. The Handsome Puerto Rican may turn out to be a taxi driver or a docker, a grocer or the girl at the cash register in a supermarket, a worker in a pharmaceutical concern or a foreman retired through injury who now keeps a bar near Cidra. Too few of these people get into our contemporary fiction and I am only partly compensated for their absence by the delightful presence of such colorful characters as La China Hereje from Luis Rafael Sánchez's *La guaracha del Macho Camacho* or Manolo the cook from Emilio Díaz Valcárcel's *Harlem todos los días*. To say it a different way: too many leading personages in Puerto Rican fiction come from the Condado and too few from Barrio Obrero, so to speak. It is as though the problematic character of the Handsome Puerto Rican—his perplexity, passivity, and bouts of defeatism; his declarations of "nada" (nothing) and "no lo sé" (I don't know)—prompted writers to concentrate their energies on characters they feel they *can* get the measure of, namely the Ugly American and the *piti-yanqui*.

This disproportion between a delighted indulgence in negative images and a comparative neglect of positive ones is itself symptomatic of the influence of colonialism in our culture. Writers in countries that have won their indulgence—Mexicans, Colombians, Peruvians—do not feel it incumbent on them to expand their talents on satirizing North Americans or *piti-yanquis*, with the result that we get stalwart examples of the Handsome Mexican, Colombian, or Brazilian in their books, ranging from decidedly heroic, outré figures like Aureliano Buendía and Antonio Conselheiro, to modest but inspiring figures like Vera in *La consagración de la primavera* or Pedro Camacho in *La tía Julia y el escribidor*. As it is, contemporary Puerto Rican literature often strikes me as in bondage to the exotic and deformed, perhaps commensurate with what José Luis González has called the "abnormal reality" of contemporary Puerto Rican life.

We should not allow our reality to be defined simply in negative terms as *not this* and *not that*; that way the ideal Puerto Rican, or what I have called the Handsome Puerto Rican, becomes merely a man or woman who dislikes the gringo and refuses to be a *piti-yanqui*. The worst of our marriage to North America perhaps lies in the fact that even in our rejections we become inextricably involved with, and modified by, the things we reject. If this is indeed the case, then the quicker we get a divorce and invest in a new set of images the better.

Notes

1. René Marqués, *La mirada* (Río Piedras: Antillana, 1976). Although I make reference to *La mirada* throughout the text, I will use the English-language translation for all further quotations. See *The Look*, trans. Charles Pilditch (New York: Senda Nueva de Ediciones, 1983), pp. 38–39.
2. Emilio Díaz Valcárcel, *Mi mamá me ama* (Barcelona: Seix Barral, 1981), p. 17.
3. "El problema de la lengua de Puerto Rico es fundamentalmente un problema político." See Arcadio Díaz Quiñones, *Conversación con José Luis González* (Río Piedras: Huracán, 1976), p. 24.
4. Luis Rafael Sánchez, *La guaracha del Macho Camacho* (Buenos Aires: Ediciones de la Flor, 1976). Although I make reference to *La guaracha del Macho Camacho* throughout the text, I have quoted the English-language translation in this case. See *Macho Camacho's Beat*, trans. Gregory Rabassa (New York: Avon, 1982), p. 53.
5. "aquí [en Puerto Rico] la población culta ha sido y sigue siendo la más afectada por la interferencia lingüística extranjera." Díaz Quiñones, *Conversación con José Luis González*, p. 14.
6. "Papi Papikins said: set a date and organize a get-together of teachers in your mama's molto bello garden: a get-together with uniformed waiters, cold cuts from La Rotisserie, barrels of Beaujolais and sparkling Lambrusco: a get-together that I'll pay for through my expense account for senatorial representation." Sánchez, *Macho Camacho's Beat*, pp. 104–5.
7. "La tipa de 306 no se sabe si es gringa o pueltorra, bródel . . . . Pide room service en inglés pero, cuando la pongo a gozal, abre la boca a grital en boricua." Ana Lydia Vega and Carmen Lugo Filippi, *Vírgenes y mártires* (Río Piedras: Antillana, 1981), p. 79.
8. Vega and Lugo Filippi, *Vírgenes y mártires*, p. 79.
9. Pedro Juan Soto, *Ardiente suelo, fría estación* (México: Universidad Veracruzana, 1961). Although I make reference to *Ardiente suelo, fría estación* throughout the text, I have quoted the English-language translation in this case. See *Hot Land, Cold Season*, trans. Helen R. Lane (New York: Dell, 1973), p. 205.
10. Marqués, *The Look*, pp. 90–91.
11. Marqués, *The Look*, p. 89.
12. "No se conoce a sí mismo a pesar de que sostiene una lucha interior por lograrlo. No sabe exactamente lo que quiere." (Río Piedras: Editorial Universitaria, 1977), p. 164.
13. See my review "The Good, the Bad and the Ugly Americans," *Sunday San Juan Star Magazine* (February 13, 1983): 12–13.

14. ''No había tomado a nadie en serio, desde que Henry la abandonara. Divertirse, a veces. Escuchar aquí y allá lo que se contaba, sin que las palabras la estimularan, por lo menos, a emitir una opinión. ¿Su posición de entonces? Neutral. Neutral en todo, y mucho más en lo que tuviera que ver con la política. Se topaba con personas de todos los bandos y ninguna creencia le hacía la menor mella. Neutral. Era mujer. Era ignorante. Era un pequeño vacío que obraba dentro de un vacío enorme.'' Pedro Juan Soto, *Un oscuro pueblo sonriente* (Havana: Casa de las Americas, 1982), p. 512.

5

Puertorriqueñidad: The Force Behind the Development of a Puerto Rican Theater

Bonnie Hildebrand Reynolds

In 1938, Emilio Belaval, at that time president of the Ateneo Puertorriqueño, delivered his famous manifesto entitled "Lo que podría ser un teatro puertorriqueño."[1] He began: "One of these days we shall come together in order to create a great theater, where everything shall be our own: the theme, the actor, the stage-set, the ideas, the aesthetics. In every people there exists an unimpeachable theatricality that must be recreated by its own artists."[2] By the decade of the 1930s, the situation of a traditionally Hispanic region controlled by a strong Anglo-Saxon nation had become a source of preoccupation for the island's intellectuals and led to the publication of Pedreira's *Insularismo* and to Albizu Campos's Nationalist Rebellion, both of whom called for the people of the island to acknowledge their Puerto Ricanness. According to Frank Dauster: "This eagerness to get to know themselves has been of prime importance in all sectors of Puerto Rican life; under the stimulus of a group of historians searching for the true character of the island, the movement became a wide-ranging probe of national reality. In the theatre, it lead to an attempt to establish a theatre which would reflect the island's reality."[3] Since the nationalist movement of the 1930s, artists and authors have become ever more concerned with the question of Puerto Rican identity, known as *puertorriqueñidad*. Through the years this concept has developed from a mere awareness of cultural differences and social and political injustices, to an overt expression of the anguish of so many years of exploitation, and finally, to a deeper probing of the validity of the ideals of liberty which often seem to lead nowhere.

The development and maturation of this search for a national identity has directly influenced the development and maturation of Puerto Rican theater as it exists today. Belaval closed his manifesto with these prophetic words: "As we transcribe our own life, a sponstaneous grace from the very earth will come forth, the Puerto Rican theater."[4] And so it came to pass. Confronted with the ever-changing world within a constant clash of cultures, those Puerto Rican dramatists who have attempted to discover and define their unique qualities as Puerto Ricans have created a durable theatre that is recognized worldwide not only as Puerto Rican, but also as Spanish American.

As we trace the theater's development since the key year of 1938, three works exemplify the transformation of the concept of *puertorriqueñidad*: *Tiempo muerto* (1940) by Méndez Ballester; *Un niño azul para esa sombra* (1958) by René Marqués; and *Revolución en el infierno* (1982) by Roberto Ramos-Perea. Each play approaches the concept with a different focus. *Tiempo muerto* is a dramatically sound play which, in a costumbristic setting demonstrates the social injustices in the life of a *jíbaro* cane cutter and his family. *Un niño azul para esa sombra* attempts to define collectively the character of the Puerto Rican island. And *Revolución en el infierno*, which had its première September 1982, questions whether the motivations behind the Nationalist Cadets' march in Ponce on Palm Sunday, 1937, and any other patriotic sacrifices made in the name of Puerto Rico, are valid in relation to the benefit accorded to the island and the resulting personal losses.

The year 1938 marks the beginning of the twentieth century for the theater in Puerto Rico for several reasons. That year, under Belaval's leadership, the Ateneo sponsored a special contest for plays written by Puerto Rican authors with Puerto Rican themes, awarding both a money prize and the promise of producing the winning plays.[5] Only two years later, in 1940, Emilio Belaval (with Marrero Núñez) founded the very important theatrical group Areyto, whose expressed purpose was to produce plays by Puerto Rican authors, thus following the Ateneo's example and responding to Belaval's own 1938 call to arms. The group, during a short life of approximately one year, was able to produce four Puerto Rican plays, among them Méndez Ballester's *Tiempo muerto* (1940). In a 1946 article appearing in *El Mundo*, René Marqués credits Méndez Ballester with being "the only author of the Areyto group that has remained loyal to the theater and whose interest in the stage has translated into various activities."[6]

Méndez Ballester's *Tiempo muerto* is a modern-day tragedy which dramatizes the miserable life of a *jíbara* family in the west coast sugarcane region. As the play progresses we witness the rapid decline of the family going from a state of abject physical poverty to a point of complete moral decline. This play is not an attempt to define *puertorriqueñidad*, but rather puts before the public the island's character of the 1930s—a class society based on authoritarianism and ruled by absentee landowners. The attitudes expressed in the play through the lives of the characters and through the stage setting are fatalistic, presenting these people as incapable of stopping their downward movement on the moral plane, but at the same time being at least partially responsible for it because of their silent acceptance of the social injustices they suffer.

The play takes place entirely in front of the run-down hut of a cane cutter, Ignacio, and his wife Juana. The author's stage directions present the scene: "The ranch, the patio, and surrounding minute vegetation convey a general impression of poverty, decay, sterility. A dried-out place, inhabited by shadows, in contrast to the green and golden sugarcane field."[7] Throughout the play, even in periods of illusory hope, this visual contrast between the world surrounding the characters and their own unproductive one, conveys constantly to the audience the futility of those illusions.

The play focuses on the family's moral decline as a result of the *jíbaro's* economic conditions in a feudal system. The old traditional values of honor and dignity are replaced by a fatalistic view of life in which there is no hope of improvement. The contrast evident between the two generations of this family symbolizes the development of this attitude and the resulting annihilation of the hopes of the younger generation.

The dramatic relationship which the play establishes between Ignacio and his son Samuel exemplifies this destructive direction. The contrast is obvious in both the physical appearance of each and the manner in which each reacts to the family's present crisis. Ignacio is a man of about sixty who suffers from tuberculosis, the immediate cause of his lack of work. The stage directions, upon his first appearance on stage, describe him as a bitter and disillusioned man. His comportment is that of a person who has no enthusiasm for life. This entrance is in direct contrast to that of Samuel earlier in the play. The son is described as a "young man of about thirty, tall, strong, full of life. . . . He is the impulsive type, nervous, and has the audacity that distinguishes the adventurer. He is affectionate. He enters with a light step . . . and greets everyone gaily."[8] This difference in countenance serves as an ever-present reminder of the kind of future to which a young man such as Samuel has to look forward.

The most dramatic contrast between the father's and son's reactions to crisis comes with the news that the foreman has dishonored Ignacio's daughter, Rosa. Ignacio himself reveals the choices each has to make as he says to his wife: "Juana, when something like this happens, one has to do either of two things: bring the bastard down with a machete, or take the matter calmly."[9] He chooses the latter when, in exchange for a job, he agrees to leave his daughter in the foreman's house as a concubine. He reveals his own desperation in a futile attempt to justify his actions when he says: "Years ago, when I was working and in good health, I would have solved a matter like this with a knife, even if I would have been riddled with bullets. But now . . . I don't know. . . . I don't know what has come over me. As you say, I've been drained out of everything. I don't even recognize myself. Sometimes I don't even know what I do.''[10] In this speech, he not only expresses his completely broken spirit, but also his total incapacity to face his problems directly.

Samuel, on the other hand, reacts to the news hysterically, and then makes the opposite choice as he goes in search of the foreman, seeking revenge with his knife. The son lays blame on the father for the turn of events because of the father's tendency to avoid the truth and his incapacity to face the situation as an honorable man. Ignacio's words to his son in combination with the play's outcome prevent Samuel's actions from taking on heroic dimensions, however, and keep the work on the level of social injustice, while proposing no solution. Ignacio says: ''When we are kids we are taught to tell the truth: that truth is God's offspring; but when you become a man you realize that you can't always tell the truth; that sometimes you must lie.''[11] He goes on to say: ''When a man finds himself, like me, without a job and with the obligation to sustain a family, to do so, one is capable not only of lying, but of stealing and killing.''[12]

The play's resolution upholds Ignacio's words but shows the actions chosen by both father and son to be futile. The foreman kills Samuel, and Ignacio then kills the foreman. Samuel's attempt at vengeance was more like an act of suicide, and Ignacio's comes too late to help either his daughter or his son. With no family left to support he resigns himself to his fate and goes off to turn himself in to the authorities. Thus, he, too, commits a kind of suicide, since it has been previously established that the *jíbaro* cannot win in a legal situation against the landowners. The final scene leaves Juana alone on stage where she expresses her family's physical and moral losses in a profound sobbing. Interestingly, the play's original version has Juana committing suicide. Méndez Ballester revised the work, however, twenty-one years after its première, and eliminated Juana's suicide. According to the author this second version was the way in which he had originally conceived the play.[13] This final version would seem to be faithful to the work's pathos and to the characters' broken spirits.

The significance of Méndez Ballester's *Tiempo muerto* lies in its choice of theme and setting. Coming on the heels of a call for recognition of *puertorriqueñidad* by the island's intellectuals, the play recognizes the social injustices of which the *jíbaro* was a victim. It represents the events in view not only of the social and moral environment within the sugarcane industry's authoritarian system, but also in view of the contrast between the natural green background of the sugarcane and the sterility that surrounds the characters. The result is a play which attempts to demonstrate dramatically the plight of the laboring classes in such a system. Because it offers no solution to the problem nor lays blame directly on any particular group, the work becomes a play of manners presenting the social, moral, and physical environment of the Puerto Rican sugarcane cutters of that period.

The Ateneo Puertorriqueño once again demonstrated its decisive leadership in the areas of the arts in the next theatrical impulse on the island, with the establishment of the Teatro Experimental del Ateneo in 1951. René Marqués, then secretary of the Ateneo, proposed the idea to the Board of Directors and, with José M. Lacomba, is credited as the founder of the Teatro Experimental. In the May 19, 1952 issue of *El Mundo* Marqués published the following reasons for the theater's establishment: "The Ateneo's Experimental Theater is an organization [created to] promote and cultivate the theatre. It has two fundamental goals: the first is to have audiences come to know Puerto Rican and foreign plays which by their very own nature would not be staged by commercial companies. The second is to place the theater within popular reach by lowering admission fees to a minimum."[14] Due to the lack of local works submitted to the group, production began with foreign works, initially with Camus's *Le Malentendu*.

The determinating impulse for the future of the theater from this organization came, however, in 1953–54 with the production of Marqués's own *La carreta*. The success of the production was such that the troupe carried the work to the stage of the Tapia Theater where they could accommodate a larger audience than was possible in the Ateneo, thus opening the door to two decades of production of works by Puerto Rican authors on Puerto Rican themes; and also opening the way for the establishment of the annual theater festivals which the Instituto de Cultura Puertorriqueña has sponsored continually since 1958.

To date René Marqués has been the author who has contributed most to theatrical activity in Puerto Rico, and all of his dramas project the conflictive Puerto Rican political-cultural reality to a universal level. In this way, besides presenting the specific and detailed problems inherent in a colonial society, he attempts to define just who is the Puerto Rican in today's world. One of Marqués's best plays and one which best furthers his concept of *puertorriqueñidad* is *Un niño azul para esa sombra*, written in 1958 and produced at the institute's Third Theater Festival in 1960. According to theatre critic Frank Dauster, not only is this play one of Marqués's best, but also "one of the best in Latin America."[15] The play tells the story of the child Michelín, caught between the liberationalist ideals of his father and the materialistic, Northamericanized world of his mother. Although the play's various elements can be dichotomized between the two sides,[16] and Michelín undoubtedly belongs on the freedom side, his position is really much more complex than would appear on the surface. The liberty for which Michelín struggles is that of the individual's right to his own unique identity. This child, however, is prevented from exercising that right because of the "shadows" that prevail in his life. His mother, Mercedes, controls his physical world and he lives in the material luxury that has resulted from the choices his mother has made in her life. His emotional, inner world, however, depends on a self-created, false relationship with a nonexistent father. This is an illusory relationship originally encouraged by his father's adopted sister, Cecilia, and later developed as an integral part of Michelín's own imagined world. Both sets of values—the mother's and the father's—so dominate Michelín's life that he is constantly torn between them with never an opportunity to develop any meaningful values that are truly his own. In the end, the only freedom which Michelín can exercise is that of choosing to create the circumstances of his own death.

Through a series of interrelated signals transmitted to the audience, the play creates an impression of temporal coetaneity which signifies a life and death crisis for the child protagonist. Michelín, who finds himself trapped between the heroic ideals of his father and the worldly values of his mother, embodies a two-dimensional crisis: that of the anguished individual within the realm of humanity; and that of the island of Puerto Rico under the shadow of a larger powerful nation. In the temporal approach which Marqués takes in this work, the second act is of prime importance. Because the action occurs as part of a child's dream, no time actually passes in the play's story. Due to the nature of the second act, past, present, and future coexist in a world of circular, rather than forward movement. This combination of circular movement and temporal coetaneity guides us to an understanding of the present, real anguish which Michelín suffers, and of the symbolic meaning behind his death.

We sense the frustration of movement as we detect strong parallels between Michelín and his father Michel. Throughout the second act, in which we seem to enter Michelín's innermost consciousness, we are made aware of the establishment of a very close symbolic relationship between the child and his father. This, in turn, leads us to perceive strong similarities in the life patterns of each one. One of the strongest relationships develops out of Mercedes' destruction of the large *quenepo* (honeyberry tree) that had once stood on the terrace, and of her similar destruction of Michel's manuscripts, which were his only hope of creating a future for himself after his release from prison. Michel's words exemplify the importance of the tree and of the manuscripts in both lives. He says of Michelin's fondness for the *quenepo*: "But in his loneliness our son made of it a companion, a confident, a . . . protector."[17] Of his own manuscripts, he says: "The only hope that I had left . . . my only foothold. . . . What a total destruction!"[18] In neither case was either father or son capable of preventing the obliteration of that last vestige of security. And, in both cases, Mercedes, representative of the materialistic world, is the person responsible for the annihilation of hope.

The accumulation of such parallels leads us to perceive the similar life patterns of Michelín and his father. The father comes from a past whose history is tied to France and to Puerto Rico during a period when his own father and grandfather were also searching for freedom. Those past worlds were not really Michel's own, however, as he is a man of thoughts, not of action.[19] His own future lies in the Bowery of New York where he dies an alcoholic. Michelín's past consists of a father who was in prison for most of his son's life, a mother who has adopted foreign values, and of Cecilia—raised a sister to Michel—who offers the child an attractive set of values related to his father's family and the past tradition, but which prove to be false because Michelín, as an individual, has no place in that world.

The final correspondence in the similar life comes with death. The father destroys himself with alcohol while the son destroys himself with another liquid—the poison used to kill the tree. Both die a lonely death, the only difference being that the father leaves a son—a sign of optimism for the future—but the son leaves no hope for a future at all. Although father and son represent two generations—normally a sign of forward movement in time—their parallel life patterns in which failures repeat themselves and ideals are lost would indicate the incidents of time to be representative and nonprogressive.

In this play, Michelín is the representative of his own society—a society whose potential is symbolized in a child on the verge of manhood. He stands for a society, however, trapped in a state of nonprogress, between the conflicting ideals of U.S. materialism and the quest for freedom and individuality—a conflict in which Puerto Rico's own identity and potential might become a victim as do Michelín's; or might be saved because of the lesson to be learned from his example. Michelín's death would seem to be a message which demonstrates the dimensions of the conflict the play portrays. This is a struggle in which the status quo relationship with the United States signals the death of a cultural identity and political progress for the island of Puerto Rico, and in which the materialistic ideals signal the destruction of artistic creativity and philosophical progress on the level of the individual.

Luis Rafael Sánchez seemed to be following the direction which Marqués had firmly set, especially with the appearance of Sánchez's *O casi el alma* (1964) and *Antígona Pérez* (1968). Unfortunately, that promising dramatist changed his course for an also promising career as a prose writer. That action as well as Marqués's stubborn reluctance to write plays after *David y Jonatán* and *Tito y Bernice* in 1970,[20] followed by his untimely death in 1979, left a void in the island's serious theater in the decade of the 1970s. Only with the appearance of Roberto Ramos-Perea, a young student of theater at the University of Puerto Rico in the 1980s, do we see what seems to be a return to well-crafted theater with serious Puerto Rican themes. Significantly, one of

Ramos-Perea's best plays to date, *Ese punto de vista*, had its première in the Ateneo's theater on May 6, 1982. In what may prove to be yet another milestone in the continuing development of Puerto Rican theater, his *Revolución en el infierno* was produced in September 1982 as part of the University Theater Department's Primer Encuentro de Dramaturgia Universitaria. Traditionally, the university's drama department has not been a patron of Puerto Rican theater as much as it has of theater from other parts of the world. As reported in *El Teatrero*, the bulletin of the University Theater Students' Association, the Primer Encuentro came about "to promote and stimulate young Puerto Rican dramatists. We need to foment the creation of a new generation of dramatists who [through their works] respond to the social, political, moral, and economic demands of our times."[21] Although there were technical problems that forced the play's date to be changed, in addition to a lack of enthusiasm on the part of the Drama Department's administration, the University Theater Department is to be commended on this activity.

Revolución en el infierno is about *puertorriqueñidad*, but it is not a political diatribe nor does it attempt to define the concept. Rather, it calls for a total reassessment of patriotic values as it questions ideals of *puertorriqueñidad*. The theme of the play is that of making choices, as exemplified by one of the victims of the Palm Sunday Massacre of March 21, 1937. The author, in his preface to the play, tells us that the characters are real and the names have not been changed. The play is divided into six impressionistic scenes with the massacre itself taking place in scene three, the very middle of the play. While there is obvious sympathy for the victims, the play does not concentrate on the ideology of the nationalists who took part in the parade that ended in disaster. Rather, it focuses on the choices that one participant, Ulpiano Perea (the author's uncle) made, his own motives, ideas, and personal anguish, and on the reactions of those who survived the massacre.

Ulpiano is torn between the patriotic loyalty advocated by his friends and his future wife, and loyalty to his family for which he is the sole provider. His friends constantly urge him to participate, giving him reasons that are rote repetitions of patriotic statements. His fiancée, Rosario, tells him: "But you must go tomorrow. Do you know why? Because if we do not protest the confirmation of the sentence, if we do not protest the incarceration, he is going to rot in jail and the struggle must go on. The more we are, the more we'll be able to accomplish. We have to show those Yankees that this is ours. We have to show them no matter how."[22] To all of the similar incitations Ulpiano responds that there must be another way, that one needs to think more before acting, rather than merely reacting.

Only after his death, does the play suggest a resolution to Ulpiano's doubts about the validity of the cadets' sacrifice. The six scenes, as well as scenes within each scene, alternate between the personal responsibility of one man to his family and to himself and the idealized, patriotic loyalty represented in martyrdom. Ulpiano reveals his personal place in the struggle as he says, more to himself than to his young sister Sarito, at the end of the first scene:

> I swear to you that it doesn't matter if I have to die. What I don't want is to die in vain, because he who dies for nothing is worth nothing. And I think that I am worth something. I think that I am someone to Don Pedro, and if not to Don Pedro, to myself.[23]

The play constantly reminds the spectator of this view as the drama alternates between the cadets' preparations for the parade and the police's preparation of the massacre, until both the ideal and the personal climax in Ulpiano's death.

Ulpiano is never presented as a coward despite his reluctance to take part in the demostration and despite his questioning of traditional heroic values. In his constant search for a valid reason for dying he becomes more of a hero than the cadets who walked into the massacre knowing that they were in a sense committing suicide but having no reasons that were personally valid for doing so. After Ulpiano's death, his friend Ramón, who finally understands Ulpiano's doubts, expresses a new view of heroism as he says to Rosario:

> Heroes don't exist. Men exist! Men of firmness and great vision. He who gives his life to serve others without spilling a drop of blood is more courageous than he who stupidly gives his own death for something that's unworthy in order to achieve that heroism that you are talking about . . . desperate people who only achieve failure and disillusionment.[24]

The play, however, does not end with Ramón's new-found understanding, and so only presents this as a suggestion (albeit a strong one) of the significance of personal choices within an idealized world. The play, rather, ends by presenting a question both to Rosario, representative of patriots who blindly follow someone else's ideals, and to the spectator, perhaps one of those so-called patriots. Rosario, who has lost her fiancée and therefore her own personal future, desperately clings to ideals meaningless to her as she seeks, but does not find, consolation. In an emotional speech which ends in a profound weeping, she tries to reaffirm her ideals:

> We know what it's like to leave life and possessions behind when patriotic duty calls upon us! We know what it means to grind our teeth when it's time to cry! We know how to shed tears of love when our men die fighting for the homeland! We know how to be good Puerto Ricans, fierce ones, because we know why we suffer![25]

Her sister Milagros quietly poses the play's final question as she responds:

"Are you sure that we know all these things? Are you sure, little sister?"[26] Thus, the final question carries the play to a personal level of the spectaror since the question is not only valid for Rosario in relation to the events of her life, but also for the Puerto Rican viewer in relation to his or her personal view of *puertorriqueñidad*.

In this view, as expressed in *Revolución en el infierno*, the old values of the so-called nationalist struggle for independence become obsolete. Ramos-Perea explains his position in the following manner:

> I do not think that our Puerto Rican theatre is in need of heroes. . . . What we do need are characters who with their conflicts and questions show us the naked face of the Puerto Rican alone; naked before his doubt and his choice. . . . The theater of nationalist struggle should use this doubt to trace the true hero, not the martyr, for the latter is only a model for a bronze statue in the middle of a plaza; the true questions which reevaluate the rotten foundations from which our aspirations to liberation sustain themselves and our most profound deliverance to struggle to eradicate the evils of domination and our own soul-tearing evils as a dominated people.[27]

Ramos-Perea, then, rather than defining *puertorriqueñidad*, calls upon his audience to make that definition by reevaluating past history and the motives behind specific choices made in confrontations with that history. He suggests that those patriots whose ideals and motivations are personally valid for them as individuals and for Puerto Rico are more valuable in the struggle for Puerto Rican ideals of liberty than are those patriots who blindly, without thinking logically, follow ideologies which have no personal validity. Finally, however, he asks that the audience consider the final question and search for just what it is that each individual really knows about himself, and thus, about his or her own *puertorriqueñidad*.

In conclusion, all three plays discussed, in some way, approach the problem of Puerto Rican identity, and at the same time as we can trace the transformation of the concept of *puertorriqueñidad* through these works, we can see that it is the constant concern for that ideal since the early part of the twentieth century that has not only initiated but sustained a theater that is truly Puerto Rican. Méndez Ballester's *Tiempo muerto* presents a "manners" view of what it was like to be Puerto Rican in the sugarcane society of the time of the play's writing. The play's portrayal of certain social injustices which would destroy the *jíbaro* in that authoritarian world dramatizes the *jíbaro's* total environment—social, moral, and physical—but neither lays direct blame nor proposes any remedy for the problem. In developing the concept of *puertorriqueñidad* as a motivator of the theater, this work is significant for its theme and setting as well as for being one of those produced by the Areyto group. We assume that its conception was due to the early incentives from

Belaval and the Ateneo, in addition to those of Areyto itself. In his masterpiece *Un niño azul para esa sombra*, René Marqués dramatically personifies his own definition of *puertorriqueñidad* in the child protagonist Michelín. Within this portrayal, Michelín embodies the entrapment of Puerto Rican identity between an idealized past and a materialistic future. This play comes from the cofounder of the Teatro Experimental del Ateneo, an author who, through his work, projected his personal preocupations about his own Puerto Rican world. In addition, he influenced those around him with his enthusiasm for identifying Puerto Rican existence. Ramos-Perea's *Revolución en el infierno* is neither a "manners" portrayal nor a dramatized definition of the concept of *puertorriqueñidad*, but rather, the play carries the idea of identity into what may perhaps be a new era. Through the dramatization of a controversial subject, the work reevaluates past ideals of Puerto Rican identity and calls for a conscious and informed choice that would make that identity personally meaningful to each individual while at the same time strengthening the patriotic loyalties of the Puerto Rican people as a whole. The success of this play as well as others by the young playwright makes a publication of his work appear to be imminent,[28] and further substantiates the importance of the *puertorriqueñidad* concept in the perpetuation of the truly Puerto Rican theater which Emilio S. Belaval envisioned in his 1938 "call to arms."

Notes

1. He delivered the talk as part of a Puerto Rican theater course which the Puerto Rican Atheneum sponsored from June 20 to June 25, 1938. Belaval's was the first lecture of the course. *Actas del Ateneo Puertorriqueño*, vol. 8, 29 December 1938, p. 127.
2. "Algún día de estos tendremos que unirnos para crear un gran teatro nuestro, donde todo nos pertenezca: el tema, el actor, los motivos decorativos, las ideas, la estética. Existe en cada pueblo una insobornable teatralidad que tiene que ser re-creada por sus propios artistas." Emilio Belaval, "Lo que podría ser un teatro puertorriqueño," reprinted in Francisco Arrivi's *Areyto mayor* (San Juan: Instituto de Cultura Puertorriqueña, 1966), p. 245.
3. "Este afán por conocerse ha sido de importancia capital en todos los sectores de la vida de Puerto Rico; bajo el estímulo de un grupo de historiadores que buscaban el verdadero ser de la isla, el movimiento se convirtió en un examen amplio de la realidad nacional. En el teatro, condujo a la tentativa de establecer un teatro que reflejara la realidad isleña." Frank Dauster, *Historia del teatro hispanoamericano: Siglos XIX y XX*, 2d ed. enlarged (Mexico, D.F.: Ediciones de Andrea, 1973), p. 74.
4. "Al copiar nuestra vida, surgirá una espontánea gracia de la tierra, el teatro puertorriqueño." Belaval reprint in *Areyto mayor*, p. 258.
5. Arriví, *Areyto mayor*, p. 18.
6. ". . . el único autor del grupo Areyto que ha permanecido fiel al teatro y cuyo interés en la escena se ha traducido en actividades varias." René Marqués, "Algo

sobre teatro puertorriqueño (Recordando un tema olvidado)," *El Mundo* (27 October 1946): 2.

7. "El rancho, el patio y la vegetación menuda de los alrededores comunica una impresión general de pobreza, de decrepitud, de esterilidad. Lugar seco, poblado de sombras, en contraste con la extensa llanura de caña, verde y dorada." Manuel Méndez Ballester, *Tiempo muerto* in *Teatro Puertorriqueño (Quinto Festival de Teatro)* (San Juan: Instituto de Cultura Puertorriqueña, 1963), p. 24. All references to this play are from this edition.
8. "Muchacho de unos treinta años, alto, fuerte, lleno de vida . . . . Es un tipo impulsivo, nervioso, y tiene esa audacia que distingue al aventurero. Es afectuoso. Entra ligeramente . . . y saluda alegremente." Méndez Ballester, p. 29.
9. "Juana, cuando sucede algo así, hay que hacer una de dos cosas: o uno matarse a machetazos con ese canalla, o coger el asunto con calma." Méndez Ballester, p. 80.
10. "En otro tiempo, cuando yo trabajaba y estaba en salud, un caso así lo hubiera arreglao a puñalá limpia, aunque me hubiese acribillao a tiros. Pero hoy . . . no sé . . . no sé lo que me pasa. To lo he ido perdiendo, como tu dices. Yo mismo no me conozco. A veces no sé ni lo que hago." Méndez Ballester, p. 83.
11. "Cuando somos niños nos enseñan a que digamos la verdad: que la verdad es hija de Dios; pero cuando uno se vuelve un hombre se da cuenta de que la verdad no se pué decir siempre; que a veces hay que mentir." Méndez Ballester, p. 106.
12. "Cuando un hombre se encuentra, como yo, sin trabajo y con una obligación de sostener una familia, pa sostenerla, uno es capaz, no digo yo de mentir, sino de robar y matar." Méndez Ballester, p. 106.
13. Notes at the end of the work. *Tiempo muerto* (San Juan: n.p., 1976), p. 127.
14. "El Teatro Experimental del Ateneo es una organización para el fomento y cultivo del teatro. Tiene dos objetivos fundamentales: El primero es dar a conocer obras extranjeras o puertorriqueñas que por su carácter no serían producidas por el teatro comercial. El segundo es poner el teatro al alcance de todo el pueblo bajando los precios de entrada a un mínimo." René Marqués, "Teatro Experimental del Ateneo se inicia con *El Malentendido*," *El Mundo* (19 May 1952): 13.
15. Frank Dauster, "New Plays of René Marqués," *Hispania* 43 (September 1960): 452.
16. See Juan Villegas's *Interpretación y análisis del texto dramático*, Colección Telón (Ottawa, Ontario: Girol, 1982), p. 68.
17. "Pero en su soledad nuestro hijo había hecho de él un compañero, un confidente, un . . . protector." René Marqués, *Un niño azul para esa sombra*, in *Teatro*, vol. 1, 2d ed. (Río Piedras: Cultural, 1970), p. 139.
18. "La única esperanza que me quedaba. . . . El único asidero . . . .¡ Qué destrucción tan total!" Marqués, p. 141.
19. Thomas Feeny discusses this attribute of Michel in his article "Women's Triumph Over Man in René Marqués' Theatre," *Hispania* 65 (May 1982): 188.
20. Marqués is said to have refused to write any more theater until *La muerte no entrará en palacio* were to be produced in Puerto Rico. (Information gathered in a private conversation with Marqués's colleague, José M. Lacomba, Summer 1981.) To date, that play has not appeared on the island's theater bills.
21. ". . . para promover y estimular la joven dramaturgia puertorriqueña. Necesitamos fomentar la creación de una nueva generación de dramaturgos que responda [a través de sus obras] al reclamo de unas necesidades sociales, políticas, morales y económicas de nuestra época." *El Teatrero* 2 (no. 1, n.d.): 5–6.

22. "Pero debes ir mañana. ¿Sabes por qué? Porque si no protestamos por la confirmación de la sentencia, si no protestamos por el encarcelamiento, se va a podrir en la cárcel y la lucha no se puede parar. Mientras más seamos, más podemos hacer. Hay que demostrarle a los yankis que esto es nuestro. Hay que demostrárselo como sea." Roberto Ramos-Perea, "Revolucion en el infierno," manuscript copy, p. 12. All subsequent references are from this copy.
23. "Te juro que si tengo que morir no importa. Lo que no quiero es morir en vano, porque el que muere por ná, no vale ná. Y yo creo que valgo algo. Yo creo que soy algo pá Don Pedro, y si no pá Don Pedro, pá mi mismo." Ramos-Perea, p. 16.
24. "Los héroes no existen. ¡Existen los hombres! Los hombres firmes y de gran visión. Más valeroso es aquél que da su vida al servicio de los demás sin derramar una gota de sangre; a aquél que estúpidamente da su muerte por algo que no vale la pena, para conseguir esa heroicidá que tú dices . . . gente desesperada que sólo consigue el fracaso y la desilusión." Ramos-Perea, p. 55.
25. "¡ Sabemos lo que es dejar atrás vida y hacienda cuando el beber patriótico es quién llama! ¡ Sabemos apretar los dientes cuando es la hora de llorar! ¡ Sabemos derramar lágrimas de amor cuando nuestro hombre muere luchando por la patria! ¡ Sabemos ser buenos puertorriqueños, puertorriqueños fieros, porque sabemos por qué sufrimos!" Ramos-Perea, p. 56.
26. "¿Estás segura de que sabemos todas esas cosas? ¿Estás segura, hermanita?" Ramos-Perea, p. 56.
27. "No creo que nuestro teatro puertorriqueño necesite de héroes. . . . Lo que sí necesitamos son personajes que con sus conflictos y sus preguntas nos muestren la cara desnuda del hombre puertorriqueño solo; desnudo frente a su duda y su elección. . . . El Teatro Nacionalista debe servirse de esta duda para trazar al verdadero héroe, no al mártir, pues esto es sólo un modelo para una estatua de bronce en medio de una plaza; sino las verdaderas preguntas que revalorizaran los podridos cimientos sobre los que se sustentan nuestras ansias de liberación y nuestra más profunda entrega a la lucha por la erradicación de los males dominadores y de nuestros propios, desgarradores males de dominados." Roberto Ramos-Perea, "Teatro de Lucha Nacionalista en Puerto Rico," *El Teatrero* 2 (no. 1, n. d.): 5–6.
28. *Revolución en el infierno* was published by Editorial Edil in September 1983. Furthermore, Ramos-Perea's *Módulo 104 (Revolución en el purgatorio)* won the Ateneo's highest theater award, the Premio René Marqués, in the spring of 1983, and that play is also slated to be published, but details are not available at present. (Private conversation with Roberto Ramos-Perea in July 1983, San Juan, Puerto Rico.)

6

Image of the City: Three Puerto Rican Generations in New York

Frank Dauster

The urban experience is usually presented in the Puerto Rican theater as an exile, whether from the land to the city or from the island to New York. This exile has been a frequent, indeed almost an obsessive theme, and there is hardly a dramatist who has not dealt with it in some fashion. A good deal of attention has been paid to some of these plays, especially to Francisco Arriví's introspective intellectuals and René Marqués's tormented visionaries of a past that never was. However, few have noted that the earliest dramatic versions of this exile are earlier than we might expect, and that there have been fundamental and important changes in the manner in which this exile is presented.

These changes are clearly visible in three plays which appeared at intervals of twenty years: Fernando Sierra Berdecía's *Esta noche juega el jóker* (1938), Manuel Méndez Ballester's *Encrucijada* (1958), and Jaime Carrero's *Caja de caudales F M* (1978). All three present the Puerto Rican experience in New York in strongly negative terms, but there are profound differences among them; they provoke very different reactions in the reader.

Esta noche juega el jóker is, if not the first, certainly one of the earliest presentations of the New York experience, and it received the Primer Premio del Ateneo de Puerto Rico for 1939. It is also of considerable historical interest in that it is one of the plays which led to the foundation of Areyto in 1940, and through Areyto and its successors to the development of the modern theater in Puerto Rico.

Esta noche juega el jóker is a sophisticated comedy which uses a stock theme of French farse to present the conflict between tradition and new forms of life encountered in the metropolis. Its characters are not all Puerto Rican; several are from other Latin countries, but they are all coping with the monstrous city. But as the play develops, it appears that some of their problems in coping look a good deal less serious today than they perhaps did forty-five years ago. Although most of the characters earn their living in fairly humble fashion, they all seem to be of rather well-to-do origins, and they certainly do not appear to have any serious economic concerns. Indeed, a good deal of their activity is simply frivolous and hardly reflects the social realities of 1938. If we recall that the United States was barely emerging from the catastrophic Great Depression, the characters seem oddly untouched by social realities, spending most of their time dancing and partying. Nor do they appear to be aware of the degree to which most of them have already become assimilated to the dominant culture.

The basic questions of the play deal with the shift in customs occasioned by the economic situation of the married protagonists, Arturo and María. Since she has been able to find a much better paid position than he, they have exchanged roles: Arturo is cook, housekeeper, shopper, etc., while María provides the paycheck. The system works perfectly well for them, and they live both happily and in comfort, but it is really more than their male Latin friends can comprehend. Inevitably, Arturo is taken to be *poco hombre* (not much of a man), and María is fair game for a new friend who fancies himself an invincible Latin lover. It is only after Arturo's daring gamble at the end and María's declaration that things become righted and all ends well.

Aside from the general question of cultural adaptation, the play really has little to do with Puerto Rico or the problems of the exile. A series of secondary romantic intrigues—resolved by abrupt marriages and the appearance from the blue of previously unknown husbands, along with the discovery that the loyal family friend is in fact himself in love with María and conniving to replace Arturo—make us realize that *Esta noche juega el jóker* is an updated comedy of intrigue, a drawing-room farse set in the barrio rather more by accident than by any necessity. It is difficult to share Francisco Arriví's vision of the play as a reflection of the terrible city's effect on the family in exile, when in fact the city itself plays almost no role.[1]

This does not deny the play's validity for today, but it is an unexpected and perhaps unintended direction from which we perceive this validity. Much more than to the Puerto Rican experience of the city, *Esta noche juega el jóker* speaks to the effect on tradition and custom of a completely different way of life, and of the terrible strains placed on these mores. Curiously, the response Arturo and María adopt is much more in tune with 1983 than with 1938. At this point in time, Capablanca's self-righteous and egotistical Don Juanism is ludicrous and faintly ridiculous, but María is a thoroughly liberated woman, long before feminism had become a social force, just as Arturo is strong enough to be able to accept his own liberation. Driven by circumstances to a drastic change in the expected patterns of life, they have made the necessary adaptation and will survive. Rather than a social problem, the play deals with an individual moral problem brought on by social circumstances.

Twenty years after *Esta noche juega el jóker*, Manuel Méndez Ballester's *Encrucijada* was staged at the First Puerto Rican Theater Festival in 1958. Again, we have a family facing the pressures of an unaccustomed environment, pressures to alter traditional ways of life, but this is a very different family. Don Alfonso and doña Patricia are an aging couple who have moved to New York to be near their children, émigrés for economic reasons, but all does not go well. Social and economic discrimination are destroying them all: One son, Felipe, is a gambler and drug dealer, the other, Mario, is a neofascist terrorist, and the daughter works as a dancing teacher in what appears to be a rather shady establishment. The younger generation is trapped in a reality very different from that inhabited by Sierra Berdecía's characters. Instead of the elegant dialogue, we have a very inelegant "Spanglish"; instead of the elegant apartment, we have a few tiny rooms made even tinier by the need to rent a room. There is constant noise, symbolizing the emotional distress caused by the dislocation: music, shouting, the noise of the police sirens, and an airshaft which is a communal garbage dump. And don Alfonso sits totally uncomprehending the radical changes which face his family, remembering his alleged triumphs as a supposed officer of the American army in 1898. The play ends on a note of total despair as Felipe returns to his pusher mistress and Mario is apprehended by the police. The monster has won and the family is destroyed.

But the problems of this family are not basically economic; rather, there is a conflict of adaptation. The play revolves around a series of moral problems created, or at least augmented, by poverty, but beneath this problem lies another: identity. This is a family waiting for assimilation to happen, with widely differing attitudes. Felipe desperately wants to be American, Mario rejects assimilation hotly, don Alfonso dreams of past assimilationist glory. Each character wears a mask, hiding behind equally useless illusions. Only the roomer Antonio penetrates to the core of the problem: Each of them is obsessed by anti-Americanism or pro-Americanism, unable to see that there are other options. They are so trapped by their individual problems and reactions to the exile that they are destroying themselves. If the city is a monster, there are other monsters, equally dangerous, hiding behind each mask.

Oddly, Méndez Ballester was unable or unwilling to accept the implications of this view of a blasted reality. He appended to his play an epilogue which is startlingly and unexpectedly optimistic. Felipe and his cohort-mistress have reformed and live happily, it is presumed, in the Bronx; Marta has finally married the persistent Antonio, and they live in Chicago; while Mario, about to be released from prison, will live in Miami with his American wife and their son. All the ends are neatly tied; even the American janitor and his archenemy Chana are to be married and go off to presumed happiness in San

Antonio. In one sense, it is as though Méndez Ballester were saying that the city cannot be defeated, we must leave and make our way elsewhere in the classic pattern of immigration and dispersal. But this is not necessarily negative; Méndez Ballester makes clear that this is life, that every family must ultimately disintegrate, as its components go their own ways to found their own families.

This is clearly true, but the epilogue seems too easy a resolution, too forced. Chicago, Miami, New York, or San Antonio, the problems of the exile cannot be that simply resolved. The experience seems to have left few scars, and we are left with the unsatisfying idyll of the enchanted grandparents playing with their grandson, discussing with which family they will live, and considering a nostalgic return to the island for their last years. Suddenly we realize that once again the play has been resolved like the classic comedy of intrigue, with all the threads happily tied.

Jaime Carrero's *La caja de caudales F M*, recipient of the Premio Eugenio Fernández García for 1978, is anything but a comedy of intrigue. It is rather a vision of the savage realities and the desperate economic scramble to which many immigrants are condemned. In a further stage in the progression of the three plays, it is written in a mixture of Spanish and English, with a heavy admixture of obscenities; the action takes place in a liquor store, and includes a considerable amount of violence, both physical and emotional. The owners of the business are Vidal and his wife Marcelina. Like don Alfonso, Vidal has seen American military service, but all the experience seems to have done for him was to exalt the false reliance on force and to destroy his confidence in himself as able to cope with the world, without the artificial aids of his braggadocio and his gun. Like so many of these characters, Vidal hides behind a mask; behind his supermacho facade, Vidal is a frightened man, on the border of hysteria. He has only hatred for the gangsters who prey on the barrio, but in his desperate drive to economic security he ignores his qualms about selling liquor and willingly violates the law by opening for business illegally.

It is Marcelina who provides the surprise of the play. She matches Vidal obscenity for obscenity, and ultimately she is stronger than he and better able to deal with the thugs who invade the store. Born in New York, Marcelina is more aware of being Puerto Rican than is Vidal; it is she who retains courage and imagination when they are apparently defeated.

Here is the greatest break with the other two plays. *Esta noche juega el jóker* is a traditional comedy of intrigue, with relatively little in the way of character development or dramatic revelation; *Encrucijada* is more a portrait of people who change drastically than an examination of the human spirit in process of change under extreme pressure. But Carrero's play, for all its bitter vision and seeming despair, shows us the power to overcome adversity. If

Encrucijada deals with the sacrifice for economic gain, in *Caja de caudales F M* Vidal and Marcelina learn that the sacrifice is too great to be tolerated. It is Marce's lead which enables Vidal to overcome his disguised cowardice, to see himself again as a man and to overcome both the enemies and himself. Marcelina does not achieve liberation only because she has always been a free spirit, and it is through her example that Vidal is able to free himself.

All three plays show their characters triumphing over the trauma of exile, but in very different ways. There is a clear development, almost certainly not accidental, from the middle class to displaced lower middle class to working class. Sierra Berdecía's mannequins go on living their adaptive lives, remote from any kind of social reality. Méndez Ballester's family is all but destroyed by the unrelenting pressure of the hostile environment, and they are saved only by some very last-minute conversions and a sort of *deus ex machina* epilogue. It is Carrero's much more negative and pessimistic view which leads paradoxically to a more positive ending, in which the characters are able to triumph over the city, which means that they are able to triumph over themselves and to establish the basis for a better kind of existence, without ever abandoning what they truly are.

Note

1. See Arriví, "Segundo festival de teatro del Instituto de Cultura Puertorriqueña," *Teatro puertorriqueño: segundo festival* (San Juan: ICP, 1960), p. 11, where he calls the play "una definición teatral del alma puertorriqueña."

7

The Puerto Rican in Popular U.S. Literature: A Culturalist Perspective

Marvin A. Lewis

In a recent essay comparing the social status of Puerto Ricans to that of other Hispanic groups in the United States, *U.S. News and World Report* makes the following remarks concerning the Puerto Rican population after stressing the progress made by Cubans:

> At the other end of the success scale are the Puerto Ricans. In New York City, where more than half of the mainland Puerto Ricans live, this group has barely begun to build the economic and political power base needed to shape their fate. Studies show that Puerto Ricans: earn less than any other ethnic group on the mainland. In 1979, more than a third of Puerto Rican families had no workers in the household; hold a higher percentage of low-level jobs than other Hispanic workers; suffer acute education and health problems. In New York City, Puerto Ricans have the highest school dropout rate of all ethnic groups, as well as a higher mortality rate than the population as a whole from cirrhosis of the liver, drug addiction, accidents, homicides and diabetes. Notes Manuel A. Bustelo, president of the National Puerto Rican Forum: "The story of Puerto Ricans on the mainland has been a history of regression over the last 21 years. It's been difficult to point out their successes."[1]

In spite of this air of negativity surrounding Puerto Rican existence in the United States, it is possible to find positive evaluations of their situation. In a controversial study, *Ethnic America*, Thomas Sowell expresses the opposite opinion from Bustelo. Sowell maintains that "most Puerto Rican adults in the continental United States today are still the first generation where they are. Few groups in American history could claim more progress in as short a span as history is measured."[2]

Puerto Ricans are one of the most studied ethnic groups in this country and subsequently have been and are targets of many popular social scientific surveys and studies. Among the most noteworthy of the past decade are *Island in the City: The World of Spanish Harlem* (1957) by Dan Wakefield; *The*

Shook Up Generation (1958) by Harrison Salisbury; *Beyond the Melting Pot* (1963) by Nathan Glazer and Daniel P. Moynihan; *Spanish Harlem: An Anatomy of Poverty* (1965) by Patricia Cayo Sexton; and *La Vida: A Puerto Rican Family in the Culture of Poverty* (1965) by Oscar Lewis.

The Wakefield book is a descriptive approach to Puerto Rican culture. The author begins with a disclaimer: "I am not a sociologist or anthropologist, and I do not have the intentions of those professions to analyze or theorize. I am a reporter and I have the intention of a reporter—to tell you what it is like" (p. 15). Wakefield concentrates on immigration, religion, chemical dependency, gangs and violence, labor, housing, and politics, from the perspective of an outsider.

Salisbury's vision of Puerto Ricans reveals them as victims—of exploitation, of dope and prostitution, of chemical dependency, of gangs and delinquency, of the educational system, and of other class struggle. He views Puerto Ricans as belonging to a peasant class striving to reach the middle class occupied by Italians and Jews. Consequently, Salisbury's paternalistic attitude results in typical stereotypes of Puerto Ricans.

Glazer and Moynihan discuss migration, community, income, school, neighborhood, culture, contributions, and color before relegating Puerto Ricans to "the culture of public welfare." They seem disturbed by Puerto Ricans' inability to become a viable part of the New York ethos surmising: "But if the prognosis for high culture is doubtful, New York's folk culture—and in time, one feels sure, its commercial culture—is already affected by the Puerto Rican migration" (p. 130).

Sexton takes a more clinical approach, since her objective is "to describe some of the patient's behavior, appearance, symptoms and then to prescribe some possible medications." This she accomplishes through tape recorded interviews with citizens of East Harlem arriving, not surprisingly, to the conclusion that the problem of the slums is primarily economic.

Lewis's study of the Bronx and San Juan which many people view as containing a great deal of fiction, comes equipped with a set of theoretical views that are still with us today. I refer to his conceptualization of the culture of poverty:

> The culture of poverty can come into being in a variety of historical contexts. However, it tends to grow and flourish in societies with the following set of conditions: (1) a cash economy, wage labor and production for profit; (2) a persistently high rate of unemployment and underemployment for unskilled labor; (3) low wages; (4) the failure to provide social, political and economic organization, either on a voluntary basis or by government imposition, for the low-income population; (5) the existence of a bilateral kinship system rather than a unilateral one; and finally, (6) the existence of a set of values in the dominant class which stresses the accumulation of wealth and property, the

> possibility of upward mobility and thrift, and explains low economic status as the result of personal inadequacy or inferiority.[3]

This conceptualization represents the sum total of a number of popular studies devoted to the Puerto Rican during the late 1950s and early 1960s. Of course, the six categories outlined here are reflective of the condition of the people described in *La Vida*. In this case the end justifies the means. To a degree, all five of these studies take the same focus of the Puerto Rican as being mired in poverty, culturally deprived, and in a hopeless state of affairs. These preliminary remarks are only to suggest that the social attitudes and images associated with Puerto Ricans in this period gained greater sophistication and applicability in the seventies to both fictional and nonfictional literature.

Two fundamental concepts are essential to this study. They are "culture" and "ideology," concepts bound together in the author's world view to accentuate both thematic and structural unity. Culture is defined by Raymond Williams as "an emphasis on the 'informing spirit' of a whole way of life, which is manifest over the whole range of social activities but is most evident in 'specifically cultural' activities—a language, styles of art, kinds of intellectual work."[4] Ideology is, according to Williams, "the characteristic *world view or general perspective* of a class or other social group, which will include formal and conscious beliefs but also less conscious, less formulated attitudes, habits and feelings or even unconscious assumptions, bearings and commitments" (p. 26).

My purpose, is to determine how ideology and world view—through literary codes—function, in Anglo writers, to adversely portray Puerto Rican culture. This discussion takes into account both fictional and nonfictional texts, although in several cases the distinction is not clear. Works to be analyzed are: *A Welfare Mother* (1976) by Susan Sheehan; *Manny: A Criminal Addict's Story* (1977) by Rettig, Torres, and Garrett; *Fort Apache: Life and Death in New York City's Most Violent Precinct* (1976) by Tom Walker; and *Benjy Lopez: A Picaresque Tale of Migration and Return* (1980) by Barry Levine. These are works that do not merely mention Puerto Ricans, but rather seek to interpret their reality.

A Welfare Mother

In *A Welfare Mother*, Susan Sheehan describes a sad state of economic dependency. This book is the fictional biography of "Mrs. Santana," a woman from Brooklyn. In the epilogue Sheehan provides an indication of how she compiled her information. She remarks: "My note taking didn't bother Mrs. Santana, but it may have been a good thing she couldn't decipher my speedwriting."[5] She adds: "Virtually all of the information in the profile was obtained at first hand'' (p. 104). The qualifier ''virtually'' implies that some of the material may have been fabricated and the fact that the woman ''couldn't decipher'' suggests deception on the biographer's part.

During the two-and-a-half-years' relationship, Sheehan demonstrates a concern not just with Santana's personal situation but with her total environment. Mrs. Santana's neighborhood is physically degrading, in a sort of poetic way:

> Children who should have been in school amused themselves by jumping on discarded mattresses; young men who could have been working souped up the motors of their Chevrolets or ogled the young women who sauntered along in threesomes and foursomes, inviting their attention; mothers wearily pushed their infants' strollers and held on to their toddlers' hands; scruffy mongrels foraged in the ubiquitous mounds of garbage, and stray cats suddenly ran out from under parked cars and from behind abandoned appliances; drug addicts shot up in vacant lots; heroin pushers went in and out of a local candy store, undisturbed by the cops on the beat, who were presumably being paid off not to disturb them; old men sipped from bottles wrapped in brown bags, or slept off last night's drunk on the sidewalk. (pp. 38–39)

This particular combination of physical and human geographies represents a personification of the culture of poverty syndrome. Neither the traditional educational system nor the system of law and order appears to be functioning. Rather, a new set of social circumstances has changed the norms to meet the needs of a population which places different demands on society. In a negative vein *A Welfare Mother* stresses the inability of Mrs. Santana to supersede a situation designed to make her dependent and to destroy every positive self-concept she might possess. This external physical description is merely a point of departure. Mrs. Santana is also unattractive:

> She makes no effort to conceal her thick neck, her big breasts, her big belly, and her enormous thighs; on the contrary she favors tight fitting, scoop-necked body shirts with Bermuda shorts or slacks. Because of her weight, she is unable to take off her fashionable platform shoes unaided. Dancing, she quickly loses breath, but she goes on dancing. She is generous and lazy. (p. 3)

In addition to being obese and lazy, Mrs. Santana is culturally deprived. She ''had never been to the Empire State Building, to Radio City Music Hall, or to any of New York City's other tourist attractions. She has never seen a play or a circus, visited a museum, or belonged to a social or political organization'' (p. 75). Mrs. Santana is, therefore, incapable of participating fully in Anglo-American culture, due to personal, environmental, and economic limitations.

Manny

This text "traces an elaborate career of deviance" while bringing into focus most of the common stereotypes concerning unlawful behavior by Puerto Ricans. Manny Torres is subjected to a thorough clinical examination by the editors who remind us that "it is important to bear in mind that the biographical narrative is essentially a report on Manny's life."[6] What the reader receives, then, is an embellishment of events surrounding the protagonist's activities.

One of the central critical issues in *Manny: A Criminal Addict's Story* is *who* speaks and from *where* the narrative voice emanates. This is apparent in comments concerning the antisocial behavior of gang members when Manny observes: "Although the theme was social clubbing at first, it seems that we soon drifted into an almost ritualistic emphasis on violence." This is precisely the route Manny follows from the age of fourteen when he is first involved with gambling and chemical dependency.

At twenty, the protagonist is "a dope fiend all screwed, and on my way by boat to Sing Sing Prison" (p. 65). Manny's subsequent prison experience becomes a cliché of sex, violence, and drugs. This is only the beginning for Manny who is on a roller coaster of violence, crime, and institutions. These experiences are summarized along with Manny's motivations at the end of this text in a dialogue with Retting, one of the editors. Subsequently, Manny provides a criminology class at Humboldt State College with living evidence of what being a "real criminal" is all about.

Certainly, if one needed an introduction to Puerto Rican criminality, Manny would be an excellent point of departure. In his career, almost every imaginable situation is accounted for, since Manny is willingly caught up in a series of events over which he loses control. This book is almost a romanticized version of deviance for in the end, Manny is rescued from total nihilism and taught how to analyze his own case using the latest sociological and psychological methods. This approach makes Manny Torres more of a projection of the editors than a true reflection of himself. This may account for the distance between protagonists and material and the manner in which Manny mouths rather than lives his experiences. As in the case of Mrs. Santana, we are dealing with a negative presentation of Puerto Ricans filtered through the blinders of another culture.

Fort Apache

Fort Apache: Life and Death in New York City's Most Violent Precinct by Tom Walker, which has been made into a popular motion picture starring Paul Newman, is a depressing view of inner city, including Puerto Rican life and culture. This is the pseudo autobiography of Walker and represents a mixture of facts and fiction in the attempt to portray life in the forty-first precinct of the South Bronx. From the moment he arrives until he is transferred, Walker is engulfed in a sea of negativity, surrounded by people without hope or aspirations. Walker is quick to arrive at judgements based on superficial first impressions and misconceptions.

His initial reaction to the people and their environment changes only for the worse, since both the human and natural orders are out of kilter on Fox Street:

> Small children played boisterous tag along the sidewalks; clusters of men sipped beer on the stoops. Burned out buildings cast eerie shadows across my path. Automobiles slumped like derelicts, abandoned, stripped of their former dignity and supported only by milk cases. The street itself was full of holes, a pockmarked face on the verge of total degeneration.[7]

This poetic description of decadence emphasizes corresponding physical situations in the animate and inanimate worlds. A state of inertia prevails over a situation of economic impotency. The automobile image becomes a metaphor for the human condition where people, too, have given up, "stripped of their former dignity." Poorly maintained streets, abandoned cars, burned-out buildings, and unemployed men implicitly pose a question concerning the children's future, which does not seem very promising.

Walker informs us that most of the responsibility for the people's plight has to be shouldered by them. The socialization process, it seems, has been a failure:

> The only vestige of civilized authority here was the Police Department. The people struck me as being rather primitive in their approach to city life. Many seemed to be travelers in a strange world. Urbanization would wait for the next generation. They didn't hesitate to throw garbage into the street, or drive without a license, or take the law into their own hands. Without any regard for the rights of others, they did what they wanted. (p. 25)

The dichotomy is drawn between "civilized" and "primitive" to demonstrate levels of social progress, with the ultimate result being a breakdown in morality. Outward manifestations of antisocial behavior reflect the internal dynamics of hopelessness and alienation when faced with an intolerable physical and social environment.

Gangs and rampant violence are two outgrowths of this situation. In one of the more graphic incidents, Pepe, a gang member, is slapped by González for making a pass at the latter's wife. The outcome is no surprise:

> Armed with shotguns and knives, they stormed into González's apartment. First they tied him to a chair and forced him to watch as they repeatedly raped his

> wife. Then they cut her savagely with their knives. Finally, they placed a shotgun between her legs and pulled the trigger. Perhaps he felt some sense of gratitude when they turned the shotgun on him and papered the wall of the apartment with parts of his arms and chest. (p. 67)

This cumulative series of events and images, physical despair, moral ineptitude, and violent solutions contributes to a negative overall perception of people and circumstances. In *Fort Apache* these attitudes are transferred into a series of linguistic symbols and signs which structure both the literary work and the readers' perception of images.

In his discussion of linguistic signs and their significance, Ferdinand de Saussure explains that "language is a system of signs that express ideas, and is therefore comparable to a system of writing, the alphabet of deaf mutes, symbolic rites, polite formulas, military signals, etc."[8] Regarding the psychological and associative dimension of linguistic signs Saussure maintains:

> The linguistic sign unites not a thing and a name, but a concept and a sound-image (that is *signified* and *signifier* respectively). The latter is not the material sound, a purely physical thing, but the psychological imprint of the sound, the impression that it makes on our senses. (p. 70)

Following Saussure's line of reasoning pertaining to language as a system of signs that express ideas, it becomes apparent in *Fort Apache* that "Puerto Rican" is associated with negativity at the level of both *signified* and *signifier*. The structural relationship between Puerto Rican and these "primitive," "lawless," "violent," "travelers in a strange world" constitutes a linguistic sign which has been fomenting since the culture of poverty days of decades past. In this literary world created by Walker, "Puerto Rican" has no positive meaning because the referential structure of the language equates this concept with adversity and only validates it when it so does.

Benjy Lopez

Benjy Lopez: A Picaresque Tale of Emigration and Return poses several serious literary questions concerning the interchange between fiction and reality. In the introduction to this narrative the editor states:

> When social scientists approach the terrain of the literary artist, this apparent contradiction becomes even more troublesome. The medium of the approach is the life history, sometimes called the personal document, the testimonial, or the first person sociology. It is not clear how different the social scientist's work in the medium is from that of the artist whose style he is approaching.[9]

This apparent contradiction between fiction and sociology is very evident in the texts we have examined thus far. Although *Benjy Lopez* has many of the literary trappings of fiction, it is not picaresque in the traditional sense of being the fictional biography (usually autobiography) of a parasitic rogue. It is, however, a very picturesque tale of the socialization of a Puerto Rican. Lopez, in the introduction, is referred to by the editor as having "many of the characteristics of these modern literary heroes, and his story reads in many ways like one of these novels" (p. xi). Of importance, ideologically, is the assertion that "Benjy Lopez is to me a Puerto Rican Augie March." From a critical perspective, it is difficult at times to determine where the editor ends and where Lopez begins.

With these observations in mind, it is necessary to approach *Benjy Lopez* as a fictional autobiography. The tale, in first person, emanates from a present-day salesman in Puerto Rico who has either experienced or witnessed many of the ills of contemporary society. Lopez, a world traveler, has been a soldier, cab driver, merchant seaman, pimp, and salesman, among other things. This experience covers a time span of twenty years, fifteen of which were spent in New York. In summary remarks, the editor views these experiences in a positive light:

> Thus when an "American-smart" Benjy Lopez, for example, returned to an "Americanized" Puerto Rico, he brought a whole host of skills and tastes that he had acquired in New York and that he was able to put to his own use back home on the island. (pp. 197–98)

These "skills and tastes" include the dominant ideology which portrays Puerto Rican attributes in a nonpositive manner. Whereas "Puerto Rican" becomes a negative linguistic sign in *Fort Apache*, the same holds true in *Benjy Lopez*. In addition, the concept of Jew assumes the opposite positive pole in this latter text. This is an interesting juxtaposition since Benjy Lopez, the protagonist, is presented in the introduction as a "Puerto Rican Augie March," the protagonist of the Jewish novelist Saul Bellow's *The Adventures of Augie March*.

Benjy Lopez subsequently proceeds to give positive qualities to almost everything associated with Jews including education, employment, and social progress in general while denigrating Puerto Ricans. An examination of the portrayal of women will demonstrate what I perceive to be one of the text's central incongruities in its presentation of the image of Puerto Ricans.

Lopez considers himself an expert womanizer since he has had, he tells us, between two and three hundred women about whom he talks freely. The Irish prostitute who Benjy's uncle lives with is described as "very tall, about six feet and she was a hustler" (p. 73). Parallel to this the narrator surmises, "I ran into a young girl at school, a Jewish girl, very beautiful with blue eyes. I forgot her name'' (pp. 74–75). Benjy, of course, respects her virginity which contrasts with his approach to other women, Irish, Cuban, Puerto Rican, who are to be pimped, made, and laid. Specially, in another parrallel episode we are told concerning Benjy's friends:

> One of them introduced me to a woman, thirty, thirty-five years old, an average looking woman. She was Puerto Rican. I found out she was a hustler. (p. 110)

Almost in the same breath Lopez maintains:

> I used to go to the student building. I had a girlfriend I would meet there. Her name was Ruth. She was a Jewish girl from New Jersey. And she was great. She was beautiful and nice, that girl, and she was so intelligent and sympathetic. (pp. 110–11)

The adjectives ''beautiful,'' ''nice,'' ''intelligent,'' and ''sympathetic'' are not applied to the many Puerto Rican women who appear in *Benjy Lopez*. Instead, these women are constantly degraded and insulted. This is evident in one of the latter episodes where Lopez reveals his true colors in portraying a woman with whom he has cohabited for some time:

> She got pregnant. I got scared. I never loved the woman, it was just that I went with her to blast. She was one of those fucked up Puerto Ricans on Welfare. (p. 148)

These attitudes are maintained on the island, where the only woman who receives much ink is described as ''one of the girls from the Barrio de Matín Peña. She wasn't bad looking and she was clearly trying to get me interested'' (p. 159). As far as Lopez is concerned, Puerto Rican women are to be used and abused. While Jews are presented as being in positions of power in regard to jobs, the professions, and education, Puerto Rican culture is totally negated. Toward the end of the book Lopez remarks: ''I was beginning to realize that the average Puerto Rican has a job, goes to work, eats, drinks and that's it. Nothing constructed. Nothing worth living for'' (p. 150). The ultimate joke comes, though, when Lopez disavows his identity: ''The end of all this is that I am not a Rican. I am not an American, I am not a Neorican. I'm a fucking international—an international who's been splashed'' (p. 185). The initial metaphor of the book, *salpicar*, now becomes clear as Lopez has been totally immersed in a culture which has caused him to hate himself and his people and to therefore reinforce negative images surrounding their existence.

In popular terms, Benjy Lopez has had the acculturation game run on him to its fullest in acquiring the dominant culture's ideology, that is, ''formal and conscious beliefs but also less conscious, less formulated attitudes, habits and feelings or even unconscious assumptions, bearings and commitments." On the surface, Benjy Lopez's comments may be taken as the ruminations of a man of the world, but when scrutinized from a Puerto Rican perspective they are damaging, to say the least.

Benjy Lopez, then, in spite of its stated intention of positively portraying Puerto Ricans, falls, to a degree, within the categories of *A Welfare Mother, Manny*, and *Fort Apache* as works which depict them as welfare cases, drug addicts, criminals, without an identity, and at the mercy of circumstances. Many of the same attitudes that grew out of the culture of poverty rhetoric still exist but at a more sophisticated level. Through a mixture of fact and fiction, sociologists, novelists, biographers, and other frustrated literary types are able to create their own version of what they think a Puerto Rican is. Ideally, this is fine, but based upon the evidence produced, their attempts end in failure.

True, we are dealing with literature and not life, but the relatability of the two depends on the audiences' perceptions. In the case of Puerto Ricans these entities happen to coincide, since often we must depend on the media, print and visual, for insights into this group of people. As far as the written and spoken word is concerned, most language, as we have seen, is charged positively or negatively with meaning. In discussing the interchange between text and reader, Terence Hawkes, the critic, comments:

> Barthes's [the French critic] later theory has developed the notion that the process involves a no less complex—even ornate—structure of codes. The codes act as agencies—whether we are conscious of them or not—which *modify, determine* and most importantly generate meaning in a manner far from innocent, far from untrammeled, and very much closer to the complicated ways in which language itself imposes its own, mediating, shaping pattern on what we like to think of as an objective world out there.[10]

Thus when Sheehan, Torres, Walker, and Lopez attempt to write their impressions, their choice of words reveals more than an innocent description of people and events. Instead, the written word conveys attitudes that are reinforced by subsequent references to reciprocal human behavior. Would it not have been as easy to stress some of the positive qualities of Puerto Rican life? Instead, what is presented in these texts is the generation, confirmation, and reinforcement of a particular view of the world in which White, mainstream U.S., bourgeois values emerge as usual, as inevitable and right at all levels. *A Welfare Mother; Manny; Fort Apache*; and *Benjy Lopez*, then, are internally structured by the dominant ideology which referentially exacts external reciprocity. Therefore, the relationship between the statistics cited at the beginning of this paper, the numerous sociological studies mentioned, and the literary texts analyzed, will continue to support each other. That is, until some profound societal changes occur.

Notes

1. "Hispanics Make Their Move," *U.S. News and World Report* (August 24, 1981):60.
2. Thomas Sowell, *Ethnic America* (New York: Basic Books, 1981), p. 243.
3. Oscar Lewis, *La Vida: A Puerto Rican Family in the Culture of Poverty—San Juan and New York* (New York: Vintage, 1965), pp. xlii–xliv.
4. Raymond Williams, *The Sociology of Culture* (New York: Schocken, 1982), p. 11.
5. Susan Sheehan, *A Welfare Mother* (Boston: Houghton Mifflin, 1976), p. 101.
6. Richard P. Rettig, Manuel J. Torres, and Gerald R. Garret, *Manny: A Criminal Addict's Story* (Boston: Houghton Mifflin, 1977), p. 4.
7. Tom Walker, *Fort Apache: Life and Death in New York City's Most Violent Precinct* (New York: Crowell, 1976), p. 8.
8. Ferdinand de Saussure, "Course in General Linguistics," in *The Structuralists: From Marx to Lévi-Strauss*, ed. Richard T. De George (Garden City: Anchor, 1972), p. 67.
9. Barry Levine (ed.), *Benjy Lopez: A Picaresque Tale of Emigration and Return* (New York: Basic Books, 1980), p. x.
10. Terence Hawkes, *Structuralism and Semiotics* (Berkeley: University of California Press, 1977), p. 110.

8

Survival, Growth, and Change in the Prose Fiction of Contemporary Puerto Rican Women Writers

Margarite Fernández Olmos

In his work *The Political Unconscious: Narrative as a Socially Symbolic Act* (1981), Frederic Jameson describes the need for a reaffirmation of marginalized and oppositional voices. These, he claims, have been stifled by the hegemonic class in its exclusive perpetuation of a single voice in the class dialogue. However, according to the author,

> the affirmation on such nonhegemonic cultural voices remains ineffective if it is limited to the merely "sociological" perspective of the pluralistic rediscovery of the isolated social group: only an ultimate rewriting of these utterances in terms of their *essentially polemic and subversive strategies* restores them to their proper place in the dialogical system of the social classes [emphasis added].[1]

By "dialogical" Jameson is referring to a form of writing which reveals the dialogue of class struggle. This rewriting, appropriation, and cooptation of the hegemonic voice to reveal oppositional messages is characteristic of the works of many contemporary Third World writers and, in the specific case of Puerto Rican literature, several of its women authors. Often this perception of literature as an action upon its reader and its world takes the form of the suggestion of alternatives to the status quo without actually representing those alternatives. In general, however, it is reflected in a concern with themes that resist ideals which are oppressive, and includes a view of history which stands in opposition to the bourgeois perspective, i.e., it portrays the human situation as one of change, and manifests the historical, material, and ideological representations and distortions of the human condition.

It is not surprising that one theme which is met with frequently is that of the qualities and conditions necessary for survival. In a country like Puerto Rico in which cultural and physical survival are constantly threatened, this is to be expected. However, the form that message takes in women authors is often unique in that an element of their deconstruction and undermining of the dominant culture includes a noncapitulation to masculinist values which are perceived as an integral part of those oppressive powers. That is to say that women in a colonial patriarchal society must deal simultaneously with cultural and economic aggression from without as well as the traditional, anachronistic, and oppressive values of machismo from within.

Nowhere are the qualities necessary for survival in a hostile atmosphere more apparent than in the character of Isabel la Negra in Rosario Ferré's well-known story "Cuando las mujeres quieren a los hombres," from the 1976 collection *Papeles de Pandora*.[2] Ferré examines the relationship between a White middle-class widow and her deceased husband's Black prostitute mistress (whose character is based on the legendary madam from Ponce). Color and class differences between the two characters are brought out from the beginning in the contrasting epigraphs which represent each of them and at the same time reveal the plot of the story: their gradual merging and face-to-face encounter at the end.

Despite their differences Ferré manages to underscore a relationship between them in their common victimization by a man of power—acquired on the basis of his sex and control of capital. What is perhaps most interesting is the irony of the situation of the "good" wife, who, in spite of the economic and social privileges she derives from her class, race, and marital status, is the weaker of the two. Her passivity and submission to the Christian view of women as advocated by Saint Paul in the opening epigraph, result in her weakness, powerlessness, and withdrawal from the world. Ironic, too, is the fact that the prostitute, whose ethics and moral choices are subservient to survival skills and directly contradict the traditional values of the chaste and obedient wife, is the one the reader comes to identify with and even admire for her frankness, energy, and determination. The story manifests the tension between the vitality of existence of Isabel la Negra and the rigidity of social myth of the widow, Isabel Luberza. It casts doubt as well on the validity of conventional views of male/female roles as practiced by "respectable" women. Real power which includes competence and economic manipulation is contrasted with an imagined, artificial one based on marital duty and "following the rules."

The story therefore examines the consequences of a false perception of the nature of power. The myth of female influence based on sexual attraction and those feminine secrets passed on from mother to daughter which are said to control a man are tried unsuccessfully by the widow on her husband.

> It was then that I decided to win you by other means, by means of that old-fashioned wisdom that I had inherited from my mother and my mother from

> her mother. I began to place daily the napkin inside the silver hoop next to your plate, to put drops of lemon in your glass, to sun your clothes over burning zinc plates myself. I would place the sheets over your bed still warm from the sun, white and soft under the palm of the hand like a wall of lime, spreading them always inside out in order to fold them right side out so as to display, and to delight you when you went to bed, an extravagant blend of roses and butterflies, loving yarns of the most tenuous pink, of a pink so fine as to remind you of the lineage of our surnames, making sure that the stems of our initials always fell exactly under the sensible underside of your forearm, in order to wake you up with their delicious touch of pure silk, the sacred fidelity owed to our union. But everything was useless. Daisies thrown at pigs. Pearls to a pile of manure.[3]

In contrast the author presents the wordly manipulations of Isabel la Negra who is described as a self-made woman with an open-eyed awareness about the nature of things.

> When you began to grow old, Ambrosio, luck turned on my side. You would only feel pleasure when watching me in bed with those young guys that you used to bring me all the time and you began to feel afraid that they would come to see me behind your back, that they would pay me more than you did, that after all I would abandon you. It was then that you made the notary come, and you wrote a new will equally benefiting your wife and me. Isabel la Negra looked at the sumptuously decorated walls of the living room and she thought that the house was perfect for her new Dancing Hall. From now on no more wasted fucks, no more in and out for ten bucks, the kings come and go and we, always poor. As long as the Dancing Hall is in the slum, even if it's a marvelous one, no one is going to pay more than ten bucks a night. But here in this house and in this neighborhood things will change. I'll hire a few gals to help me at fifty bucks a fuck or get lost. No more old whores in this house, no more lousy eating, wrinkled clitoris like orange seeds or irritated ones like dumps of salt, no more sex in the bush or in cots full of roaches . . . this is going to be a house of double the fun or nothing.[4]

The outcome of a false consciousness of power and a blind dependence for the widow is her loneliness, withdrawal from the world, and a perverse need for self-mortification. Her attempts at changing her husband's mistress are directed inwardly and are ultimaltely self-defeating.

> In time, however, I came to realize that those sacrifices were not enough, that in some way she deserved much more. I would imagine her in the cot with you, adopting the most vile positions, being caressed passionately, letting herself get fucked through the front and the back. In a way I had fun imagining her this way, like molasses, subjecting herself to those things to which a respectable woman would never submit. It was then that I began to punish myself harshly, imagining her drowned in that corruption but always forgiving her, forgiving her in every cup of hot coffee that I drank to produce blisters in my throat, forgiving her in every fresh wound that I got in my fingertips when preparing

> meat, healing them slowly with salt. But everything turned to dust Ambrosio, you destroyed everything with a single blow when you left her half of your inheritance, the right to own part of the house, at any moment she wished to do so.[5]

It is interesting to note that where Ferré's story ends—a violent encounter between the two women who had imagined each other for many years—Manuel Ramos Otero's short story "La última plena que bailó Luberza" from the collection *El cuento de la mujer del mar*[6] picks up. He portrays an old and physically grotesque Isabel la Negra whose power is of an oppressive and exploitative nature and who is no longer victim but victimizer. The fact that a male author has presented the same character in a negative light should not be confused with the misogynous image of women in such earlier writers as René Marqués, for whom machismo was a positive value, "the last cultural bulwark from which one could still combat the collective [Puerto Rican] docility."[7] Whereby Marqués's rejection of the Americanization of Puerto Rico—which he felt included the destruction of the values of an agrarian patriarchal structure, an adaptation of "Anglo-Saxon matriarchy," and unwelcome changes in the traditional role of women—"translated into the prevalence of a stereotyped or negative image of the woman as a literary character, especially when she does not conform to or breaks away from her traditional role,"[8] not all portrayals of socially unacceptable women characters have a misogynous intent. Ramos Otero's story examines another position relevant to power and survival: the belief by some that for women to attain equality they most move into a power structure and emulate "male" values of dominance and agression. Although machismo is perceived as a return to traditional Hispanic values and the method of preserving Puerto Rican nationality in authors like Marqués, the adaptation of masculinist values by Isabel la Negra in this story reveals the oppressive nature of those same ideals and a corruption of power.

The sensual clever woman of the Ferré story, dominated and exploited by men of wealth, is in the Ramos Otero story a woman who has reached the end of her life and has used her own wealth and power to dominate and exploit others, and even to purchase what can only occur to those for whom money is everything to demand: "Vengo a comprar el reino de los cielos para cuando me muera" (I am here to buy the kingdom of heaven for when I die). Her aggression is emphasized in the physical descriptions of "el pie deforme con huesos puntiagudos" (her foot deformed with pointy bones), "los dedos afilados como cuchillos" (her fingers as sharp as knives), and her Cherries Jubilee fingernails of the Ferré story are here "dos uñas color hígado de múcaro" (two fingernails as red as the liver of an owl). And if there is any doubt as to how she got that way, how her capitulation to *machista* values included a complicity in the destructive order of patriarchy, we have her own words

> that neither you nor that make-believe type of government can take on Frau Luberza, that if I would have wanted to I could have been senator and I would have done away with those full-of-shit murderers like you, but I don't have to be a senator but a lioness from head to toes to show you that no man is more of a man than Frau Luberza.[9]

An accurate historical appraisal of the changes in Puerto Rican cultural values and the changing status of women as a result of industrialization and North American political and economic domination can be found in José Luis González's essay "*El país de cuatro pisos.*" According to González, North American colonialism caused an internal upset in Puerto Rican culture: "The vacuum created by the dismantling of the culture of Puerto Ricans from 'above' has not been filled, in any sense, by the intrusion of North American culture, but rather by the ever obvious rise of the culture of Puerto Ricans from 'below'."[10] Not only is the culture of the masses replacing the values of the former landowning class, but also

> certain very important sectors of the same propertied class that have been oppressed in the midst of their own class. I am thinking, above all, of women. Can it occur to anyone to deny that the corrupt movement of feminine liberation in Puerto Rico—essentially progressive and just in spite of all of its possible limitations—is in great measure a result of the "Northamericanization" of Puerto Rican society?[11]

The integration of women into the workforce, the consciousness they developed as workers and as a result of their participation, and the fact that women availed themselves of educational opportunities, are aspects not taken into account in earlier portrayals of female characters who were often symbols of an imposed consumer-oriented lifestyle. Ana Lydia Vega's characters in the collection of short stories she coproduced with Carmen Lugo Filippi, *Vírgenes y mártires*,[12] are precisely those working women who, as a result of socioeconomic changes, have been participating in the workforce in ever greater numbers and are caught up in the consumerism of Puerto Rican colonial society. They are not the "castrating" females found in René Marqués, however, despite the fact that they have wandered far from the patriarchal values he longed to restore. There is a growth in these characters which is manifested in two ways: their economic power (limited as it is by their positions in the "pink collar" professions) and their sexual liberation, both of which are surprising and disturbing to the male characters. There is the "secretary of housing projects for Blacks," Suzie Bermiudez in "Pollito chicken,'' for example, whose political ideas are as inconsistent as her verbal switching from Spanish to English. Her perspective on the political status of Puerto Rico evolves from that of statehood to a call for independence after a sexual encounter with a Puerto Rican bartender. Or ''the Gal'' from ''Letra para salsa y tres sones por encargo'' who surprises the ''Guy'' she picks up and herself, in the motel she finds and pays for, by deciding that it is time to give up the virginity she had been guarding so jealously. After a humorous sexual encounter, ''the Gal'' tries some consciousness raising:

> The gal confronts the guy heavyduty. She sits him in bed, crosses her legs next to him, and with impressive fluency and meridian clarity she destroys the millenarian oppression, the perpetual ironing and forced cooking, comrad. Distracted by her own eloquence, she uses her bra as ashtray while emphatically claiming genital equality. Under the implacable light of reason, the guy confesses, repents, makes a strong commitment to amend, and fervently implores communion. Carried by emotion they join heads and fuse in a long equalitarian kiss. . . . Nature responds to the unisex call and the act is equally consumated.[13]

The male characters in these stories and in the one Vega co-authored with Filippi are unchanged by such experiences and cling to their machismo with ''the perseverance of Somoza, with the brazeness of the Shah.'' But Monchín, from the collectively written story ''Cuatro selecciones por una peseta (Bolero a dos voces para machos en pena, una sentida interpretación del dúo Scaldada-Cuervo),'' with his primitive analysis of female economic status and power, expresses it best:

> I gave her a chance to go to work at a bra factory because she begged me, that she got bored, that we could buy a new refrigerator, one of those that makes ice and spits water, and even change the car, hell, stupid of me to believe such a story. At first she was so sweet when she got home, baby this, baby that. Until she got into the union. It was then that my rotten luck began because when the first strike came she went to the picketing line. I let it go the first time but later she got the feel of it, and she became a professional picketeer and she wouldn't even miss a strike of dolls. She was picked up by some suspicious women, she told me that they were leaders of I don't know what. I advised her not to get mixed up in politics because this was the work of communists to me, that women belonged in the kitchen and that she shouldn't get involved in men's dealings, that she had enough taking care of the house and taking care of me. She almost swallowed me, I had never seen her so defiant, like a Black Widow, shouting and screaming: I am not a sucker, the problem is that you let yourself be pushed around because you're a Popular [party member] coward. It was then that the devil came over me and I smacked her, and the rest is history. I screamed at her, and I am not sorry for it though she brought it up at the Caguas District Court. Lesbian! You're a lesbian, like your friends. Damn those butch communists that enticed her. Because Anita was sweet and overnight she became a beast. Check it out, the next day she

> changed the locks to the house and she sued for ill-treatment. The damned woman won the case because her friends got her a lawyer; she got the house and the furniture and even a fucking child support for the kids that is eating me alive. It's a miracle they left me the car. Now they tell me that she is up and down and all around with a teamster.[14]

How do these men react to the changes in women? The final lines reveal them to be as predictable as the lament of a tango: "Pónganse a Gilberto, men. Se lo estoy diciendo hace rato: no hay como un tango pa olvidal" (play a song by Gilberto, man. I've been telling you for some time: to forget, there's nothing better than a tango).

Vega's latest collection of stories, *Encancaranublado y otros cuentos de naufragio*,[15] won her the 1982 Casa de las Américas prize in Cuba. The dialectic of power and dominance in this book evolves from the male-female relationship to an examination of the nature of survival from the perspective of the political oppression in the Caribbean and colonialism. There are, of course, elements of those themes in the first collection, just as there are similarities between colonialism and the oppression of women—economic dependence and paternalism, for example—and women are not absent from the second collection. As Vega herself says:

> Women appear by all means as theme, in the dialogues between male characters, and as heroines in two specific stories: "Despojo" and "El senador y la justicia." In this book I have attempted to work from a historical perspective on Caribbean societies and also from their myths and legends. I think that in many of the stories included in this book, women are there *without being there*. . . . And by all means, it is the feminine optic which tells the story of men from their point of view.[16]

The "feminine optic" she refers to may be found in a sensitivity to the need for a recognition of affinities and cooperation among all peoples, and *all* the people of the Caribbean; the awareness of a woman and therefore a member of what has been called "the colony within the colony."[17] This revolutionary consciousness which opposes the capitalist ideal of an exaggerated individualism recognizing the impossibility of individual resistence, also includes an awareness of the tactics of survival from the point of view of the oppressed: "subversion, indirection, and the disguise are natural tactics of the resisting weak, are social strategies for managing the most intense and most compelling rebellions."[18] *Encancaranublado* begins with a dedication to the "confederación caribeña del futuro" (Caribbean Confederation of the Future) and Vega demonstratres throughout that gender, race, and language differences can be overcome through a collective consciousness of historical affinities—and a protracted struggle—among the Caribbean peoples.

These themes were anticipated in one of her earlier works, "Puerto Príncipe abajo," from *Vírgenes y mártires*, in which a Puerto Rican tourist, a woman of color, is on holiday in Haiti. Her search for the country's heroic past brings her into direct confrontation with its devastating present. What she ultimately finds there, however, is much more valuable.

> You remember that you're missing a button and you ask for the price of the first one that comes to sight. Five dollars, he says. He is a man of a restless look. He labeled you: TOURIST. In spite of color, in spite of love. TOURIST: Like them. You say no, there is sadness in his gesture. You continue walking between voices, hands [and] eyes that call. A little girl stops you. She extends her hand as to take yours. A zombi's look. She slips something between your fingers. The five dollar button: Papa sent you this. You slip your hand in your purse to give her something. She disappears. Then an euphorical stupidity grabs you. And you return to the hotel with the relic in hand, refusing the autopsy. All puzzles of reencountered islands.[19]

The emphasis on similarities and connections among the Caribbean peoples and the anticolonial message of this story are further developed in *Encancaranublado*. Vega's choice of epigraphs is significant in this respect; quotes by such well-known anticolonial writers as Nicolás Guillén, Luis Palés Matos, and Julia de Burgos are found throughout combined with lines from popular songs and Caribbean folklore. The book is divided into two parts: "Nubosidad variable," which can be said to contain the thesis of alienation and separation, and "Probabilidad de lluvia," the antithesis of awakening and reivindication. The humor, irony, and intelligence of her first collection are present here also, as in the title story. "Encancaranublado," which contains a play on the proverbial three-men-on-a-boat tale. The inability of the men—a Haitian, a Dominican, and a Cuban—to cooperate on the Haitian's small craft headed for the United States almost results in their drowning. They are finally saved by an American ship and assisted on board by a Black Puerto Rican who dispels any illusions they may have had by informing them: "Aquí si quieren comer tienen que meter mano y duro. Estos gringos no le dan na gratis ni a su madre" (if you want to eat you better work, and hard. These gringos don't give nothing for free, not even to their mother).

Other stories from the first part include "Puerto Rican Syndrome," in which "Nuestra Señora de la Providencia" appears on Puerto Rican television to Junior, Daisy, and Mickey Colón—not as farfetched as one might believe since rumor has it that "la Virgen de la Santa Montaña" has actually appeared in Puerto Rico's Monte de Guavate and relates messages to the faithful on Saturday nights—and "Jamaica Farewell," a critique of the travesty that has been made of the ideals of a Caribbean confederation and regional independence. Delegates at a congress for "Caribbean Unity" join in a toast

> to the future of Antigua and Barbuda, to the health of Duvalier, to the memory of Somoza, to the triumph of Seaga, to the return of Balaguer, and the Free Associated State of Puerto Rico, armored showcase of the Caribbean.[20]

They conclude that

> the Caribbean was truly one country. Blacks, Chinese, mulattoes, Indians amalgamated under the protective wing of the star-spangled eagle, in an essence to join the pieces, separated by historical blows, by the old and yet always new continent of islands.[21]

"El tramo de La Muda" from the second part also deals with travelers on a journey, but this story is set in the nineteenth century and demonstrates the survival tactics of a Puerto Rican mulatto revolutionary whose cleverness and wit help him trick his wealthy fellow passengers into becoming unwitting contributors to the cause of Puerto Rican autonomy and the rebellion of 1868 known as "El Grito de Lares."

A final story which should be mentioned in the context of the themes discussed here is an allegorical tale entitled "La otra mitad de Pateco." Based on folklore and an element of Puerto Rican culture largely repressed and denied—its African heritage—this story relates the unusual birth of the primogenitor of a White plantation-owning family who is born with a White body and a Black face. The anxious father sends the child away to be put to death, but a slave takes pity on him and sends him to be raised by Mamá Ochú. The boy, José Clemente, never suspects his problem until one day he sees the beautiful Black slave María Laó and falls in love with her. After they bathe in the river and she runs away from him in fright, he glances at himself and perceives his dilemma. Asking Ogún to return him to his color, he receives this reply: "Entre los tuyos está tu color: cuando seas uno ya no serás dos" (among yours is your color: the day you become one, you will no longer be two).

The answer to the riddle comes to him one evening. A fire in the canefields has overtaken both the master's house and the slave quarters. José Clemente must decide which ones to save:

> From both sides came increasingly desperate cries for help and lamentations. As if moved by a superior strength, José Clemente headed first toward the barracks. There, jailed men and women banged against the walls with their hands full of scars. María Laó, also there, bravely pulled her father's shackles attempting to escape. A single strike with Ogún's machete broke loose the chains and set everyone free, as it is proper. Confronting the flames, they rapidly set out for the dark. The big white house blazed like an immense pot glowing in the dark.

> With the group of freed slaves following his footsteps, José Clemente got lost in the underbrush, once again. At dawn—and without setting out to do so—he found himself in front of Mamá Ochú's little house. The old woman was awaiting her protégé invocating Chango, Orula, Obatalá, and every single deity that came to mind, next to the river. She was surprised to see the young man, machete in hand, followed by his people, his body as dark as his head, and a maroon smile on his lips.[22]

Vega's writing offers a social vision which combines myth and history as a means of attaining a collective awareness and a self-apprehension of race and culture devoid of self-denial and the fantasy of "redemptive transformation in the image of alien masters."[23] Survival through personal and group consciousness of the true nature of power requires a shift from the focus on men and women as victims to that of agents of change, and an understanding that the liberation of women necessitates the liberation of all human beings. This need for an authentic, inclusive collective identity is an element of all those contemporary Puerto Rican authors who realize that in the goal of collective awareness can be found the means for a people to become the agents of their own liberation. Ultimately, there is also their recognition that "to write subversively in more than a means of exercising influence. It is a form of struggle—and power."[24]

Notes

1. Frederic Jameson, *The Political Unconscious: Narrative as a Socially Symbolic Act* (New York: Cornell University Press, 1981), p. 85.
2. Rosario Ferré, *Papeles de Pandora* (Mexico City: Joaquín Mortíz, 1976).
3. "Decidí entonces ganarte por otros medios, por medio de esa sabiduría antiquísima que había heredado de mi madre y mi madre de su madre. Comencé a colocar diariamente la servilleta dentro del aro de plata junto a tu plato, a echarle gotas de limón al agua de tu copa, a asolear yo misma tu ropa sobre planchas ardientes de zinc. Colocaba sobre tu cama las sábanas todavía tibias de sol bebido, blancas y suaves bajo la palma de la mano como un muro de cal, esparciéndolas siempre al revés para luego doblarlas al derecho y desplegar así, para deleitarte cuando te acostabas, un derroche de rosas y mariposas matizadas, los hilos amorosos del rosa más tenue, de un rosa de azúcar refinada que te recordara la alcurnia de nuestros apellidos, fijándome bien para que los sarmientos de nuestras iniciales quedaran siempre justo debajo del vientre sensible de tu antebrazo, para que te despertaran, con su roce delicioso de gusanillo de seda, la fidelidad sagrada debida a nuestra unión. Pero todo fue inútil. Margaritas arrojadas a los cerdos. Perlas al estercolero." Ferré, p. 40.
4. "Cuando te empezaste a poner viejo, Ambrosio, la suerte se me viró a favor. Sólo podías sentir placer al mirarme acostada con aquellos muchachos que me traías todo el tiempo y empezaste a temer que me vieran a escondidas de ti, que me pagaran más de lo que tú me pagabas, que un día te abandonara definitivamente. Entonces hiciste venir al notario y redactaste un testamento nuevo beneficiando por partes iguales a tu mujer y a mí. Isabel la Negra se quedó mirando

las paredes suntuosamente decoradas de la sala y pensó que aquella casa estaba perfecta para su nuevo Dancing Hall. De ahora en adelante nada de fukinato de mala muerte, del mete y saca por diez pesos, los reyes que van y vuelven y nosotros siempre pobres. Porque mientras el Dancing Hall esté en el arrabal, por más maravilloso que sea, nadie me va a querer pagar más de diez pesos la noche. Pero aquí en esta casa y en este vecindario cambiaría la cosa. Alquilaré unas cuantas gebas jóvenes que me ayuden y a cincuenta pesos el foqueo o nacarile del oriente. Se acabaron en esta casa las putas viejas, se acabó la marota seca, los clítoris arrugados como pepitas de china o irritados como vertederos de sal, se acabaron los coitos de coitre en catres de cucarachas, se acabó el tienes hambre alza la pata y lambe, ésta va a ser una casa de sún sún doble nada más.'' Ferré, pp. 37–38.

5. ''Con el tiempo, sin embargo, me dí cuenta de que aquellos sacrificios no eran suficientes, que de alguna manera ella se merecía mucho más. Me la imaginaba entonces en el catre contigo, adoptando las posiciones más soeces, dejándose cachondear todo el cuerpo, dejándose chochear por delante y por detrás. De alguna manera gozaba imaginándomela así, hecha todo un caldo de melaza, dejándose hacer de ti esas cosas que una señora bien no se dejaría hacer jamás. Comencé a castigarme entonces duramente, imaginándomela anegada en aquella corrupción pero perdonándola siempre, perdonándola en cada taza de café hirviendo que me bebía para que se me brotara de vejigas la garganta, perdonándola en cada tajo fresco que me daba en las yemas de los dedos al destelar las membranas de la carne y que me curaba lentamente con sal. Pero todo lo echaste a perder Ambrosio, lo derribaste todo de un solo golpe cuando le dejaste la mitad de tu herencia, el derecho a ser dueña, el día que se le antojara, de la mitad de esta casa.'' Ferré, pp. 42–43.
6. Manuel Ramos Otero, *El cuento de la mujer del mar* (Río Piedras, P.R.: Huracán, 1979).
7. Edna Acosta Belén, ''Ideology and Images of Women in Contemporary Puerto Rican Literature.'' In *The Puerto Rican Woman*, ed. Edna Acosta Belén (New York: Praeger, 1979), p. 99.
8. Acosta Belén, p. 94.
9. ''. . . que ni tú ni ese gobierno de pacotilla pueden con Frau Luberza que si me hubiese dado la gana hubiese sido hasta senadora y hubiese exterminado a los matones pila de mierda como tú pero no tengo que ser senadora sino leona de rabo a cabo para enseñarte que ningún macho es más macho que Frau Luberza.'' Ramos Otero, pp. 61–62.
10. José Luis González, *El país de cuatro pisos* (Río Piedras, P.R.: Huracán, 1980), p. 30.
11. González, p. 36.
12. Carmen Lugo Filippi and Ana Lydia Vega, *Vírgenes y mártires* (Río Piedras, P.R.: Antillana, 1981).
13. ''La tipa confronta heavyduty al Tipo. Lo sienta en la cama, se cruza de piernas a su lado y, con impresionante fluidez y meridiana claridad, machetea la opresión milenaria, la plancha perpetua y la cocina forzada, compañero. Distraída por su propia elocuencia, usa el brassiere de cenicero al reclamar enfática la igualdad genital. Bajo el foco implacable de la razón, el Tipo confiesa, se arrepiente, hace firme propósito de enmienda e implora fervientemente la comunión. Emocionados, juntan cabezas y se funden en un largo beso igualitario, introduciendo exactamente

la misma cantidad de lengua en las respectivas cavidas bucales. La naturaleza acude al llamado unisex y el acto queda equitativamente consumado." Lugo Filippi and Vega, pp. 87–88.

14. " La dejé il a trabajal a una fábrica de brasieres polque me lo suplicó, que si se aburría, que si podíamos compral una nevera desas que hacen hielo y escupen agua y hasta cambial el carro, carajo, tan mamao yo que me creí ese cuento. Al principio llegaba de lo más mansita, nene paquí, nene pallá. Hasta que se me unionó. Ahí empezó mi desgracia polque cuando vino la primera huelga se largó a piqueteal. Se la dejé pasal pol sel la primera pero después le cogió el gustito y se volvió una piqueteadora profesional que no se peldía ni un paro e muñeca. La venían a buscal unas mujeres medio sospechosas, ella me decía que eran líderes de nosequé. Yo la aconsejé, le dije que no se metiera en política polque a mí eso me huelía a comunismo, que la mujel era de la cocina y no debía metelse en asuntos de hombre, que bastante tenía ella con lleval la casa y atendelme. Pol poco me come. Nunca la había visto tan zafia, tan como una guabá, esgalillá, gritándome: Yo no me mamo el deo, lo que pasa es que tú te dejas mangoneal polque eres un Populal cobalde. Ahí fue que se me prendió to lo malo y le di una tanda e bofetás calle que pa qué te cuento. Le grité, y de eso no me arrepiento aunque me lo sacara en cara después en la corte e Caguas: ¡ Pata! Eres pata, como tus amigas. Ojalá y revienten esas marimachas comunistas que me la sonsacaron. Polque Anita era mansita y de la noche a la mañana se hizo una fiera. Fíjese que le cambió al otro día toas las cerraduras a la casa y me puso una demanda de divorcio pol maltrato. La condená salió ganando polque esas mujeres hasta le consiguieron abogado y se quedó con la casa y los muebles además de la jodía pensión alimenticia de los nenes que me ha sacao el vivil. Milagro que me dejaron el carro. Ahora me dicen que anda y que con un tronquista parriba y pabajo." Lugo Filippi and Vega, p. 134.
15. Ana Lydia Vega, *Encancaranublado y otros cuentos de naufragio* (Havana: Casa de las Américas, 1982).
16. "La mujer aparece como tema de todos modos, en los diálogos de los personajes masculinos y en dos cuentos específicos como heroína: "Despojo" y "El senador y la justicia." En este libro he querido trabajar a partir de la historia y las sociedades caribeñas y también de sus mitos y leyendas. Creo que en muchos cuentos de este libro, la mujer *está sin estar*. . . . Y de todos modos, es la óptica femenina la que cuenta la historia de los hombres desde su punto de vista." From personal corresponndance with the author.
17. Sheila Rowbotham, *Women, Resistance, and Revolution* (New York: Vintage, 1974), p. 206.
18. Judith Lowder Newton, *Women, Power, and Subversion* (Athens: University of Georgia Press, 1981), p. 9.
19. "Recuerdas que te falta un botón y preguntas cuánto cuesta el primero que te salta la vista. Cinco dólares, dice. Es un hombrecito de mirada inquieta. Te fichó: TURISTA. A pesar del color, a pesar del amor. TURISTA: como ellos. Le dices que no, tristeza del gesto. Sigues caminando entre el vocerío, manos ojos que llaman. Una niñita te ataja. Extiende la mano como para tomar la tuya. Mirada de zombi. Te desliza algo entre los dedos. El botón de los cinco dólares: aquí le manda Papá. Metes la mano en la cartera para darle algo. Desaparece. Entonces te agarra una idiota euforia. Y vuelves al hotel, reliquia en mano, negándote a la autopsia. Toda rompecabezas de islas reencontradas." Lugo Filippi and Vega, p. 98.

20. ". . . al futuro de Antigua y Barbuda, a la salud de Duvalier, a la memoria de Somoza, al triunfo de Seaga, al regreso de Balaguer y al Estado Libre Asociado de Puerto Rico, blindada vitrina del Caribe." Vega, p. 35.
21. "El Caribe era en verdad una sola patria. Negros, chinos, mulatos, indios se amalgamaban, bajo el ala protectora del águila estrellada, en un solo ser para juntar los pedazos, separados a golpes de historia, del viejo y siempre nuevo continente isleño." Vega, pp. 37–38.
22. "De ambas partes, salían cada vez más desesperados los socorros y las lamentaciones. Como movido por una fuerza superior, José Clemente se dirigió primero hacia el barracón. Allí, hombres y mujeres presos golpeaban las tablas con sus manos llenas de cicatrices. Allí también, María Laó, halaba bravamente los grilletes de su padre para buscar salida. Un solo golpe del machete de Ogún trituró las cadenas y puso, como es propio, a todo el mundo en libertad. Enfrentando las llamas, emprendieron todos veloz carrera hacia la oscuridad. La casona blanca ardía como inmenso anafre en la noche. Con el grupo de alegres libertos siguiéndole los pasos, José Clemente volvió a perderse en la maleza. Al amanecer — y sin proponérselo — se halló de vuelta frente a la casita de Mamá Ochú. La buena vieja aguardaba a su protegido invocando, junto al río, a Changó, Orula, Obatalá, y a cuanta divinidad se le antojó. Cuál no sería su sorpresa al ver aparecer al joven, machete en mano, seguido de su gente, con el cuerpo tan negro como la cabeza y una sonrisa cimarrona en los labios." Vega, p. 73.
23. Wole Soyinka, *Myth, Literature, and the African World* (Cambridge: Cambridge University Press, 1976), p. xii.
24. Lowder Newton, p. 22.

9

Salpicar and the Specter of Self-Hate among Puerto Ricans: On the Testimonial Literature of Modernization and Ethnicity

Barry B. Levine

For some time now I have been intellectually concerned with—and personally bothered by—the conceptual strictures that prevent observers from perceiving Puerto Ricans—as a group or as individuals—as heroic. Seeing someone as "heroic" is to see him as one who can successfully find a way to triumph over adverse conditions. Someone who is heroic is by definition not a victim, nor is he a product. Rather, he is perceived as vital, perhaps vivacious, indeed willfull, and certainly irrepressible.

This essay is a continuation of efforts to understand these restrictions; it takes off from thoughts I have expressed in *Benjy Lopez: A Picaresque Tale of Emigration and Return.*[1] What is new to my thinking are the reflections articulated here that are a result of mulling over Kurt Lewin's famous essay "Self-Hatred among Jews."[2] This paper takes its name from that essay.

As a sociologist, my interests are concerned with the social science literature, most especially that approaching the creative arts—the testimonial, first-person sociology.

Unfortunately, most sociologists begin to look at the world with specific axioms promoting cultural determinism. Having chosen neither his family of birth, his social class, his historical period, nor his society, the individual is conceived of as an unwitting victim of all that preceded him, not to say all that is above him as well. Pressured by the past and the powerful, the cards are obviously stacked against such a poor soul. Given such a vision, heroic action can be attributed only to he who changes the society in grand fashion; charisma can be found only in the hearts of new elites. Typically, sociologists thus approach the problem biased in favor of a conception of the individual as victim.

This bias has been carried forth in the testimonial literature, sometimes referred to as life history, personal document, or first-person sociology. In such testimonials individuals tell about their lives and the social conditions surrounding them. But perhaps in an attempt to avoid confusion with the genre, biography, a creative task of the humanities, as opposed to the social sciences, sociologists have deliberately stressed their duty to articulate how social conditions created, molded, indeed minted the individuals whose lives are displayed in their works. At about the time first-person sociology initially became popular, works spelling out the methodological assumptions of the new medium began to appear. One author argued in 1937 that "the problem of the life history is [to show] how the new organism becomes the victim or the resultant of this firm structure of the culture"; the life history, he continued, "is thus an account of the socialization of a person."[3] Social scientists, including those who produce testimonials, are thus obliged under such a norm to not simply articulate the social drama of human life as much as to demonstrate that this or that life is a product of these or those social circumstances. The badge of social determinism, even if it is a kind of retrospective determinism, had thus been assigned to first-person sociology as well.

Thus the methodological conditions for the possibility of the sad tale of the Puerto Rican testimonial were laid well in advance of its actual construction. Unfortunately, these conditions were fulfilled. As a result, the testimonial literature about Puerto Ricans has not been faithful to the Puerto Rican experience. The Puerto Rican has been presented as unable to take advantage of the world he lives in, unable to use it for his own purposes. Denuded of his vitality, the Puerto Rican has been made to look like a mere product of his world and is rarely portrayed as a producer of that world. There are virtually no protagonists who actively, heroically, and effectively "countermanage" the world they live in.

At first glance, one might expect to find a proud testimonial literature acknowledging the heroic aspects of the two central historical processes that have occupied contemporary Puerto Rico: the tremendous growth of the economy (even with all its problems) and the massive migration to and from the island to the continental United States (with all its consequences). Concerning the modernization of the island there is the discussion by Henry Wells in *The Modernization of Puerto Rico*.[4] Wells picks up René Marqués's characterization of the Puerto Rican as docile and explains the modernization of the island as a result of Luis Muñoz Marín's political manipulation of that docile personality. The Puerto Rican is thus portrayed as passive victim—not at all like the ascetic Protestant who was thought to fuel the emergence of modern capitalism in Western Europe; not at all like the dedicated worker of Japan; not at all like the "new man" who it was hoped would guide certain Third World societies to socialist modernity.

Consider for a moment the classic work by the sensitive anthropologist Sydney Mintz, *Worker in the Cane: A Puerto Rican Life History*.[5] It is the story of Don Taso, a rural proletarian who experienced the pressures of modernization, expressed first in his efforts as a barrio worker for the Popular Democratic Party, and then in his strivings as a convert to the Pentecostal religion. While Don Taso's conversion in a way symbolizes the impact of the processes that he lived, it always seemed to carry with it a sense of the inadequacy of his response, a vain attempt to at least do something while everything else around him was changing.

Or consider Oscar Lewis's attempts to prove the worth of his "culture of poverty" concept in *La Vida: A Puerto Rican Family in the Culture of Poverty*.[6] The Ríos family, the protagonists of the book, are presented as living proof of how internal forces prevent people from escaping poverty. Lewis tried to present his "culture of poverty" family as not simply harsh and brutalized but also as spontaneous and tolerant. Yet regardless of what one feels for the Ríos family, it remains clear that Oscar Lewis came to Puerto Rico to find losers. His protagonists do not meet modernity successfully; nor did he want them to. After all, they were chosen to demonstrate the demeaning power of the culture of poverty.

Nor has there been developed a testimonial mythology to celebrate the migrations to and from the island and the achievements of its participants. The migrants have been portrayed as devastated (Pedro Juan Soto, *Spiks*);[7] quaint (Christopher Rand, *The Puerto Ricans*).[8] Rarely have they been portrayed as heroic.

Consider Susan Sheehans's *A Welfare Mother*.[9] Her protagonist is a woman on welfare who lives amidst husbands, lovers, children, roaches, and life as "a series of accidents." In the preface to the book, Michael Harrington goes to great lengths to demonstrate that the protagonists played by the rules, "not playing the system for all she can get." But the end picture is, once again, of a Puerto Rican "unable to cope with the demands and complications of life in present-day America," unable to play the modern game, unable to take advantage of the possibilities of the modern world.

There are more such stories. Concerning the criminal gone straight one can read the testimonial by Richard P. Rettig, Manuel J. Torres, and Gerald R. Garrett, *Manny: A Criminal Addict's Story*;[10] or two autobiographies, Piri Thomas's *Down These Mean Streets*[11] or Lefty Barreto's *Nobody's Hero: A Puerto Rican Story*.[12] Whatever the positive aspects of these books, the most they show is Puerto Ricans learning lessons rather than teaching them.

In 1972, Lloyd Rogler's *Migrant in the City: The Life of a Puerto Rican Action Group*,[13] a study of a Puerto Rican civic action group in New Haven, could have presented contemporary Puerto Ricans in roles both appropriate to the modern context as well as potentially successful. But it, too, turned out to be a story of the unsuccessful and of self-defeat.

So the picture of the Puerto Rican drawn by the testimonial, whether rural worker, urban slum dweller, or immigrant to the mainland, is of the Puerto Rican not as hero but as loser. Given all the changes that Puerto Ricans have lived, one would expect to encounter a society certainly more vital, alive, and vivid than those portrayed in the testimonials discussed. Obviously, there have been biases in the selection of the protagonists to be written about.

One bias has to do with the way intellectuals appreciate, or perhaps depreciate, the bourgeois middle class. For many intellectuals, the lives of the middle class are too mundane, prosaic, and bourgeois to be interesting. They lack poetry in their lives, encounter no existential resistance to their whims, calculate for but that which already is and for that which might be. Lacking systematic adventure or tragedy, they have rarely become the focus of sociological testimonials.

One work that did try to concentrate on the Puerto Rican middle class was R. Fernández Marina, Ursula von Eckardt, and E. Maldonado Sierra's *The Sober Generation: Children of Operation Bootstrap—A Topology of Competent Adolescent Coping in Modern Puerto Rico*.[14] Of the young high-school subjects of the book the authors argued: "They are content with the imperfection and instability of human events, seeking no happiness beyond the tranquility of rational and realistic expectations. They are not impulsive, nor reckless, seeming to lack boldness and spontaneity. The sober generation is just that: cautious, prudent, and conventional—realistic and responsible." Not losers, these youngsters, however, seem to lead lives devoid of existential challenge; their successes seem unearned.

Another bias is perhaps generated by virtue of the way that change has come to Puerto Rico, introduced from without and from above. Elsewhere I have argued that the American development of Puerto Rico has come about by a process best labeled, "imperial development."[15] Owing to its political relationship with Puerto Rico, the dominant and ethnically distinct United States has controlled the ultimate prerogatives of sovereignty and has been obliged to promote economic "development" in Puerto Rico as a condition of that arrangement.

Clearly then the "development" of the island cannot be debted to any changes in the Puerto Rican personality. But even in such a circumstance of change from above, a human infrastructure below is necessary to activate such changes. Actors in such a system have to do either what is required of them or be smart enough to take advantage of what is happening around them. Thus, imperial development does not eliminate heroic possibilities or personalities from the "development" process. Rather, the hero then becomes the person who can spot possible advantage, chance it, pursue it, and develop it. Concentration on the way change has come about in Puerto Rico has often obscured that reality.

There are other reasons why this kind of personality has not been acknowledged as heroic. One reason has to do with Puerto Rican culture, where taking advantage of a situation is often confused with taking advantage of another person. Within Puerto Rican culture there is a strong moral imperative to respect others, indicating how one is supposed to deal with others: one must not violate the ceremonial code of behavior but must express deference to and protect the other, not disturb the other's self-presentation nor malign his self-image. And while there are countervailing norms—*relajo, jaibería, la pelea monga*—the moral atmosphere is overwhelmingly prorespect. Within such a context the aggressive individual seeking to maximize possibilities is more frequently seen as a wise guy, *un listo*, than as a hero.

Salpicar and Self-Hate

There are still additional reasons. Given the repeated calls for vitality from the intellectual Left in Puerto Rico, one might expect that it has located such sources of vitality. But obviously, the Left cannot locate them within the present socioeconomic system. As advocates of the independence of the island, they criticize both the Americanization of the island as well as the creation of the Puerto Rican circuit between the island and the mainland as processes to accrue only to the increasing dependence of the island to the United States. For an individual to take advantage of the possibilities created by such relations, at the expense of working toward their transcendence, would represent for the Left, not a heroic mentality but a colonial one. For the Left, then, vitality is to be found not in beating the system but in resisting its oppressive encroachment. They thus find themselves in the infelicitous intellectual position whereby they cannot deny the docility of the Puerto Rican, yet certainly cannot celebrate the world he has, if not created, at least not yet rejected either.

The question seems to be even more complicated. Frequently, given the history of Puerto Rico, socioeconomic success of individual Puerto Ricans has meant that they have learned to see themselves "as the Americans saw them."[16] Socioeconomic success in multicultural situations thus often appears as conversion to the dominant culture. Consequently, it is often avoided as a legitimate area of study by those who carry about cultural domination.

Sociologically, however, we need to ask the following questions: In a multicultural environment, have all who have become successful had to convert to the dominant culture? Put in even coarser terms, in multicultural situations, does "making it" mean "selling out?" If the answer to these questions is necessarily positive, it would be impossible to acknowledge success as heroic since it would not so much be achieved as simply purchased.

Kurt Lewin, in the essay referred to above, argues that within every underprivileged group there are forces that pull the members together and forces that push them away. "The tendency to gain status [in the privileged group]," acccording to Lewin, "means a force away from such [an underprivileged] group." But, as in the case of the Jews, there are external barriers which prevent one from simply leaving one's group and adopting membership in a new one. One possible result is a kind of introjection of externally originated hate. One's frustration with externally imposed impediments "may lead to a feeling of hatred against one's own group as the source of the frustration." This produces many types of behavior in which the actor seeks to disidentify with his own group. Lewin calls this introjection and denial, often felt by those on the way up socially, "negative chauvinism," as in the case of "100 percent Americanism," a kind of "aggression against one's own group." Lewin's essay is descriptive of one of several reactions to mobility in a multicultural context. Socioeconomic success in such multiethnic conditions raises this specter of self-hate and intellectuals, Puerto Ricans or otherwise, do not take kindly to such self-denigration. But by simple empiricism we know that socioeconomic success need not lead to either conversion or self-hate.

Moreover, a "positive chauvinism," a kind of "Mr. The Ethnic," if we can slightly alter James Joyce's image of "Mr. The Citizen," the kind of character portrayed as the Anti-Semite by Jean-Paul Sartre, seems to be as equally simplistic a psychology to adopt in multicultural circumstances. Especially in the case of the migrant, and today in Puerto Rico in the case of the return migrant, somehow cultural contact has to be appreciated in such a way that not all contact and borrowing is thought of as cultural pollution, dilution, or diminution. The image of the contemporary Puerto Rican as *jíbaro*, or even as *buen revolucionario*, to remember Carlos Rangel's biting term, can only go so far. It is worth remembering that it takes heroic energies to maintain a clear course between the dogma of Scylla and the relativism of Charybdis.

Benjy Lopez, the protagonist of *Benjy Lopez: A Picaresque Tale of Emigration and Return*, grew up on the island, was in the service in Panama and Europe, traveled the globe as a merchant seaman, worked in New York, and finally returned home to Puerto Rico. His life, a Puerto Rican odyssey of self-creation, has been one of combat and tease in which he somehow never lets his attempts at survival consume him. He lives by wit, will, and words. He sees life as a series of episodes, if not always escapades. Life involves deals, bargains, angles, short- and long-term schemes and projects. He has a great sense of the contingencies of life and makes few assumptions about continuity. Life is discontinuous, varied, episodic. What keeps it together, what gives it a semblance of continuity, is the central role that he plays.

Clearly, it is he who is the agent of happening. It is also he who gives it meaning and importance; it is he who organizes it and who gets himself through life's events. The key idea is to be able to wrap things up, to do what can be done, accomplish what there is to be accomplished, and then move on, keeping changes to a minimum.

When I asked him to try to explain his experiences—the very opposite of those that can be enjoined under the pathic concept, cultural deprivation—the concept he offered was *salpicar*, the splash. His experiences among alien cultures, in environments other than the one he had grown up in, "splashed" him, they rubbed off on him. What was the effect of all the contacts with other cultures? The following quote from Lopez should force the reader to decide for himself whether Benjy Lopez successfully passed between the dogma and the relativism that stalked him on his way:

> I know the Americans. . . . I walked with them. So I can live like an American. I can think like one too. And on the ships I also got to know a lot of other people—Germans, South Americans. . . . Don't forget the Cubans either. I can fit in with them perfectly. . . . The end of all this is that I am not a Rican. I am not an American. I am not a Neorican. I'm a fuckin' international—an international who's been splashed!

Notes

1. (New York: Basic Books, 1980).
2. Reprinted in Kurt Lewin, *Resolving Social Conflicts: Selected Papers on Group Dynamics* (New York: Harper & Row, 1948).
3. John Dollard, *Criteria for the Life History, with Analyses of Six Notable Documents* (New Haven: Yale University Press, 1935).
4. (Cambridge: Harvard University Press, 1969).
5. (New Haven: Yale University Press, 1960).
6. (New York: Random House, 1966).
7. (Río Piedras, P.R.: Cultural, 1958).
8. (New York: Oxford University Press, 1958).
9. (New York: New American Library, 1977).
10. (Boston: Houghton Mifflin, 1977).
11. (New York: Knopf, 1967).
12. (New York: New American Library, 1976).
13. (New York: Basic Books, 1972).
14. (Río Piedras: University of Puerto Rico Press, 1969).
15. See Barry B. Levine and Ralph S. Clem, "Imperial Development: The Cases of American Puerto Rico and Soviet Georgia," *Comparative Studies in Sociology* 1 (1978): 319–36.
16. Cf. Charlie Albizu and Norman Matlin, "The Death of Poetry: The '68 Puerto Rico Election," *Caribbean Review* 1 (no. 1, 1969): 2.

10

Image: The Puerto Rican in Hawaii

Norma Carr

Puerto Ricans have been in Hawaii for 82 years and have two public images: negative and nonexistent. It all depends on whom one asks, and one does have to ask. We have no barrios, no *colmados* (grocery stores), *boticas* or *botánicas* (drugstores), no *galería* (gallery), no legal defense fund, no recreation center or clinics, no Puerto Rican Studies, no famous *puertorriqueños*. In fact at the moment we do not even have an infamous Puerto Rican. Of all the labor groups recruited to serve the plantation system, the Puerto Rican is now the most invisible. How did the Puerto Rican get caught in this paradox of negative image and invisibility?

From the beginning of this historical episode the Puerto Rican was a pawn in the high stakes of the sugar industry of Hawaii which depended on cheap labor for its huge profits. The object of his recruitment was to break the back of the Japanese prounion movement. The Hawaii Sugar Planters Association (HSPA) accomplished this goal. The fact is celebrated in the Labor Commissioner's Report for 1902,[1] and in that storehouse of Hawaiian data, Thrum's *Annual*.[2] The new workers also provided some relief in the perpetual labor shortage, and good workers could count on a steady job so long as they could tolerate the oppressive plantation life. But good workers would not be rewarded with social acceptance by their betters or their peers. Their manipulation by the power system needed to continue in order to keep them and the Japanese in line.

The moment the Puerto Rican laborer came in contact with the recruiters he became the commodity of an alien power, the plantation system of Hawaii. He was subject to the judgement and control of the directors of the system. On the 6,600-mile route from Puerto Rico to Hawaii he provided economic opportunity to many interests. Much depended on his national status. If the Department of Immigration declared him a foreigner, the port of New Orleans could collect a head tax on him. But as he had been declared an expert sugar laborer, by law, he would have to be sent back to Puerto Rico. If he was declared eligible to pass through and proceed to Hawaii to work, the recruitment could continue, increasing traffic between New Orleans and Puerto Rico—providing more income for the port, the shipping line, and the Southern Pacific Railroad, all links in the passage to Hawaii. The Hawaii planters' money would circulate from the Pacific to the Caribbean. The special immigration inspector who had gone from Washington, D.C., to New Orleans for this ocassion calmly settled the matter. He declared that the Department of Immigration admitted them on the grounds that they were American citizens going from one American territory to another.[3] The business of exporting Puerto Rican bodies received a major boost.

That first little band of 114 men, women and children helped sell a lot of newspapers during its trip. Problems had arisen on the *Arkadia*, the ship which left San Juan on November 22, 1900, to carry them to New Orleans where they arrived on November 29.[4] Apparently on arrival in Louisiana some people wanted to go back to Puerto Rico. All were put on the Southern Pacific Railroad, bound for San Francisco.[5] Reports started coming out of El Paso, Texas, that the train was proceeding under armed guard.[6] Many must have been ill; the immigration inspector had remarked in New Orleans that they looked "malaria-like" and were ill-clad. Reports of the trouble persisted through New Mexico and the Territory of Arizona. At Indio, California, reporters from *The San Francisco Examiner*, along with a Spanish interpreter, joined the train. Reporter Edward Livernash interviewed the Puerto Ricans. The train had been detoured to that obscure hamlet to prevent the men from jumping train. The idea was to make a dash to San Francisco just in time to connect with the steamer, *Rio de Janeiro*, which would take the recruited laborers on the last leg of the trip to Honolulu. During the 4-day wait at Indio some Puerto Ricans did escape. The stories in *The Examiner* focused on every move made by the Puerto Ricans, all the while accusing the Hawaii planters of running a slave system and depicting the connivance of the Southern Pacific Railroad company.[7]

The *Rio de Janeiro* left San Francisco on December 14. Across its front page *The Examiner* splashed: "Threats and Force Put 66 Porto Ricans on Rio—But 50 Escape,"[8] and printed a picture to prove they were pushed on. Until December 24 stories in *The Examiner* extolled the paper's humanitarian work in teaching the planters a lesson and praised the generosity of the people of California for coming to the aid of the "little brown people" of Puerto Rico, "some of whom looked almost white."[9]

In Honolulu, *The Pacific Commercial Advertiser* received those news stories but did not print them. It prepared its own headline: "They Are a Wretched Lot, the Porto Ricans Who Are Coming to These Islands."[10] The story was printed at the bottom of the front page. The next day's issue carried a story on page 2: "Ways of Porto Ricans Topsy Turvy, So Say Americans."[11] This told how the people were rather peculiar and funny, building their houses from the top down. The "wretched" ones were on their way to Hawaii, and the remaining source of laborers was "topsy turvy."

The actual announcement of the December 23 arrival of the first little band was routine and businesslike, reported in the "Sea and Shore" column on December 24, 1900. However, a separate small item in the same issue stated that only 56 of the 134 hired hands had arrived.[12] Inexplicably, the minutes of the board of the HSPA gave the number as 118,[13] which perhaps includes the Italians recruited in Louisiana. To this day, such casual record keeping characterizes the data on the Puerto Ricans of Hawaii—namely, unavailable or unreliable.

Why did *The Pacific Commercial Advertiser* print such stories? A possible answer comes to mind when one recalls that its owner and publisher, Lorrin P. Thurston, was also a board member of the HSPA. He personally accused *The Examiner* of prejudiced journalism. Thurston had been very upset by a Hearst reporter who had cornered him in San Francisco with questions about the Puerto Ricans. William Randolph Hearst was a close associate of Claus Spreckels, a planter who supported the Hawaiian monarchy during the 1893 overthrow of the Hawaiian Kingdom, whereas Thurston had been its leading opponent.[14] This connection may explain both the interest of the Hearst papers and why *The Pacific Commercial Advertiser* would continue to carry so many harsh stories about Puerto Ricans for the next three decades.

Thus we see that Puerto Ricans were not really migrating to Hawaii, but rather were being transported to a plantation system. Their function was not only to provide labor, but also to pose a threat to the Japanese. Before their arrival they had incurred the wrath of the most powerful publisher in the islands and they were to be his employees. *The Advertiser's* third story appeared on December 27, 1900: "Porto Ricans Are Public Charge."[15]

The second group of recruits arrived on January 16, 1901. The same day they were put on board the Ke Au Hou, which was to carry them to plantations on the island of Hawaii. The next day's headline appeared to scream from the page: "Ship Captured by Porto Ricans." The article described them as dirty, tattered, with no possessions, and starved-looking. Why did they capture the ship? "Food for the entire lot of immigrants aboard had been dumped out on the forward hatch where the cattle are carried when there are any cattle going on the steamer . . . the Porto Rican who captured the vessel and compelled the captain to send for the police, said he represented the Porto Ricans on board and was carrying out the wishes of all when he held the vessel in port. He was not going to allow the vessel to go to sea until some understanding was reached with the authorities concerning food." The story continued that the Puerto Ricans were united in purpose. If their spokesman was arrested they would not go to the plantations. The Puerto Ricans all tore off the tags which both identified them and designated the plantation to which they had been assigned. Sheriff Brown and Deputy Sheriff Chillingsworth blamed the captain for not running a proper ship and failing to control the hungry Puerto Ricans.[16] Although this long account was not meant to condone the behavior of Puerto Ricans, it clearly demonstrated that dirty, tattered, tired and hungry though they were, their innate sense of human dignity was intact. No reporter could rob them of that.

Newspapers across the country carried many stories about Puerto Rico and Hawaii, the two newly acquired territories. The mainland papers often told the truth with unintentional irony. One New Orleans headline read: "Sugar Planters Hear Good News—Prof. Stubbs Talks of Agriculture in Hawaii—Where Natives Are Disappearing to Make Room for a New People."[17] How accommodating can a host society be? Hawaii's newspapers continued to chronicle the labor and social problems, of which there were many.

By March 1901 there were about 1,500 Puerto Ricans in the archipelago. As few and scattered as they were, they refused to accept standard plantation brutality. "Porto Ricans Strike on Plantations of Hawaii [the island, not throughout the territory]."[18] This news was buried on page 14. It was only for the eyes of those who could afford a newspaper and enough leisure to read it through.

The stories continued: "Thieves on Maui Isle: New Laborers Are Suspected." According to the report it was probably the Puerto Ricans who were committing the robberies. The very same issue on another page carried the story that the thieves had been caught. They were identified by race. They were not Puerto Ricans. But the story pointing the finger of suspicion at *them* had been printed anyway.[19]

The HSPA kept on issuing announcements that thousands and thousands of Puerto Rican laborers were headed for Hawaii. These served to threaten all the ethnic groups dependent on plantation employment. In their turn the Puerto Ricans felt stress, shame, sadness, and futility at the continuing stories about deteriorating conditions back on the home island. Such stories and the prohibitive cost of ship and train fares discouraged all thought of a return home.

In May, "The Board Met in Secret—Health Authorities Held Private Meeting to Discuss Porto Ricans."[20] That meeting took place in Honolulu. In June the New Orleans Board of Health suspended migration from Puerto Rico fearing the summer weather would increase the risk of epidemics.[21] The HSPA instructed the labor brokers to investigate the possibility of sending twice the number of Puerto Ricans being shipped per month—up to a total of 5,000 able-bodied male field laborers.[22] The story in the newspapers, especially in New Orleans, was that 20,000 Italians were to be recruited. Not only did Louisiana and a few other states depend on Italian labor, but Italians bound for Hawaii could just as well be shipped in through New York. The Louisiana planters faced a significant loss of workers: the port of New Orleans, the shipping line, and the Southern Pacific faced a considerable loss of business. Hawaii brought in a few Italians. The traffic in Puerto Ricans resumed in September.

Two groups recruited in September were the last to be organized during that recruitment campaign of 1900–1901. The recruiters had encountered so much opposition from the planters in Puerto Rico that they wrote to the planters in Hawaii asking them to discontinue recruitment.[23] Popular sentiment in Puerto Rico at that time supported as reasonably desirable migration to Santo Domingo and Ecuador, but not to Hawaii.

A survey of all the newspapers of the Hawaiian Islands during 1901 would show an average of one story a day about the "Porto Ricans."[24] Many were about the poor health and diseased condition of the newcomers. But most disparaging were the expressions of suspicion that it was Puerto Ricans who were committing every act of thievery and robbery throughout the territory. A cartoon showed a masked man armed with a knife and pistol. The overhead caption proclaimed: "A Growing Rural Industry." At his feet the question: "Is he a Porto Rican?"[25] Two days later "War on Vagrants"[26] was all about a Puerto Rican chicken thief, four vagrants, and a Puerto Rican employed as interpreter who "roared his explanations tumultuously." Another story, "City Full of Beggars," was about "mostly Porto Ricans and negroes . . . nothing in the appeal [for charity] but a desire to get something for nothing." Although the story could have been printed at almost any time, it happened to coincide with the arrival in September of the tenth group of Puerto Ricans. On October 19, 1901 *The Pacific Commercial Advertiser* reported that on the previous day 333 Puerto Rican and Italian laborers had arrived from Los Angeles on the steamer *City of Para*. Twenty-five were Italian, 180 men, the rest women and children. A few of the Puerto Ricans were crippled and one was partially blind. The item closed with the statement that "the importation of Porto Ricans is to be suspended for some time."[27]

It was not the sick, crippled, or partially blind immigrant laborers, nor that there were too many children to educate, nor their cultural defects which suspended the importation of Puerto Ricans. For the real reason one turns to the financial pages of the local newspapers or to *The Wall Street Journal*. Competition among foreign sugar producers had driven sugar prices down drastically. The Hawaii Sugar Planters Association had to proceed cautiously. This was not the time to continue importing laborers.

Despite the pronouncement of the special immigration officer in New Orleans in December 1900, Puerto Ricans were not American citizens until Congress passed the Jones Act in 1917, the same year that the United States entered World War I. Men in Hawaii were assigned draft numbers. Puerto Ricans were assigned numbers along with all other citizens, but when they tried to sign up to vote in a local election the country clerk claimed that the early immigrants to Hawaii were not covered by the Jones Act. Manuel Olivieri Sánchez told his fellow Puerto Ricans: "If you are not allowed to vote, don't answer the draft call."[28] He did more than that. He took a mandamus suit to court. The Lower Court ruled in favor of the county clerk. Olivieri Sánchez with his two lawyers went to the Territorial Supreme Court which reversed the decision of the Lower Court.[29]

The next group of Puerto Rican laborers for Hawaii was not recruited until 1921, after the Spanish flu epidemic of 1918 and strikes of 1918–20 had driven thousands of Japanese off the plantations.[30] The immigrants of 1900–01 still refer to the 1921 group as *los nuevos* (the new ones).

Citizenship opened the door for Puerto Rican men into many jobs in the defense industry in Hawaii, especially at Pearl Harbor. Other good things happened though they are not recorded in the newspapers. For example, two young women, both born in Hawaii, Henrietta Ortiz and Margaret Maldonado, became teachers in 1924 and 1925 respectively.[31]

For some mysterious reason, or so it appeared at the time, in late 1930 stories began to circulate that the HSPA was planning to recruit laborers in Puerto Rico. A battle of words, hot and heavy, was waged against the "unhealthy Porto Rican hookwormers," who had brought disease to Hawaii, on the pages of *The Honolulu Star Bulletin, The Honolulu Advertiser* (formerly *The Pacific Commercial Advertiser*), *The Manila Bulletin, The Hawaii Hochi*, and in newspapers on the mainland. Manuel Olivieri Sánchez had one of the last words on the matter in a letter to the editor of *The Honolulu Advertiser* in December 1931.[32] He saw all the rhetoric as a tactic by the HSPA to push all the different ethnic groups in the local labor force back to work on the plantations. He was not far off the mark. Actually the HSPA had been trying to persuade Congress to exempt the territory of Hawaii from the law, requested by California to prevent Filipinos from migrating to the United States.

In 1978 some material relating to Hawaii in the National Archives in Washington, D.C., was declassified. Most of it consisted of correspondence dating from May 1923 to October 1931, between the Department of Insular Affairs, the secretary of war, a governor of Hawaii, two governors of Puerto Rico (Towner and Roosevelt) and the HSPA. This correspondence provides a small clue as to what happened back in 1930–31.

The War Department was interested in augmenting the population of Hawaii with people who owed allegiance to the United States and who could be depended upon in an emergency. It was ready to cooperate and assist the government of Hawaii in the transfer of sufficient numbers of Puerto Ricans to Hawaii which "would create an American majority in the islands and remove the constant menace of the Japanese majority."[33] The War Department considered the Japanese undesirable and the Filipinos unreliable, since the

Philippines were demanding independence. "In time of War, and for the expansion of the Peace Garrison to the War Garrison, by use of the Military man power of the Territory, the Porto Rican will constitute a much more desirable man for induction than most of the men of the other races which now constitute the Military manpower of the Territory of Hawaii."[34]

In a letter to the secretary of war, the secretary-treasurer of the HSPA, J.K. Butler, emphasized the association's unwillingness to import Puerto Ricans to Hawaii. Not only had the previous experience been expensive and ineffective, he claimed, but the Puerto Ricans still in Hawaii "constituted by far the greatest number of those receiving assistance from social agencies in the Territory . . . [and] the Porto Rican group furnishes proportionately ten times as many mentally defective people, as for instance the Chinese group."[35] The defamation continues, attributing to the Puerto Ricans the worst criminal record, health record, and rate of juvenile delinquency in proportion to population. As usual, it was not necessary to provide any real statistics to substantiate any claims.

In 1931 the HSPA beat everybody down by convincing Congress to allow Filipinos to migrate to work in Hawaii, although they were excluded from the rest of the United States. The debate in the newspapers ended, but not the injury to the Puerto Ricans. The battle of words condemned not only the Puerto Ricans in Hawaii but also those on the island of Puerto Rico. The documents demonstrate once again that the public castigation of Puerto Ricans in the newspapers in 1930 and 1931 served the interests of the HSPA.

One response from the Puerto Rican community proved very positive and effective. In 1931 Daniel Maldonado, Baptist Figueroa, and Augusto Montiho, of the recently formed Puerto Rican Civic Club, paid a visit to Riley Allen, editor of *The Star Bulletin*. Mr. Maldonado was a highly valued employee of that newspaper. The *boricuas* (Puerto Ricans) discussed the negative image continually projected by stories in both *The Star Bulletin* and *The Advertiser*. Mr. Allen promised there would be very careful writing from then on and that every positive report given to his newspaper would be printed. He was a man of his word. From then and through the 1950s, many items about Puerto Rican civic and social activities were reported.[36]

In Puerto Rico no one could have anticipated just how thorough and complete would be the power of Hawaii's sugar kingdom on the lives of those 5,000 Puerto Ricans recruited from November 1900 to September 1901.[37] Before annexation in 1898 the HSPA had gained experience in working with foreign governments through its control of foreign nationals in the labor force on the plantations. After annexation the HSPA was ready to create any image necessary to maneuver its way through the political and economic relationships prevailing between national and island interests. Its power dominated local government decisions and its influence in Congress extended far beyond Hawaii's proportionate representation—one delegate with no vote.

It was easy for members of the HSPA to denigrate their employees, the lowly field hands. These powerful men believed completely in their own superiority and the inherent inferiority of those other races serving on their plantations. The image the HSPA projected of the Puerto Ricans determined the society's response to the Puerto Rican presence in the community. On an individual basis we can provide many instances of friendship, assistance, and mutual respect between the Puerto Ricans and the other labor groups on the plantations. But generally and in the minds of many the image became fact. In later years when they were off the plantations they forgot how much they had liked Puerto Rican music and dancing and eating *ateli* (*pasteles*, meat pies), how much they had appreciated the neighborly services of the *comadrona* (midwife), and the sharing of *gandules* (green pigeon peas) and fresh roasted coffee. Conveniently forgetting as well the suffering, humiliations, and sacrifices of their own ancestors in the plantation system, the present generation would attribute its success to the inherent superiority of its own particular culture. In their eyes the Puerto Rican culture lacked such virtues. The Puerto Rican was judged negatively for not being like the Oriental, long-suffering; not being like the Portuguese, obedient; not being like the *Haole* (Caucasian), a capitalist. He was a deviant, the product of misery and starvation. He was unorganized, and lacked social structure and traditions of industry and thrift; he lacked common sense for holding on to traditions which made him inferior; he had a history of revolution and carried weapons; he was more interested in the art of living than in working; he loved gambling, drinking, and loafing; he was not ashamed to receive welfare. He was also accused of having introduced petty thievery as a new industry in the rural areas; he was often jailed.[38] There was one factor working in his favor, but not one of his own doing: Some improvement was expected in succeeding generations, for the new environment would surely work miracles.[39]

The image was created and projected because the Puerto Rican was meant to serve the ends of the HSPA by posing a threat to the other nationalities on the plantations, especially the Japanese. He was part of the build-up of surplus labor. Instead his differences presented a threat to the HSPA. Others before them had rebelled, but none with the persistence of Puerto Ricans or in so many ways. His lack of English was supposed to keep him isolated; yet many Puerto Ricans learned not only English, but Hawaiian and Japanese in addition to pidgin, the lingua franca of the plantations. He refused to yield to the whip. He was not afraid to leave the plantations to seek jobs in urban centers. The other workers resented his disdain for the very system which held them so immobilized and sometimes hated him for that. The planters saw their investment in him going down the drain. The newspapers crucified him at every turn as a result of which the public in general read only about his supposed defects. He was described in government reports in terms more negative than those applied at that time to any group except the Japanese—the other group that had to be controlled. The image was acceptable to those workers who felt threatened by his differences.

In the 1930s when the Puerto Ricans formed their beneficial societies they were really turning inward. Their goal of self-help was admirable, but they were following the dictates of the plantation system—ethnic segregation and isolation. Self-help was not a class goal in Hawaii, it was an ethnic goal. The Puerto Rican Baseball League also took a firm stand in the early thirties, another act of segregation. Segregation was not voluntary because if such a league had not been organized, few if any Puerto Ricans would have had the opportunity to play. This same development must also be looked upon as a triumph. The Puerto Ricans had not only organized a league, but through political involvement had acquired priority rights to a playing field, Lanakila Park in Kalihi.[40] Until World War II their baseball activities were recorded on, and sometimes dominated, the sports pages of the local newspapers. A new image appeared, the great baseball player, but again, games were for good times, not serious business.

These acts of seemingly voluntary segregation, constant migration to the mainland, and one of the highest rates of amalgamation from the time of their early presence in Hawaii have contributed to the invisibility of the Puerto Ricans. Good stories make the papers all the time now, disproportionately in the sports pages. But who knows the people are Puerto Ricans? The surnames are the same as the Filipino, Portuguese, and Spanish. As for the children of mixed marriages, some may not even know they are part Puerto Rican. Some children prefer one parent's side and hardly know the other. If the mixture includes Hawaiian, that is most likely to be the chosen identity. Everyone feels the need to belong to the island of one's birth. How many generations are supposed to feel "native" to the home of some long gone ancestor, four or five generations removed, from a land they have never seen?

One reason why everyone in Hawaii still carries an outsider identity is because only people of Hawaiian blood ancestry are called Hawaiians, fourth and fifth generations of the other people in Hawaii still carry the label of origin. A fourth- or fifth-generation Puerto Rican in Hawaii does not speak Spanish, covers his *bacalao* (codfish) with soy sauce, and plays his ukelele and sings "Hawaií Ponoí" in Hawaiian as the official song of his homeland. His ancestors coped and survived successfully far beyond the credit awarded them. He worked anonymously at a steady job to pay off the mortgage on his home and sends the kids to school as far as they want to go. He cannot be told apart from other "locals" of Hawaii. He may express *aloha* for the homeland of his forefathers, or he may never give it a thought. For certain, he does not yearn "to go back" anywhere. He *is* home.

Notes

1. United States Bureau of Labor Statistics, *Report of the Commissioner of Labor on Hawaii, 1902* (Washington, 1903).
2. Thomas G. Thrum, *Hawaiian Almanac and Annual, 1902* (November 1901).
3. *The Daily Picayune* (New Orleans, 1 December 1900): 1st., p. 6, c. 4.
4. Ibid. (New Orleans, 30 November 1900): lst., p. 12, c. 2.
5. Ibid. (1 December 1900): 1st., p. 6, c. 4.
6. "Kidnapping Slaves From Puerto Rico," *The Examiner* (San Francisco, 7 December 1900): 1, c. 6.
7. *The Examiner* (San Francisco, 12, 13, 14 December 1900).
8. *The Examiner* (San Francisco, 15 December 1900): 1.
9. *The Examiner* (San Francisco, 16, 18, 24 December 1900).
10. *The Pacific Commercial Advertiser* (*PCA*) (Honolulu, 11 December 1900): 1, c. 5.
11. *PCA* (12 December 1900): 2, c. 1.
12. *PCA* (24 December 1900): 8, c. 3, p. 9.
13. From notes extracted with permission from Minutes of Meetings, Trustees, Hawaii Sugar Planters Association by HSPA librarian, covering importation of Puerto Rican laborers. Notes cover 5/1/1900 to 11/4/1901.
14. Lawrence H. Fuschs, *Hawaii Pono: A Social History* (New York: Harcourt, Brace, & World, 1961), p. 31.
15. *PCA* (27 December 1900): 3, c. 3.
16. *PCA* (17 January 1901): 1, cs. 5, 6.
17. *The Daily Picayune* (New Orleans, 16 February 1901): 7, c. 4.
18. *PCA* (18 March 1901): 14, c. 3.
19. *PCA* (26 March 1901): 14, 6.
20. *PCA* (17 May 1901): 6, c. 3.
21. *The Daily Picayune* (New Orleans, 1 July 1901): 11, c. 5.
22. Minutes of Meetings, Trustees, HSPA.
23. Same as notes 13, 22.
24. Each island had its own newspapers. There were also newspapers in the Hawaiian, Japanese, and Portuguese languages.
25. *PCA* (4 September 1901): 1, cartoon.
26. *PCA* (6 September 1901): 2, c. 3.
27. *PCA* (19 October 1901): 7, c. 3.
28. From interviews with Joseph Ayala, Daniel Maldonado, and Peter Martínez, all friends of Manuel Olivieri Sánchez.
29. *PCA* (2 May 1917, 23 October 1917): 7, c. 3.
30. Fuchs, p. 225.
31. Department of Education Directory, 1924-25, and interview with Daniel Maldonado.
32. *The Honolulu Advertiser* (formerly the PCA) (13 December 1931): editorial page, c. 4.
33. Headquarters Hawaiian Department, Office of the Department Commander, Honolulu. "A General Staff Study," p. 2. Signed by E.M. Lewis, major general.

34. "A General Staff Study," p. 10.
35. Letter to Patrick J. Hurley, secretary of war, on board *President Hoover* at Honolulu Harbor, written after a morning meeting on October 14, 1931.
36. From interviews with Daniel Maldonado and Thelma Maldonado, sister of Augusto Montiho.
37. Norma Carr, *Puerto Rican: One Identity from a Multi-Ethnic Heritage*. Office of Instructional Services/General Educational Branch. Department of Education, State of Hawaii, October 1980.
38. The faults attributted to Puerto Ricans are a partial list of the abuse heaped on them in the newspapers and official reports of the early years and perpetuated in the work of some students and faculty in the Department of Social Work and Sociology at the University of Hawaii. They took their "facts" from the early reports without questioning their validity, and without compunction condemned a whole group of people on the basis of their differences.
39. Report of the Commissioner of labor on Hawaii (1902), and repeatedly quoted in the thesis work for the Master's in Social Work, as well as in articles in *The Social Process in Hawaii*.
    It was expected that Puerto Ricans would intermarry with Portuguese. Interestingly, the problems experienced by the Portuguese in the second and third decades of this century are attributed to moral deterioration caused by intermarriage. These judgements were expressed by welfare workers.
40. Carr, *Puerto Rican: One Identity from a Multi-Ethnic Heritage*.

Part II
Authors' Voices

11

Women's Tales

Magali García Ramis

Many women have left their mark on the contemporary Puerto Rican narrative. Stories of women, a catchall-phrase which includes women who write short stories as well as women who appear in short stories and the short stories written by women, have all come to form an important and memorable part of our literary production.

When one seriously reads the narrative of the period which has come to be known as the Generation of the 1970s and the generation which we might call (if one were to follow the classification pattern based on date of publication) of the 1980s—when one first reads, motivated by a search and perhaps by pleasure, and then a second and third time to analyze and find common points of interest, the presence of the woman in the short story takes on a life of its own.

When planning a paper which in some way is to focus on the topics of image and identity, we immediately think of presenting it on women of the short story, some of whom have made an impact on us, as if by latent action, impressing us greatly as representatives of some truthful images of Puerto Rican reality.

One of these women is the woman of the sea, whose name serves as the title of a short story from the most recently published book by Manuel Ramos Otero.[1] A second is Paula, a neighbor of almost all of us, from the short story by Juan Antonio Ramos "Podando los resentimientos."[2] And the third is an anonymous woman whose identity is clearly that of the protagonist of the short story "Entre condicionales e indicativos" by Carmen Lugo Filippi.[3]

These three women of the short story acquire greater intensity as we spend more time with them. And it is not merely a coincidence that the three of them, from different perspectives, are failures. The woman of the sea is the dreamer, the one who perhaps did not exist as such but who reflects various realities, among them that of a poet from times gone by, Palmira Parés, a poet to recall the times of Juegos Florales, art deco, and "green Venetian blinds of a coastal town's uninhabited hotel." An image of the kind of poet who, a failure before the world and bourgeois respectability, takes refuge in drugs, death, a needle, love, escape, a lethal move toward New York, the cold, work—the end.

If the woman of the sea and that which she represents is a dream, then Paula, almost a caricature of the nouveau riche of a better urban development, is the plotter. Her plotting has a raison d'être: to defend the formal and moral integrity of her middle-class community; to alert citizens so that they are aware of and may deal with the crudeness, vulgarity, and spontaneity of the village family that moves into their community. Her failure as a woman, according to the canons which she shares, is obvious: Her husband feels attracted to the new and not so nice neighbor, and Paula's shortcomings as a human being, her inability to accept a woman and family with a different lifestyle, limits her in such a way that she becomes obsessed, making her lose sight of everything except the physical and psychological destruction of that other woman, of that other social class which perhaps reminds her, with too much intensity, of her own class origin.

Compared to Palmira Parés, moved across the sea which bears her name while mortally wounded, and to Paula, drowned in her own resentment by keeping up social appearances with the woman whom she helps to destroy, we find an exquisite and painful portrayal of a virtuous and Catholic woman from Yauco, frustrated and resentful, cold, hard-working, elegant and, in a lucid moment, doubtful and judgmental of class, state, and religion. In spite of the faults some find with this short story, the representation of that woman is one of the most authentic in our society: The woman who was in bloom a generation ago, fearful of God and observant of religious laws, is incapable of divorce and of breaking away from a failed marriage, and is therefore destined to the solitude of those irrational people who comply with mores and norms.

These three women of the contemporary Puerto Rican short story are secondary characters, and we maintain that it is not merely a coincidence that they are failures, because they are true examples of women asphyxiated on different terms by the same peculiar ideology which limits their development as human beings.

What image and identity can these women have and what image and identity do they reflect to us? The three of them indicate one of the common points of interest among contemporary Puerto Rican narrators—the representation, in all its facets, of the Puerto Rican middle class and of the aspirations of becoming middle class held by the suburban masses that have not yet come to economic power.

These women of the short stories force us to see the Puerto Rican world in a new light. The true-to-life image which they present, without recourse to an obsolete naturalism, and the common, yet not boring daily occurrences of that class, lead us to ask ourselves what they are looking at and what Puerto Rican narrators of today are trying to represent.

Due to organizational and analytical motives, there is a group of Puerto Rican narrators which we have classified as the Generation of the 1970s. When we look at ourselves and read and reread one another, we immediately find vast differences in style, approach, and ways of seeing reality.

Nevertheless, when we compare ourselves to previous generations, we realize that the differences among us are not that great and that our group has a particular interest in representing the urban and suburban Puerto Rican man and woman in all their facets: the middle class, from the poorest and most alienated, doing the best they can in forget-it-all bars and food stamp lines, to the richest and most isolated who make the best of it between trips to Disney World and college in the North for their children. With the middle class we go from the sublime to the ridiculous. We not only represent it in a denunciatory perspective, but in a loving one as well, with the same love with which natural scientists study sharks and remoras which concern them, or the ecosystem which permits their survival.

This representation is important because the foothold this narrative acquires is due to the fact that what it has to say is both authentic and compassionate. Its denouncement of oppression is no less because death blows have not been dealt to the bourgeoisie, but it is even greater, showing the bourgeoisie in all its tragedy, manifesting its contradictions and pointing out the causes of its eventual transformation. There are similarities and, to some degree, differences between us and our predecessors. But how do you begin to locate them?

When those of us of the Generation of the 1970s read "El escritor," a short story which José Luis González dedicates in one edition to Luis Rafael Sánchez,[4] we found after only a few minutes of reading and an eternity of introspection that we had completed a cycle of that which has been interpreted as three generations of Puerto Rican narrators, or two generations and one intermediate (one being transitional), and which perhaps only represent moments and different perspectives of the same place.

In that short story a well-to-do intellectual writer, abusive of his seductive power with the servants and of his economic power with his friends, regrets that there is nothing to write about in the country, while outside his house workers stage a strike and a police threat closes in on them. It is a compact, accusatory short story, and depicts many alienated intellectuals of our country, a short story in black and white, as were the first Fellini films, and just as realistic and allegorical. José Luis, as we all know, belongs to the Generation of the 1940s together with Emilio Díaz Valcárcel and Pedro Juan Soto and to one side, René Marqués. Usually placed alone between the Generation of the 1950s and us, is Luis Rafael Sánchez, who at first made himself known as a dramatist, as did Marqués.

When we reexamine our narrative work, we see that in some way we have all been identifying with a social problem and with the need to find a human, not metaphysical solution which is socially and economically just; one which is founded in the dignity that only the taking of individual and collective power brings, not in the simple solution of always remaining a colony where because one makes no decisions, one becomes acritical, weak, and sterile. What makes us different is the where: where we want to focus our attention, where we see the problem. Edwin Reyes has said that he is an uprooted person because he is between a rural infancy and an urban adulthood, between two worlds without definitively belonging to either, and he does not say this like those supporters of a free state in the sense of a loss, but rather as a representative of a period which required him to live a period of grasping transition.

And we—when I say "we" I try to include all those narrators of the new generation, from Manuel Ramos Otero to Ana Lydia Vega, Juan Antonio Ramos, Rosario Ferré, Carmen Lugo Filippi, Carmelo Rodríguez Torres, Edgardo Sanabria Santaliz, and many others—those of us who began to publish in the present decade, are also in most cases in that transition, in that duplicity, in that we have racial, cultural, class, and societal blocks and trends to follow.

I am not going to deal with the generalization about whether we are or not patriots, since it is well known that in Puerto Rico in the field of literature there is not at this moment a single valued narrator writing who does not have a social conscience and pride in his Puerto Rican identity. The assimilative groups have in their ranks two or three people who at some former time were influential, but nowadays, as they die off, no others have emerged from those parties and groups. And while this happens in almost all the arts, in literary production, the narrative in particular, it is a substantiated fact.

We have in common, then, a consciousness of place of origin and of the nation we represent, in different ways; our differences arise from different historical moments which each one of us had to live and hence the answer that we have given to the proposals of that moment.

For example, the Puerto Rican narrators of today are not as influenced by the brutal change from the rural areas to the city as were those of the Generation of the 1940s because we live it from different perpectives: Either we were born in the city to start with, or we came to suburban life as youngsters and we finished growing up there. We did not see ourselves as having to rebel as much against the docile image René Marqués wished to present of us because when the time came for us to look at ourselves, the historical reality of the Cuban Revolution, the war in Vietnam, and mandatory military service already had us marching to the sound of conga drums by the thousands at university campuses, singing "Mírala que linda viene," and shouting "Out with the ROTC." We looked for links with revolutionaries throughout the world and we argued loudly, even shouted, when we saw the film "La Batalla de Argel," and we asked ourselves why Puerto Rico could not gain national liberation in the same way that it was gained by that French colony. Many of us passed by the MPI, or the PIP, or the PSP, or the MSP, or the study circles, or the socialists' Jornadas de Cristiandad, or Iván Illich's seminars in Cuernavaca, or all of that at once, and we read Marcuse, Che and Régis Debray, who seemed too intellectual for us; and we refused to listen for some time when the great change came. The relationship with the most advanced empire in the world brought us a brotherhood with the minorities in North America, we identified with Eldridge Cleaver and, in imitation of the Black militants, we began to raise our left fist because we were leftists in our estimation, while the leftists of the rest of the world raised their right fist, the one of battle.

When the time came for us to look at Puerto Rico we wanted to apply, despite all the obstacles, the new mores of the feminist revolution, the sexual revolution, and the student revolution to our society. When we began to analyze our economic, cultural, and political problems we were tuned-in to the entire world, to the Beatles and Roy Brown. Mao's China was a total cultural revolution and the teachers were paper tigers, and the paper was bought not only to write on but also to roll prohibited cigarettes.

We saw René Marqués represented in the Tapia as something cultural, whereas Luis Rafael was seen in the Café Teatro La Tea when Abelardo allowed them to put on "Los ángeles se han fatigado" and Esther Sandoval made the place tremble. Afterwards we went on a pilgrimage to number 13 Sol Street and thought, "Here is where everything happened, thus, it was true."

The link between literature and reality made more sense for the narrators when we began to hear from other Latin American latitudes the words which had already been paired forever, magic realism, and read back in time to discover Alejo Carpentier who, when we were very small or not even born, one fine day wrote *El reino de este mundo*, as one who gets up and sits down to breakfast. We were Isabel la Negra and Monchín del Alma, if heaven would allow it, and the mayors of the town and the snow that Felisa brought at Christmas. We were able to see ourselves from many different perspectives; to feel a brotherhood with a progressive Chile; to cry for Allende and Neruda; to hope again after knowing Benedetti; to cry for the liberation of our five nationalists; to fight to have the navy removed from Vieques and to feel desperate anguish over the death of Pinochet. Upon seeing ourselves reflected in a thousand neighboring villages from the Caribbean and Central America, to the world of the Andes and from all of America, our differences were no longer, as we played one last time before growing up, *Rayuela*, with Cortázar, and once and for all, we sat down to write.

What did we write about then? How were we different? The country was not the same. They had taken away the trains, there were fewer if any blazing fires, no Blacks at the border of the ghetto which they cleaned almost completely, so as not to besmear the entrance to a financial goldmine, which never came to be except in the form of scraps of plastic.

We were different in our not so accusatory but, perhaps for a moment, more pamphletary tone. The ties with political groups and the need to define our culture forced us many times into a closed compromise which was translated for some time into a straightjacket for all the artists who would drown their feelings, characters, or verses on some ocassion because they did not appear as orthodox Puerto Ricans who were as they were required to be, by others and by themselves. For the sake of that definition, enthusiastic about everything Puerto Rican with a capital ''P,'' we took the criteria of excellence and of creative job discipline beyond the desirable limits and accepted much of that which was only mediocre as good, simply for having a fighting bird, a crowing rooster and a waving Puerto Rican flag, and, by the magic of the nation, this became an exquisite an orthodox representative of our culture.

We rediscovered the Taino Indians and began to call our children not only Guarionex, as had been done at the beginning of the century for its connotation of a fighting leader, but a variety of precious- sounding words such as Atabey, Urayoán, Turey; these were destined to become Papito, Pucho, and Chiqui only a few weeks after our innocent ones were baptized.

But that was one stage. And precisely because we were able to overcome it, we, the so-called young narrators, began to exercise a critical sense over some representative short stories, which truly motivated us, concerned us, sprang from us, and made us create literature. Many of us then went to live and study abroad. Abroad to New York and to small-town cities in Mexico and Spain; some to Paris, though few; and that separation helped us to reexamine ourselves and project ourselves in a different way, much like the aviators did, who, raising themselves above the ground, discovered to their surprise that rainbows are not as they had thought, but rather are perfect circles which those of us standing on earth are unable to see, but this does not stop them in our eyes from being magic circles called rainbows.

We were born as a generation of narrators from different lifestyles but with similiar social, cultural, and political focuses. And upon examining our chronological origins, we find some families have been through not one, but three wars, unimaginable hurricanes, and economic hard times which were nothing like any of us had ever known. We discovered that great middle class and that great class which wanted to be middle class and, with their songs and pains, divorces and credit cards, we begin to shape them in a different narrative. Our collective lifestyle remained in our narration as authentic as it was, and the representative characters were for us as valuable as they were for the previous generations of farmers and landholders, those who emigrated to New York and the new millionaires, and the soldiers who returned in lead boxes which could not be opened.

The middle class and the women of the middle-class short stories took on a different life. And those women of the short story are only one of the themes which unite us and it is through them that we may focus on a piece of our national reality. The Paulas who are resentful, who want to dominate everything; the castrating and terrible women, products of local consumption and exportation; the "you" second persons, as secondary sexes, humiliated and enclosed in a shady imitation of the Christian and European heritage; and especially the women of the sea of poetry, life itself, drugs and estrangement, through which one sometimes arrives at greater lucidity; these are women who are cursed from the start and sought after, with a suitcase in hand, and a train that never leaves in their eyes; they point toward a rich trajectory of possibilities which we have barely begun to narrate.

Speaking for myself, although perhaps some of my colleagues would agree with me, this is a terrible and agonizing labor, but when the literary creation of narrative allows for it, it becomes the greatest passion, one which takes everything from us, while giving us everything we have, such as the "Maestra Vida" by Rubén Blades. The critical sense in ourselves sometimes ties us down for years to some short stories which we never dare to show, but by force of making ourselves into narrators, by intimidation and at the same time because a social, political, ethical, and aesthetic responsibility, which signifies what it is to write and to be read in a nonsovereign country, we continue to work exiled from ourselves and one hundred out of a thousand times share with you, as today, the labor of the Puerto Rican narrative. Of the short story we can say what Manuel Ramos Otero says of a character in the story "El cuento de la mujer del mar": "one goes creating it with dreams and words, hands and footsteps, submitting it to the slow custom of love."

Notes

1. *El cuento de la mujer del mar* (Río Piedras: Huracán, 1979).
2. *Pactos de silencio y algunas erratas de fé* (Río Piedras: Cultural, 1980).
3. *Vírgenes y mártires*, with Ana Lydia Vega (Río Piedras: Antillana, 1981).
4. *En Nueva York y otras desgracias* (Mexico City: Siglo XXI, 1973).

12

At the Middle of the Road

Edgardo Rodríguez Juliá

To assume the role of a writer is always a daring act. To place one's own scant talent before a tradition more than three thousand years old is, to put it mildly, an excess of vanity. But here I am, responsible for an incipient work which is, at times, an excessively harsh accusatory finger. At eighteen years of age—it was at that age that I seriously began to practice this pretended occupation—one attempts to take the literary heavens by force. We already know that ignorance is bold; in the case of the writer, ignorance also has pride to give unsound advice. At that age I had read little; and I had rather be measured in terms of my neighbors than by my heroic grandparents who, because they had lived so long, appeared unreachable. Dante, Tolstoy, and Cervantes often seemed boring; anyone claiming the opposite is probably fibbing. I preferred the story about the young madman of Prague who was transformed into an insect to Tolstoy's three hermits (a tale which, for all its wisdom, is somewhat sentimental). If one does not know life, one ignores the greatness of those hands which have touched it so tenderly and yet so terribly.

I am astonished above all by the literary cunning and artful intelligence involved in telling and narrating. Cortázar seems more profound than Chekhov; that old, fiendishly astute Borges seems superior even to the sometimes clumsy hand of Melville. Between Baudelaire and Rimbaud, I pick the cursed adolescent. Quevedo's cruelties fascinate more than advice from the *Curioso impertinente*. What happens to this young writer who always makes mistakes? He is a poor fugitive of his feelings, still guided only by his intelligence.

Every writer is also a reader, at times a voracious one, and at times (as in my case) a crazily selective one. It has already been said that taking on the literary tradition is a bold move. But so too, though to a lesser extent, is the rescuing of a portion of the solemn history of music or plastic arts. The pulse of whoever calls himself an artist must tremble at the sight of a da Vinci drawing. It seems difficult to believe that Beethoven and Willie Colón share the same 7-note tradition. Now the plastic arts require a workshop or academic apprenticeship in the same way that music does; this promotes the artist's command of, or at least his minimal competence in his profession. It is not so in the case of literature. The writer learns on his own by reading the great and not so great masters. It is a matter of having Conrad, Joyce, Cervantes, and Borges as speaker and teacher. Learning the profession of a writer is often a solitary undertaking; we can only bargain for a dialogue in which one of the interested parties remains silent. This dialogue with the eloquent silence of the greats can lead us astray. Every young writer is somewhat inclined to vain solipsism as he interprets his own talent only from the point of view of its virtues. What is lacking is the resistance of craftsmanship which is mastered in the humility of the workshop. This security only begins to falter when a mature writer who points out defects and applauds virtues is found. Lucky is the young writer who finds himself a teacher who points out grammatical horrors as well as errors in characterization.

Who have my close teachers been? When I was young I used to submit manuscripts to the closest literature teacher I ever had, Rafael Añeses, who guided my first literary steps at the Colegio San José. It was he who had the unfortunate job of reading some poems in prose, in the fashion of Baudelaire, which painstakingly attempted to become short stories. He caught me by surprise one afternoon back in 1963 on the corner of streets Arzuaga and Padre Rufo. I had just bought a critical anthology on Kafka at the university bookstore. I was walking aimlessly through the streets of Río Piedras with the Jew of Prague between my brows. That meeting with the Spanish teacher was for me rather like that of a father meeting his adolescent son who had just bought a pornographic magazine. I guess by around that time we must have been reading *El Quijote*. I did not want to give the impression that I was being unfaithful to Cervantes so I could go and eat plums with the boy of the tormented eyes. I mumbled something about *The Metamorphosis*, but Añeses understood. At his famous hideaway in Santa Rita, he was to give me a volume of Proust as a gift, while at the same time assigning *Doña Bárbara* to me in his course. In my second year at the university, Héctor Estades and José María Bulnes patiently read my first essay; a confused treatise on Artaud where the dense profusion of ideas drowned every possibility for a well-placed comma. It was Pepe Bulnes, that inspired Chilean, who first taught me that commas and accents are not at odds with intelligence. I owe him my reading of a book which obsessed me for years; *Perceval* by Chrétien de Troyes. During those years I read Vallejo and Neruda, Cortázar and Octavio Paz. In Puerto Rican literature I was to discover the solid work of Laguerre, the inspiration of Palés Matos, the brilliance of Andreu Iglesias in *Los derrotados*. I even had a terrible intuition as to what my obscure destiny as a Puerto Rican writer would be: My Puerto Rican literature teacher read us a book by Manrique as she fanned herself between yawns over there in Pedreira's old cellar. I appreciated the comments made by Margot Arce after reading my first short stories. She pointed out that the road to becoming a writer is difficult. I realized that a well-learned profession is the best counselor of talent. José Luis Vivas Maldonando read my manuscripts of those years. He also showed me the road to self-improvement. Pedro Juan Soto read my works with enthusiasm, and with the same patient craftsmanship for which he is known, he made his comments about two short stories that were a bridge between my first book and my first novel. I must admit that our meeting was not cordial, but in the long run it proved enormously beneficial. It was Pedro Juan Soto who pointed out something which I had long suspected: My short stories were becoming exceedingly long, tirelessly struggling to reach the bounds of the novel. Pedro Juan Soto advised me: "You are a long-winded writer." I interpreted that comment with little modesty. I said to myself: I am a novelist. Even today I can still remember the advice he voiced in my house. That afternoon I had the privilege of sharing with Carlos Soto Arriví the tender severity of Pedro Juan. While the future martyr of Cerro Maravilla played in the hammock on the balcony, his father insisted the he tie his laces; that afternoon the mystery of parenthood was crossed with that of literary apprenticeship. It is true, Pedro Juan, that before walking your shoes should be securely fastened; your insistence on professionalism is sane advice to any young writer. Another teacher was Charles Rosario, my dear Charles; but Charles was always the lenient father, inclined to exaggerate virtues and cover up defects.

Then there appeared our literature's great missing person, José Luis González. José Luis, an avowed Communist, will forgive me the following anticlerical affrontery: When I was a child I thought that all bishops were tall men with round bellies; Jaime Pedro Davis visited my town and that prejudice was happily confirmed to me. Perhaps from that wild, childish imagination sprang the governing bishops of my novels and my affection for José Luis González. How did this great friend of mine come across my work? It was by way of Mexico, his beloved second country. Allow me to explain myself: Miguel Donoso Pareja, the Ecuadorian writer, asked me in August 1976 to collaborate with him on the magazine *Cambio*. He had read *La renuncia del héroe Baltasar* and was somewhat mysteriously impressed. José Luis read a fragment of *La noche oscura del Niño Avilés* in *Cambio*. On his next visit to Puerto Rico he wanted to visit with me. When he met Vivas Maldonado in the El Patio restaurant of Río Piedras—in those days both writers lived in the hotel of the university—José Luis asked about me; Vivas arranged a meeting. So this was how one evening in 1977 I received one-fourth of the generation of the 1940s at my apartment in the El Monte condominium complex. To cap it all, both were called José Luis. That night I read long and extensively to them from the manuscript of *La noche oscura*. I was wearing my British navy shirt, the one for good luck; José Luis González would not stop praising me when I served a bowl of seedless grapes as an appetizer. Soon after the room filled with smoke and praise: my Camels overwhelmed the Marlboros and Winstons of the others while my voice, choked by emotion and shyness, strained to keep up with the rhythm of Avilés's long baroque sentences. When I finished I looked anxiously at José Luis González; I became my own critic before the frugal, meticulous, and exacting writer of the short story "La carta." I demonstrated my dissatisfaction with the excessively elaborate texture of my prose. José Luis shook his head from side to side and said, "That is what you are capable of for now and it is very good; we will see what happens later on." A younger writer's insecurities are many when he is confronted with another's established respectability.

Shortly afterwards I invited Luis Rafael Sánchez to my house. Güico has always insisted that I be true to my own voice, to my particular way of seeing and expressing reality. He has been one of my principal mentors since the very generous letter he wrote me after reading the manuscript of *La renuncia*. I read new fragments of *La noche oscura* to him; between chapters we ate marinated fish; he was still just as enthusiastic as he had been when he first read my work. Others involved in my learning of the craft whom in all fairness I must mention are: Juan Antonio Corretjer who, while sitting in his warlike Rambler as we were leaving his house in Guaynabo, said one Saturday afternoon years ago, "I have had to go against my ideology to appreciate what you write"; José Luis Vega who has also been one of my readers over the years; and Juan Sáez Burgos took the first manuscript of *La renuncia* to Arcadio Díaz. After all, learning how to write, as we have seen, is a dialogue between masters both immortally faraway and nearby and between eternal and silent books and their patient readers. I cannot complain, I have had an abundance of both. I have never been short of advice to listen to, nor of teachings to read.

It is through these paths of appreciation that I come to my book. Talking about one's own work is an exercise in futility, conceited at times, and almost always deceitful. When a writer talks about his own work, most of the time he is moving on the dangerous turf of his intentions and not his accomplishments. What a writer has accomplished with his work is a matter for the critics. But, do you not think it is also interesting to explore that unclear, labyrinthian place, that region where the writer traces the Utopia of his talent, that place which is upsetting at times, but where one's works are more a project than an end result, and more a plan of attack than a conquered city? There is a critic turned inside out in every writer; that voice which traces intentions and forms according to the limits of talent is the imagination. Forms seek to justify themselves; those are the intentions we are talking about, the poetics of the creator. I would like to say something about this. But I am also interested in revealing something which is contained in the imagination. This is the seed of one's work, as it were, that particular way of inciting one's imagination—what we might call the way a writer approaches reality.

It just so happened that one afternoon in 1972, while I was studying in Madrid on the street called Sainz de Baranda, seated on a green sofa next to a window overlooking a typical Madrid-like interior patio, the sum total of forms that I needed to write a book was revealed to me. Put another way, that particular organization of form and feeling which we call individual style hit me as if by divine inspiration. It was perhaps the most authentic moment of inspiration that I have had since I began to write. I was not very clear at the time that it was to be a novel; I remember perfectly that I had conceived that form as some new literary machinery, halfway between the long narrative and meditation. I perversely had thought that it was possible to narrate an idea, to relate subtly the perfection of a syllogism. After all, having already read almost all of Borges' works, it was not difficult for me to figure it out. But I must confess that at that particular moment influences began to fecundate my originality. The fact that this book was later affiliated with the genre of the novel is purely accidental. Perhaps I did not think about a novel because at that time it would have terrified me to begin to write one. This psychological trick relieved me from having to face the task of writing "my" first novel. Nevertheless, very Hispanic and solemn, "I headed for the office," without Unamuno's cane or Ortega y Gasset's cigarette holder. In that cold corner of Madrid's spring I wanted to write about my warm faraway island, and about times and men even more remote. Two months later the book was written. I discovered with *La renuncia del héroe Baltasar* a way of exercising a fantasy-filled imagination. For me the imagination is the faculty for transforming experience into a work of art, whether it be realistic or fantastic. Fantasy is a more specific ability which transforms the visible into the invisible, experience into hallucinations, nightmares, or dreams. There is a gratuitous, "ludicrous," mysterious, and lustful inclination involved in fantasy; this slightly diabolical inclination of talent is that which in the eighteenth century was referred to as "capriccio." *La renuncia del héroe Baltasar* is a capriccio. When I wrote it I was passionately interested in El Bosco, Goya, Fuseli, Piranesi (even before I knew any of his work), the erotic literature of the eighteenth century, parody, mannerism, linguistic textures, virtuosity, the chronicles, and the eighteenth century and the exercise of power. It has been almost ten years since I wrote that book. As time passes, writers do look down on their first work. I do not plan to comply with this. I hold that book in high esteem, which is why I published it, despite the fact that prior to its composition I had written a book of short stories. What are its virtues? These are inextricably linked to its defects. It is an astute work, with a complex structure which still astonishes me today. There is complexity in the texture of the prose and even in the way that this prose is organized. But the subtleties of the text made characterization more difficult. The characters of *La renuncia* are men known through the written word, from what they write, from their memoirs, diaries, and letters. Characterization is achieved by transforming the characters into unrepentant scholars. This gimick required an eye for details and gestures in order to become fully effective art. But, as it happens, the writer of *La renuncia* was an extremely brainy young man, dazzled by Borges and Cavafis and a little frightened by the prospect of having to come to grips with the fact that in addition to an ingenious intellect, fantasy, and other lesser virtues, the writer needs to learn how to look at reality. That is the most difficult thing for a writer like myself; it is without a doubt the thing which has been most difficult for me. To look at reality is to learn how to characterize through situations and things, gestures and details. That is what seems to have been missing ten years ago. That is why it is a work which is more astute than intelligent, more ingenious than wise, more celebral than emotional, often cold in its characterization, with a firm though schematic plot. *La renuncia* is a work written under the label of fantasy, that virtue all too overrated since the appearance of García Márquez. It is a fancy design created by dazzling trickery which is only partially touching.

But what was I trying to accomplish with that work? No more and no less than to go to the seed of our nationality, to that blurred eighteenth century where the birth of our shared living is hidden. I did not wish to resort to history or documents. I decided to invent my own eighteenth century that would be like a nightmare of Puerto Rican history. Nightmares also say something about reality. Every nocturnal hallucination is the key to understanding hidden fears. Whoever reads this superficially will think that I am talking about Haiti. Go back and read it as you would read a nightmare, guessing the front side from the reverse, this from that, history from imagined myth, the truth from a lie. What has been more real in the long run: the chronicle's view of Ledrú which shows Black slaves and White Creoles living in harmony, or mine, showing that even today a disturbing restlessness exists on the hasty marriage of that young child Josefina to the renegade Baltasar? Somehow that novel expresses the deepest repression of our collective consciousness, which explains our racial complexities and the internalized colonialism in which we are up to our necks, our second skin. I know I am in the realm of myth, and I am not sorry. I never confessed to being a Marxist, even though José Luis González has proven me right in *El país de cuatro pisos*. But *La renuncia* is something more: It is the beginning of a theme which comes from my dark side. *La renuncia* is a novel about parenthood. Up until now that has been the great demon of everything I have written. My work of art is a dialogue between a young and an old man, between illusion and disillusion, between ignorance and maturity, between Utopia and imperfection, between desire and reality, between life and fear. Well, enough of that, for I risk converting this statement into a confession.

Now something else about imagination being seduced by fantasy, the true emblem of my youthful works. For many years I valued excessively the ability to imagine the almost invisible, and this was something compulsive in me, as if my talent—or perhaps my melancholia—had no other option than to exceed continually the bounds of what was lived and observed. This inferior mode of literary talent was imposed on my craft; I was a young, astute, and capable writer, with no other option than to convert my weaknesses into somewhat dazzling virtues. Often this is the cause of the young writer's deceit; he confuses his skills with originality and ease with talent.

Now I will tell you about an unpublished work, one which perhaps justifies my participation in this conference, and show the plans for my second novel, *La noche oscura del Niño Avilés.*[1] After finishing *La renuncia*, Charles Rosario advised me to take a break. I was twenty-six years old and very impatient. I undertook to write my second novel, the second part of a trilogy projected to cover eighteenth-century Puerto Rico. I confess quite candidly my innocence in the year 1972, when I began to write it: I set out to write no more and no less than a masterpiece. What a task! It took me six years. It is 1,500 pages long, possibly the longest work in our literature. Almost ten years after its conception, I can assure you that, instead of a masterpiece, I am simply holding a very long work, unpublishable to date: a literary white elephant which clumsily travels among my manuscripts, making things impossible, placing its enormous cheeks on new projects, since I am afraid to complete this trilogy of the eighteenth century without an editorial outlet. What is it about? I described it in the following way to José Luis González in Febraury 1979, five months after its completion (note the insecurity in the titles and the blind faith that it would soon be published):

> Well, here it goes. The novel's tentative title is *Crónicas de Nueva Venecia.* The first part, which I am checking and typing, will be ready in the summer and will have the title of "Pandemonium." I realize that it is intimidating. I do not like it very much either, but it is all I have been able to come up with so far (the truth is, titles are difficult for me!). Why "Pandemonium?" It deals with the many demons and devils which Bishop Larra unleashed, the great battle between the rebellious slaves and the ominous Bishop Trespalacios, where the great exorcism of the city of San Juan Bautista by said bishop is also told; the flight of all the little devils except one, the Gran Leviatán, future founder and governor of New Venice.
>
> The second part was to be called "El camino de Yyaloide." It deals with Niño Avilés's education by Bishop Trespalacios and Modotti, an Italian adventurer "who knows every trick and every angle." It deals also with the "maiden

voyage'' of Avilés to the mangrove, where, in the Arcadia, the adolescent boy falls in love with (how did you guess?) the pretty little Creole girl. After these trails and tribulations, his spirit tempered by love's dissillusionment, he embarks on a philosophical voyage to Havana, where he studies canons, lives on his monthly allowance from old Trespalacios and his skill at the gambling table, and gets involved in a thousand fights for being ''smart and a good fencer.'' But all this is also about the trials and tribulations of Bishop Trespalacios due to the absence of his godchild. Avilés comes back to Puerto Rico; the motives for his desertion to the English side during the attack of 1797 are told. The last part of this second volume will be occupied principally by the English siege and the different battles.

The third part has the title which I like best: ''La noche oscura del Niño Avilés.'' It deals with the foundation of New Venice by Niño Avilés and his group of madmen and dreamers. It deals also with the two moves of the Utopian city erected in the mangrove, a true ''lacustrine phalanstery.'' All the sacred cows of the novel die in these places: Trespalacios dies on a key; Modotti, Avilés's fencing teacher and a furious Venetian, travels to his meeting with Death from Cartagena de Indias, dragged along by the fame of New Venice, the city where he wishes to die, since ''the real Venice is at a distance half way around the globe.'' The chronicler Gracián, one of the most accomplished characters of the novel, dies also; and finally, the work concludes with the solitude of Avilés in the last place in New Venice, a row of little towers built by the dreamer architect, Silvestre Andino Campeche on Goat Island, which is related to the ''historical'' Campeche.

I would like to take advantage of this letter to talk to you about the theme of that strange novel which is now on the verge of publication and about to leave my imagination, to test its fate in that of other men. What is the theme of this work? Which is the clear side? (I am unable to talk to you about its darker side.) This novel deals with a Utopia. It is a novel about the perfect space which men long for; but it is also about the need which makes them indebted to time, war, death, and all that which subdues our precarious freedom, making it ''too human,'' transforming it into a caricature of the angelic will implied in all human efforts. (Not only is sainthood angelic, but the demonic is also a child of light!) New Venice, founded in *Las ciudades invisibles*, contains all imaginable cities: the infernal, Pandemonium, the Arcadian, God's and Leviathan's, the city for dreamers, the one for the powerful, the hope of the oppressed. Might this Utopia be the *state* which is still lacking from our nationality? But, a novel about Utopia must be by definition a treatise on pride. In this case it is about the pride of a young man scarcely over the narcissism of his first youth, who launches himself into politics, into the ''organization of hope,'' as Bishop Trespalacios puts it. Avilés is a youngster who has barely become an adult owing to his inability to overcome his childhood necrophilia and ''romantic anxieties.'' He is unable to free himself from the identifying traits of his personality: impudent aesthetics and the perverse fascination he feels for death. Avilés has very little aptitude for life: He is never born to ethical life; he never accepts choice as an unavoidable reality of human need. The Utopia arises from there, which is precisely an attempt to attain the city of God in ''the kingdom of this world.'' That is where my Niño Avilés is! He is tangled up in the word and prophecy, wanting to reach perfection, ''happiness,'' without realizing that

> we men only have a choice between the human and the demonic. "It was a dark night, and now I have left it behind; but I believe that it has sweetened my life."
>
> I am going to quote to you from Hostos in *La peregrinación de Bayoán*—he will shed some light on that which my clumsiness darkens—so that you may better understand the road taken from *La renuncia del héroe Baltasar*: "And transforming pain, from an obstacle into leverage, and subordinating the problem of happiness to the one of obligation, and preferring the battle of reason to the triumph of the heart, *I submerged myself in the study of history*."

La renuncia del héroe Baltasar placed me within the limits of my imagination. After that effort, I wanted to acquire a more temperate style. I had to reeducate my talent. But I discovered that I had already done it; those six years of work on this novel had transformed my craft. In what way? In the first place, in spite of the parodical use of language in *La noche oscura* and the desire to emphasize the surface of prose, I was able to come up with much more profound characterization, meaning the texture did not take away as much from the humanity of the characters as it had done in *La renuncia*. The narrative space was not accomplished through linking anecdotes, but rather with organically articulated situations. The result was a more vital structure. The characters lived and the space of the novel breathed. I became more meticulous in the art of blending situations with gestures and details. Gestures observed in the street or the barber shop were included in the novel about the eighteenth century. The relationship between characters and things became an obsession, symbols began to be based more and more on experience and observed gestures. While symbols became more necessary, visions abound, but their sense is embodied more in imagery. While the visionary and symbolic are magnified, a precision almost lacking in *La renuncia* is established. I am within the limits of my fantasy; but the "whims" of my fantasy become increasingly meaningful, less "ludicrous" and unfounded. The privy relationship of the visionary grows with the plot. I take more chances than I did in the previous novel, but the fruits are more numerous; I flirt with allegory, but this in turn does not abandon anecdote. The writer has changed, because the man has changed. Once I had overcome the narcissism of my first youth, I longed to take a closer look at life. As the writer conquers his personal neurosis—the same demon which put pen in hand—so does the approach attain a more complete and total vision of the human condition. I was acquiring, at last, a balance between observation and fantasy. Literature was already, as Hemingway pointed out, knowledge transformed into imagination.

I would like to mention the development of a technical element in this second novel. The point of view in *La renuncia* tries for a false omniscience. A first novel is almost always autobiographical. In some ways *La renuncia* also is, but in the most indirect way possible, for it uses some subtle distancing mechanisms, and in a most complicated way avoids the first person which would point toward the author. I achieve an authentic, omniscient voice in *La noche oscura* without recourse to absolute distance, which in *La renuncia* is achieved with the speaker. I also insist on an acquired omniscience on behalf of the different first person voices. But I am not satisfied. That multitude of voices which I have within me, that multitude of writers which are like the different voices of a parodist long for, as Vivas Maldonado pointed out to me, a unique voice. I feel comfortable with the first person and the illusion of a third; but perhaps my technique needs a totally omniscient story in the third person to purge itself of what a writer such as Hemingway would call a "straight novel."

I learned the value of observation of details and gestures with *La noche oscura*. I learned to base the symbolic on the common, as well as the unusual and fantastic. I stretched my imagination to the limits, creating a work of metafiction where the fantastic never abandons realism. I wrote compulsively for six years. My daily task prepared me to appreciate new readings and to permit new influences. I discovered the outstanding quality of three great novelists: Malcolm Lowry, Alejo Carpentier and Joseph Conrad. Reading Lowry reaffirmed my belief in the effectiveness of a rigorously symbolic realism. Carpentier showed me the possibilities of a critical history. Conrad confirmed to me the supreme lesson of situations and things, details and gestures. Even in high school I read some short novels by the brilliant Pole. Now I was to discover, in *The Nigger of the "Narcissus"* (in that passage where the trapped Black man tries to get out through an opening between two planks), the eloquence of detail which captures an emotional situation—in this case, fear. I did read a lot of Thomas Mann during these years, and it is perhaps he who is responsible for such long inspiration.

La noche oscura was my real apprenticeship. I owe to it almost my entire craft as a writer. Even if it is never published it will continue to be the most important work in my development as a writer. It is perhaps for that same reason that destiny has condemned it to silence; it is too aware of my weaknesses and failures, my desires and efforts. Perhaps with its silence that very wise work is pardoning my life. What will be the inevitably dark fate of this second novel? I do not know. Perhaps its future lies more in the ups and downs of the cost of paper than in any action on my part; in these inflationary times publishing houses prefer small narrative accounts and big bucks.

Now we come to *Las tribulaciones de Jonás*. I wrote this book in one stroke, without any difficulties, in less than a month. The apprenticeship which I assimilated from *La noche oscura* allowed me uncommon ease. Again, it is a dialogue between the old man and the youngster; but now the personal anecdote and the social interrelate in the most perfect way. The book is my dialogue with the patriarch; it is also a loving conversation with that mural of our complex baroque humanity, the people at the funeral, at which time the leader's profile is completed with that of his countryman. Personal obsession intersects with that of the masses, and a fan of meanings opens which transforms this book into my most accomplished work. All modesty aside, there are few traits about *puertorriqueñidad* (what it means to be a Puerto Rican) which are not at least sketched in that book. The book is an inventory of our vital and political complexity, an intensely effective charm to adjust to the pattern of our shared living and the gestures of our conduct; what is missing from this is that which only the most stubborn love prevents us from seeing. I do not want to talk much about this book. I prefer to leave that to the critics, for it was only recently published and they are the ones who must explain it. But I shall say something about it.

This work starts a dialogue which was previously missing. I am referring to the couple's dialogue. I have always considered *El coronel no tiene quien le escriba* to be the most accomplished work of García Márquez. A writer's most accomplished work does not necessarily have to be his masterpiece. This refers to the most complete exercise of the imagination, to that most perfect realization of one's abilities with the fewest number of resources. *El coronel* is a long conversation between an elderly woman and an elderly man, a definite contribution to the literature about marriage which goes from *The Odyssey* to *Macbeth* and *Under the Volcano*. *Las tribulaciones* is also a book about marriage; a great man and a passionate woman dispute the protagonist's role. Until *Las tribulaciones* female characters were for me a totally unexplored area. It is perhaps a cliché to say that female characters require more effort than male characters; men are complex, while women are mysterious. In my case this is a perfectly true statement. With the characterization of Doña Inés, I have achieved my greatest female character. If she is consistent with her characterization in the book, I suppose she will hate me. If she does not hate me, I suppose she deserves another book. For now let this one do. And let it be known to her that in spite of her silence upon receiving my book, I am still in love with her human complexity, with her inevitable condition of being an intensely Puerto Rican woman.

What other than less expressive greetings and a few invitations to the living rooms of politicians have I gained? Nothing less than a new way of expression. The chronicles, diaries, letters, and gossip implacably captured in words are the preferred voices of my heroes and villains, from Bishop Trespalacios and Garcián to Niño Avilés, Baltasar, and Bishop Larra. These chronicles of the eighteenth century have taught me to be a witness to present day-events. I learned with them to look at reality, to fall in love with it, and to transform observation into a constant labor of the pen. By listening to them, that linking of contradictory extremes, of a baroque ablaze with complexities, of the exaltation of the absurd which we breathe in all the air of this country, developed in me. Without the chorus and the macabre dances described by Gracián in *La noche oscura*, I would have never been able to accomplish the mishmash movement of Muñoz Marín's funeral. But, what is the chronicle for the contemporary writer? I offer this definition which I owe more to my own experience than to another's manual. Let us first distinguish between the chronicle and the aged tales of customs: tales of customs are static and the chronicle is dynamic; the chronicle deals with capturing a single event just as it happens through a situation of shared living, whether this be a wake in Ehret or a beach fry in Piñones, a meeting of the Popular Party or a visit from Juan Mari Bras to the Exchange Club of Summit Hills. If Rubén Berríos were to sample the corn feast and *pinchos* (shish kebabs) of the coast, I would come running to write that chronicle, even though this would launch me headfirst into a difficult genre of science fiction. What position should the chronicler adopt under such privileged circumstances? Maybe that cursed book has made me highly visible; in the chronicle part the efficiency of the burial of Muñoz is due to my desire to make myself invisible, that is, seeing a lot and greeting little. Since the book's publication many people have become nervously aware of my presence, some have run the risk of inviting me to their homes, others overwhelm me with assignments to write the chronicle of this or that, as if I alone were able to make the sociology and literature of the damned country. Now, since I am fairly well known, this profession of chronicler seems ironically to be dead at birth, though my presence will undoubtedly help to improve the general behavior of the country.

What other fruits have I harvested from this book? I believe I have acquired the appropriate vocabulary to tell of my time; it is a prose which does not avoid expressive Anglicisms, the crude word of a vulgar saying; gossip transformed into art, the merriment of the streets livens up formal syntax, the tasteless stands side by side with the sublime—I am expressing the gaudy. When a writer is mature he no longer fears sentimentality, and so I go on killing that sober Civil Guard which is the curse of so many Puerto Rican writers, a ruthless guardian who left us the imperial language and who even today looks over our shoulder to pry into our writings. The liberation of language implies a freeing of sensitivities. I want to be a witness both of the *pinchos* of the coast as well as the chromatic excellences of Campeche. All Puerto Rican reality impassions me, from brother Manuel's song with his conga drum before swimming across the bay of Guánica to the pastoral visit of Bishop Arizmendi in the year 1812.

Who am I? A Puerto Rican writer beginning his thirty-sixth year. If I had realized my first dream—to be a baseball player in the big leagues—I would now be on the verge of retirement. In Puerto Rico, a tenderly patriarchial society, I am still a young novelist. That is gratifying but not consoling. I am neither a young nor mature writer. Rather I am a writer in crisis who finds himself between the enthusiasm and innocence of *La noche oscura* and the compassionate precision of *Las tribulaciones*, between the faith of youth and the dark hope of maturity, between the myth of the first two novels and the history of a third which I hope to begin some day. Once the demons of youth are recognized and almost expelled, I am tempted to become a mere reader; the compulsion to write is tempered; my destiny as a writer will be dependent upon the passion with which I receive another's wound. I have discovered that happiness is more difficult to express than misfortune. I would like my novels to have four unavoidable elements: comical, lyrical, tragic, and erotic. It is in this way that Santayana defines literature. I have added the erotic because without this conversion of sexuality into fantasy the novel would be the final point of literature, our survival as a species would be kidnapped by obstetics. I am sometimes taken in by the image of the solitary creator: Simón Rodia who constructed on the patio of his house in the Watts ghetto his incredible towers, decorating them with broken windows and shells, the bottoms of Seven Up bottles and little mirrors. No one paid any attention to him, thinking him more a nut than an artist, and when they did remember him it was to shower him with stones. But not a day went by without this stubborn dreamer going to work on his towers, with a bottle of wine always at hand and his illusion ablaze. When he finished the towers he simply disappeared, without pain or glory. Nothing more was ever heard from him. To write in Puerto Rico is something like parodying poor old Simón Rodia. Every Puerto Rican writer has experienced the intimate desolation of knowing that there are very few who listen. But it is for them, the deaf, that we build these towers. Very well aware of this were Zeno Gandía and my great-uncle, Ramón Juliá Marín, whose novels *Tierra adentro* and *La gleba* have undeservedly been forgotten. Laguerre, Díaz Valcárcel, Pedro Juan Soto, and José Luis González are well aware of this today. Our intellectual and literary tradition is still unripe; we Puerto Ricans prefer *salsa* to the short story, baseball to the novel; the Puerto Rican writer is not hailed as a part of our national pride, despite the thousands of students that have graduated from our university. The Western tradition of "higher learning" has become middle-aged between basketball games at Roberto Clemente stadium and traffic jams in the fifth extension of suburban Santa Juanita. The generation of Platero and Juan Ramón which strolls with "the peripatetic" through campus is today undecided whether to read *Hombre de mundo* or *Vanidades*. What does destiny have in store for that generation which fervently applauded Jorge Luis Borges's honorary doctoral degree? Let us not fool ourselves; in spite of the war of the galaxies and ancestral nosiness, our life continues to be excessively commonplace. That is what our calling has been. But we must forge ahead with those towers besieged by indifference; if we were to abandon them, we would betray the little that we can have in this abject colony, that is to say, an image of ourselves. I wish to explain myself and my country, come to terms with personal demons and eradicate the collective ones. For me literature is not the pleasure of the text, but a road to salvation, which is the same as searching for a road to life and liberty. It was that which initially brought me to literature. It is in that ethical dimension that all its greatness lies. That is why I considered literature to be important when I was eighteen years old. The day that faith in its greatness dies in me, I will have died as a writer. Literature has nothing to do with doctoral titles and palace receptions; it has something to do with critics, but really very little to do with universities. Literature has to do with life and how we come to grips with its terror and come to deserve its beauty. I do not pretend to advance Puerto Rican independence with my writing. I only wish to understand why we are like we are, and why we are where we are. In the worst moments when cynicism scrapes the bottom of our dark hope I conceive of my country only as a curious object of knowledge; but that is only in the worst moments. I am always at war between the most intense love and the most rancorous anger. That is the way it should be, until we shed more light on hope.

Note

1. Edgardo Rodríguez Juliá, *La noche oscura del Niño Avilés* (Río Piedras, P.R.: Huracán, 1984).

13

The Two Lived-In Houses

Edgardo Sanabria Santaliz

When I was less than one year old my parents moved from the town where I was born to the city of Río Piedras, where my father studied accounting at the university and where the three of us lived in an old boarding house with an echoing staircase and walls covered with water paint that stained one's fingers when brushing them against the surface, and rooms with overhangs so high that they appeared to have been constructed to house elephants under the poor solitary light bulb which anointed everything in an oily yellow when turned on. That place would not remain in my memory because I was still very little and because my father completed his studies in less than a year; he obtained a good government job and the family moved again, full of hopes, this time to an urban development. I would remember that other place, since it was there that I spent the rest of my childhood, my adolescence, and the first ten years of my coming of age.

That which comes to my mind before anything else is the vision of the street without trees which seemed to lose itself in the horizon, a new tarless street, made of wrinkly grey cement. The sidewalks had rounded edges such that they ended at an almost nonexistent groove that made up for the gutter and which, upon going around the corner, emptied into a kind of subterranean prison, a bottomless black pit with thick bars where the sound of the drops echoed, wetting the darkness, and where I believed an enormous and repulsive frog took shelter and swallowed everything going in there. In the center of the street, spaced out at intervals like the Our Fathers of a rosary, the circular manhole covers shone beneath the hot sun and rattled as the cars, shaped like birds and insects, passed over them. The only signs of vegetation were the small Maltese cross bushes and red poppies which unknown neighbors, also recently moved in, had planted. And in front of the houses, in every squared plot, stood small tufts of scanty grass in rows which were hosed down in the afternoon, under the illusion that this would make the flora (with caterpillar tractors had leveled off when building the urban development) grow again. All the houses were exactly alike; perhaps one was distinguishable from another by being a different color, but the great majority were different from one another by a letter and a number on some part of the cubic frontage. They were duplex houses which repeated themselves inside as if there had been a mirror in place of a dividing wall between them. Inside, five rooms with limited space and a very low ceiling were crammed: living room-dining room, kitchen, bath, and two bedrooms. Everything seemed immense to me: the roof, as high as the sky itself; the Venetian blinds (with narrow, bright green strips of aluminum) extremely wide, when in reality they were no more than three-by-six feet rectangles which kept the light from penetrating through; the step from the living room to the balcony, a precipice which I feared when it was no more than a little jump for the crickets on their first attempt. Since no one had put up fences yet between the patios, the animals which many people brought with them—dogs, chickens, and even goats and pigs—entered placidly through the doors that had been left open.

Time passed and my sisters were born. One day my father parked his first Chevrolet next to the house. On another occasion he appeared with a large and heavy box from which he removed, before the round and surprised eyes of his children, a television set: Behind the greenish black, silent screen, crouching figures were hiding ready to jump into our eyes and hearts—the Lone Ranger, Tarzan, Lassie, Rin Tin Tin, Superman, Laurel and Hardy, the Three Stooges—heroes and antiheroes to be added to those populating the comic books: Little Lulu, Batman and Robin, the Fox and the Crow, Chanoc, and the saintly protagonists of "Exemplary Lives." Also stopping once a year at the weed-filled lot on the corner was a humble circus—two melancholy clowns, a lion, some clumsy trapeze artist, and a few long-tailed screaming monkeys—which to my mind was the most sensational spectacle on earth. But all of these events were no more than that: singular events distributed scantly throughout the months and years, happenings that came along once in a while, each of them leaving a mark on my soul. As far as everything else is concerned, my life was regulated for the most part by the comings and goings between my house and the school where I was educated. Today the only recollection I have of this school is my fear of and respect for the nuns dressed in white and the bliss I experienced as I sat for hours on some bench in the empty church, inhaling the smell of incense left behind from the Masses and looking at the stations of the cross, the altars, the images which pointed with their fingers to the stained-glass windows filtering the light.

However, at least three times a year—during Christmas, Easter, and summer vacation—an undeniable miracle happened to me: my family packed their suitcases and left for the town. Crossing the island always consisted of a series of interlinked excitements—the landscape on the left, vaporizing rain from the faraway mountain range; the narrow and extremely long bridge that crossed the delta padded with aquatic plants at the entrance to Arecibo; the unexpected appearance of the postcard-like panorama of Guajataca; the blue meeting with the Pasaje de Mona and the graceful descent from Agaudilla to Mayagüez—surprises which paved the way for the most notable of all: Climbing the hill on Luna Street once we arrived to the town and getting to the top where Mother would point out a hospital and say to me: "That's where you were born."

A long, long time afterwards, when I was growing up, I would feel the need to write stories, and one of the shortest, a sketch, was to end in the following manner: "Up the stairs in a jiffy and in a moment the wonder of the house takes effect once more, the marvel of the nine rooms which gather the substance of our dreams." That would be the only way to describe what happened when we arrived at my grandparents' house. This house occupied two floors above a business divided into a travel agency and a gift shop belonging to Giusseppe, a naturalized Italian who, in addition to selling trinkets, was a photographer and a magician. It was a spacious house which faced one side of the mayor's office and the main square; it was an old turn-of-the-century house with a vestibule and living room separated by an elaborate centerpiece supported by attractive columns; and tall French windows with shutters and stained-glass arches which dyed the rooms three colors; and a turret flooded with the shrillness of light and air from which one could catch a view of most of the town: To the south stood the ancient Porta Coeli church facing a second square, the oldest, made of bricks and with streetlamps and wood and steel benches; to the north, the view of the peeling tower of the parish church crowning the cubist perspective of graded roofs. The space in the house that especially absorbed my attention was the balcony which stretched across the dark pink façade from one end of the house to the other. Through the silver-plated ironwork of the railing, reminiscent of fans and flowers in bloom, I used to comtemplate the events which brought the townspeople together every year in the square, from the sad processions of Holy Week to the feasts of the patron saint, when a giant net of light bulbs, strung out over the crowd, expelled with its pointillism a great portion of the night; and the floats of the giant Ferris wheel erected in front of the house almost rubbed as they were propelled against the balcony handrail. Below, the merry-go-round whirled infinitely to the sound of waltzes. Creating the fright that spoiled my dreams was the sudden explosion of fireworks (during the feasts) and the endless scream of the mayoral siren (when announcing a cyclone), events which forced me to take refuge in the most secret hiding place in the house, with my hands over my ears and my heart trembling. Those were the only fears I suffered while visiting the town. On the other hand, the two pleasurable images which I was to keep alive in my memory, filling me with amazement again and again, are the return of the swallows at sunset and their alighting on the electric cables running parallel to the balcony (the birds settled there, black like musical notes on a staff). That, and the time when I went down to Giusseppe's back room with my grandparents in order to witness the most extraordinary of his magic acts: His wife squeezed into a 12-inch flower pot, only her beautiful head showing, her hair combed and face nicely made-up, greeting everyone and speaking with all those who entered as if her usual self were standing there.

Such was the town. There, cats meowed like hungry babies before lashing each other with their claws in the shadow of the alleyways which lined off the houses, from where they were shooed away with pots of boiling water which left scraps of fur, still warm and bristly, along the streets. There the neighbors asked one another with complete naturalness which three it would be today, because destiny had irrevocably decreed, in some fateful moment, the demise of three inhabitants every day. There, mighty showers would fall all of a sudden and make one sleepy, showers which sounded like hundreds of crabs running around the zinc rooftops, or as if someone had been throwing stones from the sky. There, in the evenings, met four dishevelled aunts, dressed in mourning and sitting around the dining room table—in the center of the table stood glowing a glass container filled halfway with water—with their hands joined so as to invoke the spirits of dead relatives from years ago, so that they could find out the luck each one had had in the other world. The town was a hogdepodge of old houses and narrow streets through which there passed automobiles, wooden carts pushed by men yelling ''Fish!'' or ''Fruit!'' and trucks, uncommonly overloaded with sugarcane, which one could gather from the gutters as they shook on by. There were bells that struck the hour and quarter hour, and went crazy on Sundays, calling the six daily Masses; and also a commotion of bats complaining in the dusk as they emerged from the holes in the rotten planks of the eaves. In the town there was always a barefoot madman loose on the streets, and people had old names that glittered like gold when pronounced; and in the evenings the women rocked and fanned themselves with tambourines on the balconies as they watched the people pass by, while the men went to the square to smoke and talk of cock fights and a million other things.

The return to the urban development was always a sad affair, and the nostalgia only let up when my grandparents came to visit, bringing with them a small piece of the town. With the passing of the years, nevertheless, that return would be progressively more discouraging because things in the town would continue to change, while the urban development had multiplied with the persistence of cells throughout the length and width of the island, sprouting up in the outskirts of cities and towns and finally encircling them, after destroying all the greenery to replace it with rows and more rows of concrete houses, endlessly repeated. The world of the town, on the contrary, would continue to decompose until it disappeared the moment my grandparents sold the house with the long balcony and tall French windows in order to move, they too, into an urban development. From that time on we were not to return as frequently to the town (except to say hello to my aunt, uncle, and cousins who remained behind), and when we did go back we were to find that everything had been strangely modernized. The streets were wider than usual; a countless number of concrete houses had replaced the wooden ones, which were leaning and too rotted away; feasts were no longer celebrated in the square, but rather in some suburban terrain at the entrance to a brand new housing development; and the square itself and the church were eventually remodeled. In place of the lovely arbor where the band used to play music, stood a concrete block of questionable acoustical properties; instead of the giant oaks, there were half a dozen sickly little tress burning under a desert sun; and inside the church, the ancient walls were covered with Formica panels in imitation of marble, and in place of the old golden altarpiece stood a large, ornamental stone wall rising up to the cupola illuminated with neon tubes.

In my short stories, though not in all of them, the worlds of the housing project and the town stand out because they are both settings of experiences that have touched me deeply, experiences which, at some time in my life, I have felt the need to commit to paper, whether for purposes of clarifying them to myself, or to find or assign a meaning to them. The town and the urban development are the two houses inhabited by placid or nightmarish visions which give me the impulse to write. I do not belittle one house to go and occupy the other, but I do recognize that the town is a more spacious dwelling, with more nooks and crannies to explore, where there are figures and objects and splendors and darkness whose textures are closer to the warp and shadings of a dream. Curiously enough, with the passing of time the other house has been taking on the appearance of the town; or perhaps it was I who imposed the image of the town upon that other place which is already shadowed by trees, where there is a church that scatters the chimes of its bell throughout the air on Sunday, and where every neighbor has at least been able to individualize with details and additions the standard house they first acquired.

In our literature, the urban development has played an increasingly important role over the years, along with scenes from the city and the town, and rightfully so since this is a phenomenon that has been affecting our identity for almost four decades. The housing project is present in novels such as *Ardiente suelo, fría estación, Figuraciones en el mes de marzo* and *La guaracha del Macho Camacho*. As far as the genre of the short story is concerned, we find notable examples in books such as *La familia de todos nosotros* and in the collections published by a young writer who declares he belongs only and exclusively to the world of the urban development: Juan Antonio Ramos. This author allows us to see the space of the housing project from within, from its asphyxiating, dehumanizing, violent, and prosaic center; a perspective which, nevertheless, does not exclude the compassion hidden behind his dramas which seem to say: This is the way my world is, take it or leave it; I denounce it because I love it and grew up in it and it contains many of the best moments of my life. Paradoxically, while reading his short stories, one thinks at times of the town, or rather, of an outline of a town, and this is due in the final analysis to that which I have already suggested: The capacity for survival of our idiosyncracy despite the fact that we may be moved from one place to another, in this case from the town to the urban development, which we have to a certain degree transformed into a town. It is significant that the last short story of the previously mentioned book by Magali García Ramis, ''Guión de todas las casas,'' deals with an urban development and closes a book which explores family ties on a personal as well as a wider level: that which makes a large family of our country. I believe such a line as ''Y se sentirán un poco en comunidad'' (thus they would feel somewhat like a community), in spite of the ironic understones it may contain within the context in which it is expressed, redeems the neighbors of Villa Atenas somewhat from their everyday life.

I said before that as far as I am concerned, the town has disappeared. That is not true. The town, as I was lucky enough to have known it, remains alive and unchanged in my memory, requiring me to set down—as far as possible—the chronicle of its fall, before it is erased by time. In the final analysis, the reason why I tell stories, the reason which—keeping a respectable distance—compelled one of the great writers of this century: Marcel Proust. In the first volume of his monumental work, we find the following words which I quote because they summarize the basis of my literary vocation:

> But when from a long-distant past nothing subsists, after the people are dead, after the things are broken and scattered, still, alone, more fragile, but with more vitality, more unsubstantial, more persistent, more faithful, the smell and taste of things remain poised a long time, like souls, ready to remind us, waiting and hoping for their moment, amid the ruins of all the rest; and bear unfaltering, in the tiny an almost impalpable drop of their essence, the vast structure of recollection.

A smell and a taste. It is the famous scene of the little madeleine soaked in lime-flower tea. Sensations as humble as an odor and a taste are capable of calling together a universe. That is what memory is made of: odors and tastes, things heard and seen and felt. That is what literature is made of.

14

Dope Themes and Other Highs

Juan Antonio Ramos

It is said that the industrialization process in Puerto Rico in the decades of the 1940s and 1950s brought a disturbance in all orders, and that the short stories that appear during these years by the so called Generation of 1940 properly attest to this. Treatment of this new theme demands new techniques and stylistic recourses that will adjust to the chaotic and confused nature of the urban world. The fringe areas, the corner bar, the newsstand, the house of prostitution, the Latino barrio in New York, the battlefield in Korea serve as settings for the stories of José Luis González, René Marqués, Pedro Juan Soto, Emilio Díaz Valcárcel, and the people connected with these places—the unemployed, the alcoholic, the prostitute, the spik, the handicapped veteran—are called marginal beings. The drug addict, the so-called *tecato* (junky) is not included in this group since drug addiction is not perceived as one of the great social calamities of the aforementioned period. I think that it is with "Que sabe a paraíso" by Luis Rafael Sánchez that the character and theme of the drug addict begin to take on real importance in the Puerto Rican short story.[1]

Writing on social themes is sometimes dangerous for the narrator, particularly if he possesses ideologically progressive concerns (as I think is the case with the writers I include in this paper), since indignation before a world filled with injustice and abuse could induce one to moralizing or to presenting a simplistic portrait of reality. Because of this one cannot lose sight of esthetic considerations, since they will determine the literary worth of the work. The stories I study here, while having different focuses, are a good example of the balance that should be sought between the thematic presentation (the message) and the expressive (or formal) aspect.

Luis Rafael Sánchez approaches the subject of the drug addict with astute caution. He opts for an omniscient narration (in third person), and a festive irony is the tone that prevails in the story that begins like this:

> The dance was slow, slow the entrance to paradise. He had lain down mouth opened to enjoy the disappearance of the light, hands behind his neck, the body and the legs free. But the light did not go away, it remained intact in its plain sky of rafters, downright slow in the dance obligated by the wind that came up from the Marina. His head fascinated by this slow movement also executed a minimum of motion, motion that squinted his eyes and brought on the small and dear laziness that anticipated the outburst of pleasure.[2]

We surrender to the pleasure that the drug addict derives from the hallucinating experience of the drug, and the narrator describes it as a slow dance, a paradise, a relaxing joy that leaves us, disconnects our body, divides feelings and realities, is slow movement, a vibration that causes the eyes to close, divine pleasure. An inept, sententious writer would speak of the slavery that befalls those who embrace drugs, but Sánchez, without contradicting this, equates the exclusive, fantastic dependency of the addict on drugs with that of a believer and religion. We encounter this irreverent, parodoxic note beginning from the time that we reach the title of the story (''Que sabe a paraíso''), and it continues to accompany us throughout the body of the text '': . . . sap of paradise to be offered to the God of the veins, prudent most prudent needle, venerable needle, laudable needle, powerful needle, honorable needle, needle of the highest devotion, needle of protection and refuge,''[3] until at the end of the story ''Delia crossed the room and knelt beside him, her hands buried in her breast, like a deity about to initiate a ritual. He did not understand the ceremony . . . . Nor Delia's ascension over his body while she played in a rapture. Tomorrow you will be with me in paradise!''[4]

The action of the story lasts the length of the ''high'' undergone by the unnamed protagonist, and we experience it through the nebulous and lethargic images that float in his suspended and unstable mind. From that slow, divine dance the reader infers all the addict's tragedy, in its most sordid and miserable expression, and Sánchez has been able to convey that impression to us without engaging in bothersome diatribes. His handling of the proverbs increases and strengthens the rhythmic and sensuous pulse that gives form and meaning to the text. In addition, the author has taken advantage of certain terminology proper to the drug addict subculture to color his story with realism. This is the element that best identifies this literature; the use of the language of the addict, his slang as expressive instrument, key that the reader will have to decipher in order to enter the ''high'' story.

The protagonist of ''Que sabe a paraíso'' ''had spent the morning *working his connection* but *the last haul had half of humanity in hock*.''[5] His dead eyes denounced lack of ''sweet herb, savory dope, the savory dope and the saving stimulant.''[6] His old buddy angers him by showing off because ''I have a high . . . I have it man, I have it. . . . Let me live it richly elevated, let me live it, let me live it.''[7] The narrator from time to time slips into drug addict slang words or expressions, roundly and precisely seasoning this first "high" in Puerto Rican short stories.

The drug addict, who enters uninvited, has tried to take over the situation after becoming the center of attention when he claims the street name Papo Impala. He tells us that he is trying to break the drug habit, and he assures us that he will not fall back into it again: "No brother," he insists, "I swear to you that what I get into me is just one or another 'supor' . . . an occasional grass, but you know that's no vice, I do it undercover, but brother I am going straight, and I'll get a 'detox' so people don't bother me no more." Then he gets involved in Eddie Palmieri and "salsa" music and then we come to realize that he has told us his entire story.[8]

After listening to him, we do not know whether he will really break the habit or end up in jail, or worse, whether they will have to pick him up from the gutter and get him into an ambulance. It is simply a brief impression taken out of an ordinary day in the life of Papo Impala with no pretense of selecting or finding solutions.

The dominant tone of the story is one of roguish humor, neither bitter nor skeptical. This is an oral, rhythmic story—the protagonist is a salsa musician—where the abrupt image is common and on ocassions the direct and grotesque crudeness with which the character expresses himself is overwhelming.

In "Cráneo de una noche de verano" by Ana Lydia Vega[9] a guy narrates what happened to Güilson (no doubt a pal of Papo Impala) as a warning to his audience—drug addicts are individuals who in one way or another "are in the struggle." His story will serve "so that they become aware and try to kick the habit if they can. If not the dirty old horse will have you for lunch."[10]

There are some revealing differences between this story and the last two. The character created by Sánchez simply gives in to the pleasure of drugs without pretentions of wanting to break the habit. Papo Impala is frank: "I am not going to deny that the damned trip isn't good because if I say that to be stoned like a dog is bad, I am lying"; however, he realizes that one's mind "ferments" and worst, "one must hustle for money and you even pawn your balls to get dope."[11] Finally, the narrator of "Cráneo de una noche de verano" fights drug addiction without pretexts and uses Güilson's story to serve as a warning. Ana Lydia Vega wages a fierce attack against drug addiction, harshly satirizing her character, recourse that was also utilized in the aforementioned stories, but in a less direct manner. I say now "Ana Lydia" and not "the narrator" because the plot is dotted with comments of a voice of an ideological conscience that we do not conceive of in a repentant drug addict. The political implications suggest an allusion to statehood, declared and supported by the people and all the colonial parties of Puerto Rico.

The supreme act of national surrender is perceived through Güilson's "trip" from which one could infer that, according to the author, the social evil of drug addiction, to a great degree, is the product of a system debased by an unconditional dependency and a collective alienation that idolizes the dehumanizing comfort invented by North American power. Thus we see "the big gringo flag unfolded in the air, teasing him, slapping him with air blows, pinching his ribs with its mast."[12]

The risk Ana Lydia takes in openly presenting her position with respect to the social evils of drugs and their political implications does not reduce the literary value of the story, thanks to the artistic skill in its conception. What prevents this story from being a political diatribe is Vega's excellent control of the difficult art of satire, which she executes through the unfolding of a very particular language. Contrary to that observed in the previous stories, Ana Lydia rarely utilizes the slang of drug addicts; in its place she selects the use of an equally vigorous and colorful language, consisting also of coarse phrases and exchanges which are clearly associated with the common people. The following examples help understand this point:

> The sun was as it was born at the point of bursting.
>
> Do you know what it's like to see yourself pale and more shriveled than an asshole and in addition to shriveled, toothless?
>
> Then he got so hungry that he wouldn't even be satisfied with a barbecued dinosaur.
>
> Because of the sun and the hunger he felt that midday was coming like a patient in a bus of the AMA.
>
> Then things began to smell like Martín Peña Bridge.
>
> The whole avenue was filled with a crowd resembling an Ayatollah's rally.
>
> They played so bad that one knew it had to be the police band playing, something like the American anthem with a merengue beat, men.[13]

In this story as in "Papo Impala está quitao," the oral character of the narration noticeably stands out, but the emphatic satiric intention renders the drug addict a true human refuse, a human bug clearly undergoing spiritual and physical deterioration. The humor and roguish irony of "Papo Impala" here becomes a sustained mordancy and the descriptions of the character and his environment reach intense levels of grotesque crudeness, thanks to the utilization of images of a certain plasticity. After reading and rereading the story, one arrives at the conclusion that the narrator makes a commendable effort to warn his audience: He who insists on continuing with the "vice," if he is addicted, does so because he truly wishes that "the old dirty horse have him for lunch."

As we know, three stories do not make a trend in literature, but they can initiate one. The drug addiction theme offers good literary possibilities since, in addition to examining a stirring human problem, it also requires a distinctive formal treatment. Up to now satire, parody, and humor seem to be the fitting vehicles for working with the themes and character of the drug addict. This does not mean that the authors of these stories purport to ridicule narcotism, to the contrary, they attack the system that propels it, with its pressures and false values, to its moral destruction without offering real alternatives for rehabilitation. On the other hand, one has to understand that satire and laughter prevent the writer from falling to a pathetic and melodramatic level that would esthetically debilitate the story.

It is curious to see how much of the drug addict lingo has slowly been extending to the rest of the Puerto Rican population, especially but not exclusively among young people without social status considerations. Thus we have *gufiar* (to goof), *nítido* (neat), *bufiar* (to make fun of), *tener una nota* (to be high), *juquiar* (play hooky), *estar en la brega* (to be in the struggle), *janguiar* (to hang out), *buscar la cura* (to get a fix), *bróder* (brother), *broqui* (broke), *pana* (buddy), and many other expressions that we sometimes identify with the addict but that can be used by any ordinary citizen, or if he does not use them, at least he understands them or they are in some way familiar to him.

It would be encouraging to think that this phenomenon is a signal of a process of justification of our language, where new words would be added to the list of those we ordinarily manipulate. It would be worrisome, however, if the opposite were true: that the Puerto Rican, accustomed to using the new and comfortable vocabulary, would become careless, come to disdain and even forget the words that Spanish provides to express the same ideas we intend to communicate with "el gufeo de lo último" words that will then fall into disuse due to the fact that they are not heard or spoken regularly in the appropriate contexts, limiting in this way our expressive recourses.

The literary treatment of the drug addict theme presents a great challenge for the writer, since it demands the investigation of the grotesque web woven by the addict and the deciphering of the key peculiarities in his communicative acts. The representation of this disheartening portrait should be realized, taking into account the esthetic factor independently of the focus adopted. Art is the best option available when trying to obtain the pertinence and persistence of any literary work.

Translated by Lourdes Torres and Marvin A. Lewis

Notes

1. The story belongs to the collection *En cuerpo de camisa* (Puerto Rico: Lugar, 1966).
2. ''Era lenta la danza, lenta la entrada al paraíso. Se había tendido boca arriba para gozar la desaparición de la luz, las manos bajo la nuca, sueltas del cuerpo y las piernas. Pero la luz no se marchaba, seguía intacta en su vulgar cielo de vigas, solemne de lenta en la danza a que obligaba el viento que subía de La Marina. La cabeza fascinada por el despacioso movimiento ejecutaba también un mínimo de vaivén, vaivén que achinaba los ojos y traía el pequeño y querido mareo que anticipaba el desembarco del placer. Aunque esta vez, la milésima en una larga aritmética de jeringuillas, el mate divino se hacía esperar.'' Sánchez, p. 9.
3. ''. . . savia de paraíso para ofrendar al dios de las venas, puya prudentísima, puya venerable, puya laudable, puya poderosa, puya honorable, puya de insigne devoción, puya que ampara y protege.'' Sánchez, p. 14.
4. ''Delia atravesó el cuarto y fue a arrodillarse junto a él, sembradas las manos por el pecho, como una deidad que iniciara el sacrificio. No entendía el ceremonial. . . . Ni entendía la ascensión de Delia por sobre su cuerpo, mientras rezaba transportada. ¡Mañana estarás conmigo en el paraíso!'' Sánchez, p. 15.
5. ''Había echado la mañana *trabajando la conexión* pero la *última redada tenía en chirola a media humanidad*'' (my emphasis). Sánchez, p. 10.
6. ''[La] yerba dulzona, la tecata sabrosa y la puya salvadora.'' Sánchez, p. 10.
7. La tiene arriba . . . la tengo man, la tengo . . . víveme ricamente elavado, víveme víveme.'' Sánchez, p. 10.
8. ''noo mi pana . . . por lo más santo que lo que me tiro al cuerpo es una que otra supor y uno que otro tabacón, pero que tú sabe, eso no es vicio y es guillaíto, pero que mi pana estoy en la perfecta, y me voy a dar una limpieza paque no molesten más.'' I make a brief reference to my story ''Papo Impala está quitao'' (*Démosle luz verde a la nostalgia*, Río Piedras, P.R.: Editorial Cultural, 1978, p. 127) with the intention of placing it within the drug addiction theme.
9. This story is part of the collection *Encancaranublado y otros cuentos de naufragios* (Puerto Rico: Editorial Antillana, 1983). For this paper I have used the literary journal *Plaza* (nos. 5–6, Fall 1981–Spring 1982):34–39.
10. ''Pa que le den cabeza y metan mano si es que pueden. Si no se los almuerza a uno el viejo caballo mellao.'' Vega, p. 34.
11. ''esa pendejá no te voy a negar que no sea buena, porque si te digo que estar arrebatao común perro co nun cantazo bien sólido es malo testoy metiendo un paquete,'' ''hay que buscarse el billete y empeñas hasta los güevos por conseguirte la tecata.'' Ramos, p. 128.
12. ''la banderota gringa se puso a dar bandazos en el aire, cucándolo [a Güilson], jartándolo a galletas de viento, pullándolo en las costillas con el asta.'' Vega, p. 39.
13. El sol estaba como nacío a punto de reventar [Vega, p. 34].

    ¿Tú sabe lo que es verse a uno mismo jincho y más plegao que un culo y tras de plegao sin dientes? [p. 35].

    Entonces le entró una canina que no se le hubiera quitao ni con un barbiquúe dinosaurio [p. 35].

    Por el sol y el hambre se sentía que el mediodía venía pancima como enfermito en guagua de la AMA [p. 36].

Ahí fue que empezaron a güelerle las cosas a Puente e Martín Peña [p. 36].

Un gentío de Ayatola cubría la avenida entera [p. 36].

Por el desentono se sabía que era la Banda e la Policía, men, tocando algo así como el himno americano en tiempo e merengue [p. 38].

15

Juan Antonio Ramos: A Feminist Writer?

Carmen Lugo Filippi and Ana Lydia Vega

Juan Angel Silén points out in his book *La generación de escritores del 70* that one of the characteristics of the world view of that "generation" is the problem of the "double exploitation of women."[1] Books such as *La lucha obrera en Puerto Rico* (1971) by Angel Quintero Rivera, *Hacia una visión positiva del puertorriqueño* (1972) by Silén and *La mujer en la lucha de hoy* (1973) contribute to an "ideological alienation between the young writers and the generation of the 1950s in regard to the problem of the exploitation of women."[2] The speakers at a recent forum on the short story sponsored by the Pen Club of Puerto Rico agreed that the new focus on the woman question is perhaps one of the cohesive elements of the so-called Generation of the 1970s.[3]

In that same decade, the impact of Puerto Rican female writers who had been developing a forceful poetry and narrative began to be noticed. Rosario Ferré's first book found a favorable sociohistorical climate to promote some already effervescent ideas and a burning controversy at the same time as the feminist liberation movements, the international university students' protests, and the antiwar movement in the United States. A Pandora's box is opened from which will emerge a group of male and female writers of feminist orientation, that is to say, whose literature postulates that the integral development of women is inseparable from that of humanity.[4]

We wish to speak of one of these writers. It is the man who published in 1978 *Démosle luz verde a la nostalgia*, in 1980 *Pactos de silencio*, and who with his third book *Hilando mortajas* is already an established short story author in his own right: Juan Antonio Ramos.[5] Like Manuel Ramos Otero and Roberto Cruz Barreto, this writer of the 1970s puts women in the forefront of his narrative, creating psychologically complex characters. On this subject, Ramos himself, in an interview conducted by Ana Lydia Vega and Dalilih Jiménez, states: "Woman is a heroic figure for being agonic. She fights to be more than what her husband wants: the respected and respectful mother, the self-denying wife."

Seed of change, forger of the language that is transmitted, the woman is the fundamental nucleus of the short story writer Juan Antonio Ramos. In this paper we propose to examine the role and image of some of the heroines in the anguished universe of *Démosle luz verde a la nostalgia* and *Pactos de silencio*. We will contrast male and female images and present some conclusions that will contribute, we hope, to a better understanding of the work of this author within his social context and that of the generation of writers of the 1970s.

Horrors of Machismo and Other Evils

Evil mockers from Bayamón, veteran "crackpots," and punishing patresfamilias populate the pages of Ramos's violent stories where "nothing can flourish but the grotesque, the wretched."[6] When the man is not an active aggressor, he is a passive accomplice to the status quo of domination. His world is one of dubious privileges inside a moral whirlwind that accentuates the human misery of both oppressors and oppressed. None of Ramos's stories attacks machismo with more fury than "Latidos telefónicos" (winner of the *Zona de Carga y Descarga* prize in 1975). The protagonist, prototype of the sly seducer, expert Don Juan of direct dialing and other technological advances, discovers by means of his favorite pastime, the tapping of telephone conversations, that his long-suffering wife has beaten him at his own game. Overwhelmed by the Othellian furor that consumes him, he returns to his house drunk and sexually abuses his wife, releasing his vengeful lasciviousness in the very telephone receiver which he identifies with the absent lover. A more clear ring could not be heard. The crude scene that, to heighten the catastrophe, is viewed by the couple's children, is only the climax of a series of insults attributed to a phallical situation in what may well be a moral story of warning to impenitent machistas.

These monsters of insensibility who lash out without pity at the women of the stories lack, nonetheless, the moral stature of the traditional evil character of the movies. They are insignificant beings, prisoners of the taboos and prejudices of a guilty society. They live unauthentic lives, do not know how to love, even if they cry on women's shoulders as does Don Enrique (in the story "Elpidia Figueroa"), big baby of unconscious cruelties, responsible for the mutilation of his son. It is because of this that there is no artificial Male-evil/Female-good polarization. The evil are only evil because they do not recognize the price of their privileges, because their mothers have helped perpetuate the value of machismo, "they justify it and they transmit it."[7] And the good women are not all that good, as is shown below.

Witches and Witches' Brew

Entangled in their hell of gossip and conspiracies, resting behind the mythical "me generation" attitudes of the middle class suburbs of the decadent Commonwealth, many of the protagonists spin their webs of malediction and make others drink their hate potions amidst their brew of frustrations. Jealousy and envy reign in this underworld where love is prohibited. The only escape is the turbulence of emotions as can be attested to by Paula from "Podando los resentimientos"[8] or Miguelina Lorenzana from "Miguelina Lorenzana se despechó sin la bendición."[9] With an almost sleuth-like intelligence, these women play all kinds of games, mental doings and undoings in order to release the inhibitions and frustrations of the petit bourgeois lifestyle without any greater emotional outlet than that of attending Mass on Sunday. Some resort to infidelity, as in "Latidos telefónicos," "Scrabble," or "Adivina quién vino a verte,"[10] but those who do not dare, those who cannot invent interior worlds contrive Pandorian vengeance against scapegoats.

The story that best presents the Machiavellian mentality of this type of woman is "Podando los resentimientos."[11] It is narrated with a magnificent manipulation of points of view, the stories of Paula and Merche, whose lives intersect as neighbors of the same suburb. Merche comes from a hamlet, and her family is the black sheep of the respectable little world where Paula lives. The intrigues of Merche end in Paula's destruction, in what is a class struggle with sexual nuances that at times acquires epic dimensions.[12]

The same confrontation between classes is found in stories like "El espejo" and "El bautismo de un despojo," where marginal characters are simultaneously complementary and contradictory to other middle-class characters. The marginal character, as Ramos states, "is the split that nobody dares to undertake, the oppressed person is the true I struggling to burst out, the authentic, that which torments the other."[13] Asked if that *true I* is associated with sexual liberation the author comments without hesitation: "Yes, because that is the first liberation that one must achieve."[14]

The female binomial, repressed women/liberated women also appears in the story "Cuaresma."[15] Here the generation battle between mother and daughter is treated in the style of a less populated "Casa de Bernarda Alba."

Play of Mirrors: Masculine Paralysis and Stagnation versus Dynamic Feminine Unfoldings

This panoramic view of the gallery of females populating Ramos's stories would be incomplete if we did not concentrate on a specific text to point out in detail how he proceeds in the narrative with the literary treatment of female protagonists. The selection of point of view that Ramos makes in various stories whose protagonists are women is significant. The angle of vision or narrative focus in which the narrator places himself to tell his story determines, to a great extent, the type of relationships that are to exist between the author and narrator, between the narrator and what he narrates, and between the author and narrator, and the subject of the story. This has been corroborated by numerous studies, beginning with Perry Lubbock and continuing with Norman Friedman, Wayne C. Booth, Thomas Uzzell, Bourneuf et Ovellet, and Jean Pouillon, among others. For our particular purpose, showing the degree of distance the narrative voice adopts in the story "Elpidia Figueroa,"[16] we frequently refer to the theoretical postulates developed by Jean Pouillon in *Temps et roman*.[17] We agree with Pouillon that the problem of comprehension in the novel or short story is twofold: (1) What is the author's position in relation to his characters? (2) What is the nature of that reached by such comprehension? We are interested in exploring these two categories specifically in "Elpidia Figueroa" because the position adopted by one who wants to understand is influenced by what one wants to understand.

It is highly suspected that in "Elpidia Figueroa," as well as in "Podando los resentimientos" and in "Así son las cosas," a single feminine character is selected and then moved to the central position of the story, and that it is from this position that we always see the others. Assuming this position with respect to what is narrated has been called by Poullion "the view with" because it is through the main character that "we see the other protagonists, we live related events and, undoubtedly, we see clearly what happens in him, but only to the extent that what happens in someone is apparent to this someone."[18]

Such a vision requires an imagination that will bring us closer to that which we desire to be. Consequently this type of narrator demands from his writer as well as from his reader an empathic type of comprehension. An understanding which, as Pouillon suggests, "makes me put the others in me, understanding them, attributing to them my own feelings or ideas and for that reason, diminishing them or raising them according to the event."[19]

Various immediate consequences follow once one has adopted this position. For example, because the reader cannot separate himself from the narrative voice, he will find himself forced to know others through that central voice and will only be able to "see them" and "understand them" in the way they are captured and represented by the protagonist narrator.

Such is the case in "Elpidia Figueroa," where information about others is gleaned from a young servant girl who has emigrated from Naranjito to Bayamón in order to work in the home of Rosita Fonseca, a woman from her same town, because she preferred to do this type of honorable work "before having to become a prostitute."[20]

Rosita, her husband Enrique, and their son Raulito exist only as an image, since they are only projections of the protagonist-narrator, who irradiates a description of them so that they exist only as a reflected product of the comprehension the narrative voice has of them. Paradoxically, we have an embracing, almost profound understanding of these character-images conveyed to us through Elpidia's comprehension, the only guide in the analysis of others, but we lack these same resources when trying to understand her. Nevertheless, what is revealed in Elpidia's analysis of others helps us to formulate her image, because in the image she presents of others lies the key to her own.

Elpidia's narration centers on the disgrace that falls upon the name of Rosita Fonseca, the proud ex-small-town dweller who has married well and been able to escape the suffocating small-town environment by moving to a middle-class suburb in an urban zone of Bayamón. Husband, son, and house come to be the symbols of success attained by that Naranjito emigrant.

The uninterrupted discourse of the protagonist-narrator establishes from the beginning a complex play of mirrors where the image of a fat Rosita, enthusiastic spokesperson for the false values imposed by her own new social class, and unfortunately a prisoner of the most ominous bourgeois defects, is in opposition to the implicit image of an unaffected Elpidia, defender of the pure Creole customs. Nonetheless, the candidly objective discourse of the narrator reveals her resentment. Rosita has obtained what she was denied, indeed her position as servant is proof of her failure. While Elpidia never directly articulates her misgivings, we deduce that an image of another possible Elpidia that might have come into existence under more favorable circumstances is reflected in her married friend. Because of this, Rosita constitutes the antithesis of Elpidia, a frustrated old maid without a home, husband, or children. Now, if what is inferred from Elpidia's narrative contained only hidden frustrations, her character would lack the subtle complexities making her interesting. The presentation of absorbed possibilities, mere nostalgic potential, would have reduced her to an immobile stereotype. Fortunately we find ourselves before a narrative that conceals, behind ingenious descriptions and opinions, a network of dialectical connotations that transform the character through a dynamic force from which change emerges. Elpidia Figueroa is not limited to looking at herself in a mirror of jealousy, rather, in her narrative, an implacable criticism is directed at the deteriorating condition of the family relations of her employers. She is not dazzled by the false values of the nouveaux riches, she perceives the alienation of the women, the cruel innocence of the man, and the lack of affection of the child, who by the way becomes the object of all her attention and kindness. From the world of the other, Elpidia values only the child and the house, since these represent to her the yearned-for home, while she detests the duplicity of the man and the stupidity of the woman. This hatred reaches its culminating point when Rosita's jealousy and Enrique's insensibility provoke a catastrophe where Raulito ends up the scapegoat. As a result of a cruel beating by his father, the boy loses his right hand in an operation. This event acts as a catalyst so that the undeclared war between the servant and what the other represents gives way to a subtle confrontation, a dialectical process that is resolved in favor of Elpidia. And Elpidia does not have to make much of an effort to realize her unconscious desires: By virtue of its own contradictions the couple slowly destroys itself. The woman ends up in a mental hospital and her husband is driven to suicide by remorse. Elpidia's conscious omissions toward the end of the text are extremely significant: Although fully aware of Enrique's intent to commit suicide, she does not lift a finger to prevent him from doing so. Her position with regard to the others is clear: They are undeserving of any compassion. Because deep down, between what is said and what is left unsaid, between the information supplied to us by the text and what we discover between the lines, we understand that Elpidia's ambition is to remain with the best of the two worlds it has been her lot to live. We see outlined the task of creating another image that will be neither the marginal Elpidia nor the alienated Rosita, a happy synthesis that will give way to a new woman and a new reality; a reality from which stagnant and unauthentic beings have disappeared. From the moment Elpidia takes over the house, a new era begins in which the child and she will live "with tranquility" because it will be Elpidia and only Elpidia who will impose her vision of the world, free of tricks and wretchedness.

As in so many stories of Ramos, the woman is presented in all the complexity of the process of change: from subdued victim to rebel, including wielder of recently acquired power. She turns out to be an active, dynamic force, both thesis and antithesis. Elpidia Figueroa constitutes a clear example of a synthesis of those protean forms of women. From servant to owner of the house, the trajectory of this narrator-participant symbolizes woman's ascent from subordination to taking possession of her universe.

Translated by Lourdes Torres and Marvin A. Lewis

Notes

1. Juan A. Silén, *La generación de escritores del 70* (San Juan, P.R.: Editorial Cultural, 1971), p. 97.
2. Ibid.
3. Juan Antonio Ramos was one of the participants in the alluded forum.
4. Ramos Otero and López Rámirez have made use of female characters since 1971.
5. Both books were published by Editorial Cultural, San Juan, Puerto Rico.

6. Notes from the aforementioned interview published in *Reintegro* (no. 2, 1980).
7. Ibid.
8. In *Pactos de silencio*.
9. In *Démosle luz verde a la nostalgia*.
10. In *Pactos de silencio*.
11. In *Démosle luz verde a la nostalgia*.
12. Ibid.
13. Cited interview.
14. Ibid.
15. In *Démosle luz verde a la nostalgia*.
16. Ibid.
17. Jean Pouillon, *Temps et roman* (Paris: Gallimard, 1946).
18. Jean Pouillon, *Tiempo y novela* (Buenos Aires: Paidós, 1970), p. 62.
19. Ibid.
20. In *Démosle luz verde a la nostalgia*, p. 157.

Part III

Puerto Rican Literature Written in English

16

A Neorican in Puerto Rico: Or Coming Home

Piri Thomas

I was born on September 30, 1928 in Harlem Hospital. My mother, Dolores Montañez, was born in Bayamón, Puerto Rico. My father, Juan Tomás, was born in Oriente, Cuba. My name at birth was supposed to be Juan Pedro Tomás Montañez. However, when I grew up and looked at my birth certificate I discovered that it said John Thomas. And, whoever heard of a *puertorriqueño* named John Thomas? I wondered at the time about the reasons behind this: Was it a planned program on the part of the hospital authorities for assimilation? Or had they convinced my parents that to have a name like John Thomas would give me a better chance in the United States of America?

I believe every child regardless of color, race, sex, or geographic location is born with a sense of either identifying with or being identified with others. When I was a child I would sit in a little corner because at that time the young ones were not to be seen or heard. I have always disagreed with this idea. How else can you learn if you cannot ask? I would listen to imaginal projections of Puerto Rico from my parents. My mother, Aunt Angelita, Aunt Otilia, neighbors, and friends would talk about the fantastic island in the Caribbean, using terms such as "Island of Enchantment" and "Borinquen," talking about its beaches, palm trees, and mountains. It never snowed there. I would look out the window while they were talking and as I looked at the gray streets below I wondered—why do we live here? I would ask the question: Hey, what are we doing here, Ma? and what I would get in return was a little funny look. Of course, the situation was, and is, like it has been for every other immigrant that has come to this so-called Promised Land—it is always an economic problem. Believe me, those who have money in Puerto Rico only come here temporarily. They take a look and then they go back. It is only the poor who come here with a dream of someday going back to Puerto Rico, although they never quite make it in this sense.

When I was a child, like many others I wanted to "identify." I lived in three worlds: The world of the home; the world of the school; and the world of the street. At home, of course, it was very beautiful in many ways because Mami was a very spiritual woman.

I want all of you to know that I have written *Down These Mean Streets*. I could have written about Puerto Ricans living in penthouses, but Puerto Ricans were not living in penthouses on Fifth Avenue. If they were anywhere near the penthouses they were working as doormen.

Children are born with dignity and perceptiveness, and understanding, and they sense when they are loved or not loved. I am a human being who has not allowed the childlike qualities in me to be slaughtered by anyone. If you lose your childlike qualities, and this has nothing to do with childishness, you then lose that beautiful identity, your own personal dignity. That is what identity is all about, your sense of dignity.

I remember wanting to "identify" in school. I would dress in a white shirt, blue trousers, and a red tie. Doesn't that remind you of a walking flag? I did not mind at all. I would put my hand over my heart and pledge allegiance to the flag of the United States because it did say "with liberty and justice for all." I would sing just as loud the national anthem. I was a child and I wanted to belong.

Out in the streets, it was different. Racists could not make up their minds whether to call me a "nigger" or a "spik." I would say, "Hey you so-and-so, I am a human being, man. I'm beautiful, can't you see?" Like many children I was born very beautiful and natural, into a most unnatural atmosphere. I do not feel any shame or guilt for the things I wrote in *Down These Mean Streets* and my other book. I have learned within myself that I was not born a criminal from my mother's womb. I was born a very beautiful child in a very unnatural, criminal society, a society filled with racism, exploitation, and a complete lack of caring for human dignity.

It was not until I reached the age of thirty-two that I had a few revealing experiences. At times I thought that my youth would kill me, but one thing I had in my heart all the time was to see Puerto Rico. To visit Puerto Rico would be like a homecoming. In New York I felt that most of the time I would only be identifying with a fire hydrant. I could jump high over it but the funny thing was that many times I did not make it. I say this with humor because if I were to say it in the way it should be said, with the rage of emotion at the outrages and all the things that our people as a people have had to endure, my goodness!

I arrived in Puerto Rico in 1960, and once I got off the plane and felt the breeze I was dumbfounded. I got out of the tourist area and once I got past the Dorado Beach Club and the Hilton, I began to see that Puerto Rico was as beautiful as its people. I found out that in Puerto Rico there were green ghettos; there were grey ones here too, but I found beauty and dignity. Our country is beautiful because there is love and affection.

In Puerto Rico I discovered that my Spanish was atrocious. I spoke Spanish badly, but regardless of this fact I decided to go ahead because I was a Rican. Whenever I made a mistake someone would correct me without making me feel ashamed. One day I was talking and a little girl approached me and said, "Excuse me," and I said, "Don't mention it." She suddenly turned to me and asked: "Excuse me, are you from the North?" I said, "Hum." She added: "Are you from New York?" And when I asked her how she knew, she replied that it was because of the way I spoke Spanish. When she noticed my sadness, she asked for my forgiveness since she had not meant any offense. I only added that I wanted her to know that although I had been born in New York, my soul was Puerto Rican. And that I was proud of speaking the Spanish that I had learned from my mother.

I remember being in Puerto Rico in 1960 and working on a drug addiction program with Dr. Ramírez. I was exposed to a radio station where we could bring in parents for information. I remember my pride every Sunday morning when I got to that radio station. I sat in front of the microphone and said: "Buenos días, pueblo puertorriqueño. Este es Piri Thomas y con zapatos o sin zapatos, hablándoles en español" (Good morning Puerto Rico. This is Piri Thomas, with or without shoes, talking to you in Spanish). I was so proud to be in my country! I was born hung up in the middle, with no place to go. If you asked me now whether I have been accepted in Puerto Rico wholeheartedly, my goodness gracious! There is no way that I as a Puerto Rican here can be the same as a Puerto Rican from there. But one thing for sure is that we can certainly share, because being bilingual is not a crime, it is a knowledge, a way of flow, a means whereby we can defend each other to the best of our abilities and to the best of our souls.

In my young fifty-four years, I want to continuously be able to identify with that which is positive. I have found out that we will never have unity unless we can have a unity that is born of truth, without hypocrisy, without envy. We are not to deal with greed, that exploits men, women, and children of all colors. I have learned to identify with the feeling of being universal. Wherever my feet are, that is my turf. I am an earth being, part of the earth and the universe. This way I can reach out more and I do not feel confined by being defined and thereby diminished. I am proud to be the mixture that I am, and I am proud to be part of a family. The worst thing in the world for any child is not to belong or to be completely kept from belonging. I have learned that in order for us as humans—and I speak to you, the young ones of all ages—to know where we are going, we also have to know from where we come. That is part of our dignity. My enemy is not color, sex, or geographic location. My enemy is the enemy of all children: indifference to human need. I have learned to be very careful with words and feelings. I have learned to say what I mean and mean what I say because it is very important how your behavior can modify children's minds in the name of love. The children, young people, all of you were born highly perceptive, psychic if you will. When somebody says to me that we are a minority I take it as an offense. I get very angry because to me the word *minority* is just another synonym for "nigger" or "spik." *Minority* means less than and whoever heard of a child being born "less than"? I speak as a majority of one, similar to everyone but with different fingerprints.

If you ask me what I have learned about "identifying," it is that identification comes from within oneself. If you know what is inside of you, then you can relate to others. Relations begin at home, men-women relations, feelings. I come from a long line of machos and machismo and most big-mouthed macho mistakes. It is from good women that I have been able to learn. I had to first go in and check out the women spirit that is in me, that spirit that comes from my mother and will always last in my soul.

17

Puerto Ricans in New York: Cultural Evolution and Identity

Nicholasa Mohr

The European culture that has dominated these United States since its beginning is continually being imbued with the cultures of the people of color, and most recently by Hispanics. This infusion is the start of a new epoch, one that will be unique to the New World. Hispanic culture is now sweeping across three thousand miles: from the West Coast, Southwest, and Midwest, where huge areas are densely populated by Chicanos, to the South, where Cubans have turned Miami into a minor Hispanic capital. Finally, there is the East Coast and New York City, cultural capital of the Western World, populated by the greatest concentration of Puerto Ricans living outside of the island of Puerto Rico.

New York's cultural preeminence—both nationally and internationally—must reckon with its Puerto Rican community. This turn of events typifies the impact the Hispanics are having on North American culture as a whole. The Big Apple is undergoing changes. It is expanding, growing, and may yet become an Avocado—a brilliant one! A new group of people in large numbers, from a particular ethnic group, who struggle to retain their cultural heritage and at the same time will not remain cast outside the mainstream, inevitably alter their dominating ruling society.

A peculiar example of this process can be seen in almost any given area of this city where one sees bold brilliant spray paint exclaiming, "Chico-153 lives here!" Graffiti splattered in powerful swirling strokes announce that "Willie H/49 and Concha 703" are also part of this city. Rich in color, using symbols, numbers, and names, the graffiti decorates billboards, public vehicles, buildings, and, most dramatically, the subway system. The immensity of this visual vocabulary covers such huge areas that at times architecture seems to take on a design other than the one originally intended. Entire trains appear to be swallowed by silhouettes of color and pattern. This graffiti is put there by the young. They are the children of the people of color; for the most part Hispanic and Black. These young people are waging a war, shouting, "Look, *look at me!* Recognize I am here, I exist. I demand the right to be and will not be ignored." They defy a powerful threat—one that would seek to insure their immobility and eventually destroy their identity—the threat of invisibility.

Millions of dollars are being spent on clean-up campaigns, police and dog patrols, in efforts to stop this underground army of protestors. Embarrassed city officials and an offended public want the young people prosecuted and their images erased. No sooner is a section of the city or subway system repainted and cleaned that the images reappear. The tenacity of these youngsters and their energy and ability to continue in the face of such hostility is remarkable. Even more remarkable is that this graffiti war has been going on and growing for over a decade. It is still being handed down from one youngster to the next. A comparison can be made to classical guerrilla warfare, when the most sophisticated weaponry and troops do not defeat the people. This war, however, is not being fought with guns, but with one of modern society's most commonplace products, affordable cans of spray paint. Easy to buy—easy to steal. With this simple tool, combined with imagination and daring, the war against invisibility continues.

Beyond this kind of confrontational expression, there are other forms of visibility for the Puerto Rican. One has only to walk through neighborhoods in the boroughs that make up the city, and almost everyone sees *cuchifrito* (deep-fried pork ennard) stands and small Caribbean restaurants. The stands are laden with *alcapurrias* (fried food made out of ground plantain and pork wrapped in butter), *pastelitos* (native dish stuffed with ground pork wrapped in plantain leaves), and other delights of Puerto Rican soul food. We see *botánicas* (stores that cater to the needs of spiritualists) selling small images and statues of saints and African deities, potions to help in love, cure ills, prayers for luck; all to support the community in its daily survival. Advertisements, subway posters, instructions in public areas, notices and pamphlets are now printed in Spanish as well as in English. "Aquí se habla español" ("We Speak Spanish") signs, so prevalent in the 1960s and 1970s, are now obsolete. Of course, you had better speak Spanish, or you are a fool in business not to recognize who your best customers are. Even a Spanish business telephone directory is now available. Nearly everywhere one turns, Spanish is heard, spoken, and read. The Hispanics who are not Puerto Rican, adapt to Puerto Rican food, music, and even the colloquialisms. In spite of the hostility and concerted bureaucratic fight against bilingual education, New York is indeed a bilingual city. All this is being intrinsically woven into the daily lives of all New Yorkers, and is now a part of the fabric of this city. And even those who do not want to accept the changing pattern find themselves touched, greeted, and sometimes offended. But they cannot remain unaware.

The struggle for visibility of the Puerto Ricans had its beginnings when the first wave of migrants arrived in small numbers after World War I. I am the daughter of such a family who arrived here in 1927 with four children; they settled in the area that came to be known as El Barrio, Spanish Harlem. Later three of us were born during the Great Depression. Growing up, I remember that outside my immediate neighborhood I learned that being myself meant hardships and discrimination. For example, speaking Spanish in school resulted in punishment from my teachers. Visibility often evoked hostility and violence upon oneself and one's family. I remember no such graffiti then. No such boldness. The bits of graffiti that existed were to be found only in our neighborhood; so were the few restaurants, stands, *bodegas*, and *botánicas*. There were no public ads, signs, or displays in Spanish. "Rivera," when one went to rent an apartment, became "Rivers," and "Colón," when one went to work, was pronounced "Collin."

The impact of the great migration that followed my parents, arriving during the post-World War II era, was to bring about lasting changes, not only on the general character of this city, but for those of us who had been living here for a generation. They came by the tens of thousands, and in a short time the Puerto Rican population exploded.

Jobs, shelter, clothing, the basics, had to be provided for these newcomers. Relatives and friends doubled and tripled inside already crowded quarters. These newcomers faced the difficult adjustment to a cold climate, another language, and an alien atmosphere. Their presence disturbed not only the non-Hispanics who reacted with hostility and fear, but unsettled those of us who had deluded ourselves into thinking we had attained a peaceful and worthwhile coexistence with the White society that dictated our destiny. We had, in fact, only achieved a most tenuous arrangement. Fair-skinned Puerto Ricans were seeking a life alongside other White ethnic groups. Dark-skinned Puerto Ricans were becoming resigned to life alongside Black Americans. This polarization of racial identification permeated right into one's immediate family.

The arrival of this new wave of migrants was a rude awakening for us. They came wearing the flamboyant colors of the tropics and speaking their working class Spanish, loud and clear. These people with their unabashed ways were our sisters, brothers, aunts, uncles, cousins, parents, and grandparents. "*Jíbaros* . . . greenhorns . . . marine tigers," we whispered, and made fun of their accents. There were those of us who had never been to Puerto Rico, fantasized about Anglo-assimilation, and had developed a disdain for poverty. In some instances, our elders, who were themselves victims of the colonized class system from the island, abetted us in these values. Suddenly, we found ourselves surrounded by the poorest of the working class from the island. Consequently, we were awakened much like a semiconscious patient recieving a life-saving shot of adrenalin. These workers came here full of hope and promise, eager to work, creating an ambience which maintained the quintessence of their values and culture. We second-generation Puerto Ricans absorbed many of their mannerisms, adopting their speech patterns and integrating their music and folklore into our New York lifestyle. And in the end we accepted our kinfolk. From this time on we began to develop a greater sense of identity.

In the 1960s the civil rights movement and the Black social revolution brought us even more self-awareness. The question of whether Puerto Ricans were Black or White was posed. Color became not just a question of how White your physical countenance appeared, it symbolized a political and social philosophy. At that time we aligned ourselves politically with the Blacks, thereby defining ourselves as a people of color. Out of this time of frustration and anger came a sense of pride and self-worth. For the first time in decades we were motivated to political action. Programs such as Affirmative Action, bilingual education, and open enrollment in colleges and universities were implemented. Puerto Rican politicians began to strive and campaign for a voice in city politics. Toward the end of this decade there emerged poets, writers, visual artists, performers, musicians, and composers from within our community.

"Nuyorican," a term coined in the 1970s, is now used to describe those of Puerto Rican origin, born or raised in New York. Our poets and writers express themselves often in both Spanish and English. Our visual artists for the most part are deeply involved in the graphic interpretation of our daily existence. Musicians and composers are performing, creating, and experimenting with the rhythms of the Caribbean, classical Western music, and Afro-American jazz.

With the founding of Hispanic art and cultural associations, dance companies, bilingual theaters, small presses, and a museum located in our oldest community of Spanish Harlem, we have made inroads. The visibility of Puerto Ricans grows more evident with the passage of time as all our accomplishments begin to crystallize. Certainly not enough to fully meet our needs or help develop and accommodate the potential young talent in our community. But a benchmark has surely been carved into New York culture. What is happening here is being echoed throughout the nation wherever there is a concentration of Hispanics.

We, Nuyoricans are the descendants of *tabaqueros* (cigarmakers) and other skilled and unskilled workers who were the pioneers that arrived early on, as well as the migrants who followed a generation later. For seven decades our development as a people has evolved a set of values and traditions unique to the Puerto Rican here. We are no longer an island people. This reality has become increasingly incomprehensible to the Puerto Rican from the island. This new world, which we are still creating, is the source of our strength and the cradle of our future.

18
Nuyorican Aesthetics

Miguel Algarín

The 400-year-plus history of Puerto Rico is really a very simple story of greed and amorality. The men who ventured to cross the great Atlantic arrived greedy for gold and the acquisition of land, and in their wake they left whole generations of people, whole tribes of people, dead and without any semblance of a history because all historical records were destroyed. And then, in 1917, we were all made U.S. citizens by the Jones Law so that by 1946 Puerto Rico was allowed to have its first Puerto Rican-born governor. With appropriate reforms in the Jones Law it was possible for Puerto Ricans from the lower classes to come to the mainland looking for bread, land, and liberty. This maxim really is the thing under which the idealized trip up North is sold, and so, in 1948, the Department of Labor initiated the migration to the North that was to result in a mass evacuation of the island of Puerto Rico.

What does it mean, then, to the New York Puerto Rican to have been moved to the North and to find once he gets there that there is no real hot opportunity going on—that the dollars are really hard to get to, that the jobs are demeaning, and the historical continuity has been totally severed? It means that only a heroic act can save what becomes the Nuyorican—the Puerto Rican caught in the urban ghettos, where the population that is economically mobile is evacuated and businesses have long left, and housing is falling apart, and all semblance of hope seems to be in the direction of Uncle Sam's welfare check. That leaves us with a situation where we must perpetuate rituals and habits that are the remnants of an already badly weakened historical consciousness or historical self.

The first generation of Puerto Ricans in the 1930s and 1940s boldly and heroically maintained family traditions as intact as they could, with as much fervor as they could. However, the economic situation made it very difficult for the family to hold together, and dissolution of the family seems to be the living threat we now face. At the heart of all that there is a loss of trust that leaves us aimless and looking for love in empty spaces. The generations have been badly stripped of all historical conciousness what is left is a heroic attempt at a continuity which is really pale in comparison to what it could have been.

What are the roots of the New York Puerto Rican or Northern Puerto Rican? Those roots are really the débris of the ghettos, the tar and concrete that covers the land, the dependence on manual labor that is merely brute force, the force-feeding of the young in schools that kills their initiative rather than nourishes it, and the loss of trust.

On the more positive side, we have maintained our music, we have put down in New York something that is called "salsa," and we have carried forward into the 1980s the Black man's religion, a mixture of Catholicism and African religions, and most importantly, we carry on the oral tradition—the tradition of expressing self in front of the tribe, in front of the family. The holding force in that expression is a feeling and commitment that becomes the deepest bond of trust that we have going at the moment. The conflicts are many. Languages are struggling to possess us; English wants to own us completely; Spanish wants to own us completely. We have mixed them both.

The acculturation is happening very quickly, but the bilingualism is helping curb it. We create poems for ourselves; poverty keeps us away from the space and time that composing long prose pieces requires, but that is changing too. So what does the future hold? The future will be procured by what we do that is cultural in the present, so that we are not so much chasing the tradition of a culture as we are putting it down. We do not so much look to the historical development of Puerto Rican literature as much as we just lay down the poem on the page. Our usage and our new content is going to struggle with the forms and the old meanings, but that is again nothing new, and we will continue to wage that struggle.

Puerto Rican literature is alive and well in New York. Its vibrancy stems from Point Zero. When you have nothing and can expect nothing, anything you do is something, so that our experience makes it possible for us to write poems that describe our condition without fearing that they might be too personal or too lost in the detail of the day and not metaphysical enough. The consequence of having that content freed of standards that kept White American writers enslaved for so many years brings with it a blessing, and the blessing is that language can be worn again and it can be worn as feeling; you can feel it all over again, since it is something you have just learned.

The persistence of Spanish as a live form of expression makes it even richer because like all European tongues, this mixing of Spanish and English is an old phenomenon, and at the edges of the Latin empire—French, Portuguese, Rumanian, Italian were all considered the vulgar languages—and they were really just reflecting constant and daily usage, so that their irregular verbs or irregular usages became dialects which in the ultimate passage of time made the formal respected languages of today. We expect to be able to do the same by mixing Spanish and English and not fearing the present insistence on the part of those who fear it—they claim that if we go the route of mixing languages, we will be ignorant in both and control neither. That is nonsense—language is serviceable on the streets, not in compositions for expository writing, and everyone knows that. If language functions on the street and is useful in conducting the economy of the tribe, it will grow. So the roots of Puerto Rican literature are in the New World in the urban centers now being evacuated by the White part of society, and we are inheriting dead cities with no industry and no money to rehabilitate them or start business again. So the attitude must be something about the future, something about establishing patterns of survival all over again.

The Nuyorican aesthetic has three elements to it. The first is the expression of the self orally and the domination of one language or both to a degree that makes it possible to be accurate about one's present condition: psychic, economic, or historical—and I think the first steps are always oral. The second reality of the Nuyorican aesthetic is that if we are to safeguard the future, we must create a dialogue among ourselves about setting up systems of protection and mutual benefits. The urban centers of the Northeast present the greatest challenge, but if we ignore it, we will find that in the next ten to fifteen years there will be roving urban youth gangs in numbers of fifteen to twenty, all self-dependent, but both mutually aggressive and aggressive against any other gangs. We need to lay down a groundwork for the future by establishing a constitution for survival on top of tar and concrete.

Regarding the ways in which we use the languages: English has a stress system; Spanish has a syllabic system. I think that Nuyorican verse is a combination of both and it is also doing something that Charles Olson took great pains in his essay on projective verse to clarify, which is that the kingpin of English written verse is the syllable. I do not know why he decided to say that in the 1950s, but it is accurate, and we can prove it by our poems and the Black man in America can prove it, because the more he depends on the syllable, the more the language can become his.

The last thing about the Nuyorican aesthetic has to do with art: transformations before the public eye are a very important way of psychic cure. In other words, the creation of places where people can express themselves—expressly created for that purpose. People will come, and they will bring their writings. And if you, as guide of the place, have generosity of spirit, you will find that you will have created a center for the expression of self and for people to transform themselves before the public eye.

Note

This essay was first published under the title "Nuyorican Literature," in *Melus* 8 (Summer 1981).

19

Ambivalence or Activism from the Nuyorican Perspective in Poetry

Sandra María Estéves

When discussing the term *Nuyorican*[1] (or any of its variations, Neorican,[2] New Rican,[3] or *nuevayorquino*[4] *puertorriqueño*) what is simply meant is the Puerto Rican experience as it exists in the United States. We will begin this investigation by examining the Nuyorican image of itself, its daily realities as a people, as a vibrant living community trying to survive within the confines of mainland America.

By Miguel Algarín's[5] definition, the New York Puerto Rican has three survival choices: to labor for slave wages, to become independent and risk the law, or to create "alternative behavioral habits."[6] For him, the work of the poet is to express a vocabulary of alternatives for taking over the immediate environment. He sees the Nuyorican as an outlaw battling against the institution which the English language represents. Every Nuyorican is forced by the need of survival to risk taking a stand against the law, just as the Puerto Rican, the Indian, the African, the South American, and the Mexican have been forced by the same requirements of survival to migrate from their own lands. It is a forced confrontation, a fierce one, but one which, nevertheless, involves the deepest aspects of the soul.

In one sense, the Nuyorican is the new *jíbaro*. The language of the Nuyorican is essentially street-rooted and evolves from the natural mixing of multiethnic people.[7] Still in its infancy, this language is a lyrical blending of English and Spanish with *bomba* African rhythm and tropical variations. But it is also more. Nuyorican writers are angry. They see themselves as "victims of a universal process of displacement," driven from the homeland to a strange metropolis.[8] "The cultural identity and racial discrimination and the adverse economic conditions which the Puerto Rican has experienced in mainland North America have politicized the general mass of middle-class Puerto Ricans."[9]

According to Wolfgang Binder in *Los puertorriqueños en Nueva York*, the major problems facing the Nuyorican are to retain their culture amidst a general hostile environment in a different world, to establish economic well-being, and to mesh into the mainstream American culture. Binder adds: "The Puerto Ricans in New York must deal with a brutal reality that exists in the monstrous society where being poor is sad, traumatic, and dramatic."[10] Now that we have considered some of the realities confronting this new generation of Puerto Ricans, let us attempt to analyze their poetry.

Two poems by Miguel Algarín, "Mongo Affair"[11] and "Inside Control: My Tongue"[12] reveal the humiliation and demoralization of the Nuyorican as a result of an existence dependent on begging, handouts, and welfare. This dependency leads to an impotency which cripples one's ability to take control of one's own environment. In these two poems Algarín shows migrating *borinqueños* in Chicago getting ripped off for slave wages; he presents them as exploited consumers in department stores; he depicts the streets of the Lower East Side of Manhattan as the fields of Vietnam or Nazi Germany; he portrays the Puerto Rican as a defenseless minority in his own land; he points out the nomadic condition of the Puerto Rican and the exploitation of Puerto Rico by the North American capitalists. These confrontations, in his words, will only be resolved when the principles of unity and trust prevail.

Louis Reyes Rivera, poet, historian, editor of Shamal Books, and lecturer, in his poem "Grito de Lares" describes the Spanish invasion of Lares[13] in a forceful rhythmic epic on the military attack of September 23, 1868, in Lares, Puerto Rico. In another work entitled *Who Pays the Cost*,[14] the militant historian deals with other subjects from the viewpoint of the sensitive husband and affectionate father. In "A Place I Never Been,"[15] the poet recounts the incident of the death of Malcolm X. In both poems he recreates moments from the past and creates an immediate and urgent confrontation. Throughout his work, Reyes Rivera critically explores human conditions. He points an accusatory finger toward North American oppression and acts as the revolutionary conscience in favor of universal liberation.

In "Reconnaissance" by Roberto Márquez[16] the confrontation arises from the immediate defense of his land, or perhaps it is the plundering of another's, since both concepts coexist. His tone is both defensive and offensive.

In Lucky Cienfuegos's, "Lolita Lebrón, Recuerdos te Mandamos"[17] there is a clash between the ideals of freedom and the delayed liberation of Lolita Lebrón, Puerto Rican Nationalist and political prisoner for twenty-five years in North American prisons.

Confrontation is a major theme in Nuyorican poets and it is viewed and portrayed from different perspectives. For Miguel Piñero, in "The Book of Genesis According to Saint Miguelito,"[18] the confrontation is the dirt and filth of the ghettos and slums; it is the trauma of methadone and drug withdrawal, of disease; it is "running scared"; it is the realization of a Godless existence, controlled by "capitalism . . . racism . . . exploitation . . . male chauvinism . . . machismo . . . imperialism . . . colonialism . . . wall street . . . [and] foreign wars." In this poem God is no more than a dictator-president ignoring the needs of the people, who "called in sick, collected his overtime pay, a paid vacation . . . [on] the sunny beaches of Puerto Rico." It is Joey's "mami" trying to make ends meet by illegally selling *cuchifritos* (deep-fried pork ennard) in Central Park; it is the need to seek a "cause" for living instead of dying, to discover that the self is the cause for survival.

Dadi Piñero's challenge in "Puerto Rico's Reply"[19] is to discover an overwhelming number of American capitalist interests in Puerto Rico on his first visit. He makes the symbolic exaggerated statement that "there are no more Puerto Ricans in Puerto Rico."[20]

In T.C. García's "Message of My People" the confrontation is poverty, hunger, forced slave labor, drug abuse, and loss of identity, land, and cultural pride. For him, the poet and *borinqueño*, the solution is "*boricua* Revolution!"

Angel Berrocales, in "The Teacher of Life"[21] and "Situation Heavy,"[22] criticizes the educational system. He feels that this institution does not fulfill its goals. Jorge López's "About the Rats"[23] deals with another social problem, the heavy drug traffic which exists in the streets. Like "DDT" and "Rat Poison," he, the poet, will take a stand in the battle.

In his poem "Viet-Nam,"[24] Archie Martínez faces the confrontation when his father returns from fighting the Vietnamese ("who have never done nothing to him") in a coffin blown up by a grenade, another man's leg in place of his own.

Martita Morales in "The Sound of Sixth Street"[25] criticizes bleaching out blackness from the skin, an attitude produced by colonial circumstances. She, the poet, "fights and rebels," and is eventually expelled from a "hunky Ass-bourgeoisie" school which does not understand her cultural pride.

Colonial violence in 8-year-old children, the unnatural industrialization of the land, the every day condition of marshal law which exists for some and not for others; living "in midtown office congestions . . . with mucus on the lips of colonial imposition/y un negrito [who] committed suicide/choking on paranoia" are the preoccupations of Américo Casiano in "A Day When Clinkers, Sparrows and Canaries Jitterbugged Down the Street with a Latin Accent."[26]

For Bimbo Rivas, in "A Job,"[27] the confrontation is the need for work in order to be able to organize his life in a healthy mind and body, instead of wandering aimlessly "lost in the labyrinth of HELL."

In Tato Laviera, who has published two major volumes entitled *La Carreta Made a U-Turn*[28] and *Enclave*,[29] we find a variety of themes representative of a broad range of Nuyorican ethics from the many lives of Puerto Ricans in New York. Laviera is one of the few Nuyoricans to express a strong literary fluency in bilingual combinations of imagery. He shatters English grammatical rules in strong poetic statements which symbolize the condition of his immediate environment. He paints the Nuyorican world in real pictures, phrases, and gestures similar to the natural rhythms of dialect, music, and style established in the earlier writings of Luis Palés Matos (1898–1959). For Tato Laviera, the major confrontation is to retain his cultural being in a Northernized setting, and to evolve artistically as a true poetic voice despite numerous obstacles.

Pedro Pietri, who is among the most existential of the Puerto Rican poets in New York, confronts in *Puerto Rican Obituary*[30] the brutality of the surreal condition. He explores the absurdities of mainland United States in a guidebook of sorts for the newly arrived Puerto Rican. His images are a direct contrast to the lush tropical images from the island and a sharp criticism of the colonial condition in New York. In "Telephone Booth Number 420"[31] we find the philosopher who is able to divinate his future from the furniture. Here the poet's challenge is to exist as a person and maintain his identity and dignity.

In Norma Iris Hernández' *Precious Moments*[32] we find a woman reacting to her environment and redefining her values. The verses are a declaration against male oppression and a voice on behalf of female liberation.[33]

In "Puerto Rican Graffiti,"[34] "149th Street, Winter,"[35] and "Welcome to San Juan, Oldest City in the U.S.,"[36] Amina Muñoz addresses problems such as the cultural shock of living and adjusting to New York City's lifestyle and the struggle of the Puerto Rican in such a hostile environment.

Luz Marina Rodríguez[37] writes about women, motherhood, and the growing awareness of her own feminism. Her poems are written in the rhythm and lyric of the traditional folkloric Puerto Rican music of the *bomba* and *plena*.

Lorraine Sutton, in *SAYcred LAYdy*[38] (sic), is one of the first Puerto Rican women to publish a volume of poetry in the Nuyorican style, a natural English dialect. Her work encompasses a different range of experiences and disillusion. In "Oye Gloria"[39] we hear an everyday conversation which takes place over the kitchen table. The information, similar to the broadcasting of the day's news, is tragic: The neighbor's son is dead from a drug overdose, the welfare check is not paying the bills, the electricity has been cut off, the college youths are selling their souls for material goals in an attempt to become middle-class North Americans, substituting their own culture for another, desperately searching for a way out of the colonial degradation, attempting to establish a security of financial independence from a poverty-stricken way of life. In her poems "You Snatched"[40] and "Oh Say Can Ju Lay"[41] Sutton portrays women as sexual objects, used and abused, similar to the victimization of Puerto Rico by North American financial interests.

These are only fragments of a literature, drops from a river that travels from the rain forests of Puerto Rico, through the Iberian Peninsula, the valleys of Africa, the mountains of South America, to the streets of North America, into the Nuyorican ocean of language.

Ambivalence is a constant political condition that goes beyond the boundaries of our Puerto Rican identity. We are always caught up in our choices for living, trying to survive somewhere between Yin and Yang, Heaven and hell, the Right and the Left, the New York Puerto Rican and the Caribbean Puerto Rican, English and Spanish, poverty and technology, oppression and expression, the self and the soul. At every turn there is a new confrontation awaiting us. The challenge is to find the solution, to uncover, discover, recover, and recreate it. It is both a social and individual priority, and one of the many reasons why we are here. Ultimately, we make choices, we focus on the confrontations and "deal," manipulate, change, and work toward logical solutions.

Whether Nuyorican, Neorican, New Rican, or *nuevayorquino puertorriqueño*, it is not my intention to reject or accept the validity of these terms or what they represent. Rather, I am attempting to shed light on their nature, peculiarities, sociohistorical contexts, without debasing them with any of the usual bias apparent in certain sectors of the intellectual community who would rather dismiss the Nuyorican as insubstantial or irrelevant, or as being something other than what they are: Puerto Ricans.[42] It is my intention to defend our people, and to take offense against those who would deny us our cultural birthright.

The Nuyorican poetry of today is an affirmation of political struggle. It is an acute awareness of the North American condition which manifests itself at the core of every individual. Ultimately, it is a statement of determination, to dream, perhaps to hope, to determine, to give birth, to mold, to survive that confrontation victoriously.

Let it be known that despite our lingual deviations, despite our geographic separation, despite the varieties of our color and interchange of blood, we will continue to persevere and cultivate our existence, in the perpetuation and understanding of our history and the evolution of our identity as a people who in body, mind, and soul have remained a nation undivided.

Notes

1. Miguel Algarín and Miguel Piñero (eds.), *Nuyorican Poetry* (New York: Morrow, 1975).

2. Piri Thomas, "Images and Identities: The Puerto Rican in Literature" (Newark, N.J.: Rutgers University, April 7–9, 1983). National Public Conference.
3. The New Rican Village was a popular cultural center in the Lower East Side of New York City, which began sometime around 1976 and came to prominence for featuring upcoming Latin Jazz musicians and poets from this genre.
4. Grupo Folklórico y Experimental Nuyorquino, *Lo Dice Todo*. (Salsoul Records, SAL-4110 Stereo, 1976), jacket notes.
5. Miguel Algarín is the founder and director of the Nuyorican Poets Café in New York.
6. Nuyorican Poetry, p. 9.
7. Ibid.
8. Alfredo Matilla and Iván Silén (eds.), *The Puerto Rican Poets/Los Poetas Puertorriqueños* (New York: Bantam, 1972), p. xiii.
9. Wolfgang Binder, *Los puertorriqueños en Nueva York* (Erlangen, Germany: Universidad de Erlangen, 1979).
10. Ibid.
11. *Nuyorican Poetry*, p. 52.
12. Ibid., p. 58.
13. Efraín Barradas and Rafael Rodríguez (eds.), *Herejes y mitificadores* (Río Piedras, P.R.: Huracán, , 1980), p. 68.
14. Louis Reyes Rivera, *Who Pays the Cost*. (New York: Shamal, 1977).
15. Ibid., p. 25.
16. *Herejes y mitificadores*, p. 50.
17. *Nuyorican Poetry*, p. 59.
18. Ibid., pp. 62–75.
19. Ibid., p. 84.
20. Ibid., pp. 76–77.
21. Ibid., p. 79.
22. Ibid., p. 81.
23. Ibid., p. 42.
24. Ibid., p. 48.
25. Ibid., p. 49.
26. Ibid., p. 82.
27. Ibid., pp. 93–94.
28. Tato Laviera, *La Carreta Made a U-Turn* (Gary, Ind.: Arte Público, 1979).
29. Tato Laviera, *Enclave* (Houston, Tex.: Arte Público, 1981).
30. Pedro Pietri, *Puerto Rican Obituary* (New York: Monthly Review Press, 1973).
31. *Herejes y mitificadores*, p. 52.
32. Norma Iris Hernández, *Precious Moments* (New York: Parnaso, 1981).
33. Ibid., jacket notes.
34. *Nuyorican Poetry*, p. 107.
35. Ibid., p. 108.
36. Ibid., p. 109.
37. *Voices from the Belly: Spring 1980 Poetry Series* (New York: El Grupo Moriviví, 2 May 1980).
38. Lorraine Sutton, *SAYcred LAYdy* (New York: Sunbury, 1975).
39. Ibid., p. 3.
40. Ibid., p. 8.
41. Ibid., p. 9.

42. Discussions and conclusions from The Puerto Rican Forum on Poetry, "The Political, Cultural and Social Implications of the Term 'Nuyorican'" (New York: Hunter College, May 16, 1979). Panel discussion.

Bibliography

Algarín, Miguel, and Miguel Piñero (eds.). *Nuyorican Poetry*. New York: Morrow, 1975.

Barradas, Efraín, and Rafael Rodríguez (eds.). *Herejes y mitificadores*. Río Piedras, P.R.: Huracán, 1980.

Binder, Wolfgang. *Los puertorriqueños en Nueva York*. Erlangen, Germany: Universidad de Erlangen, 1979.

Grupo Folklórico y Experimental Nuevayorquino. *Lo Dice Todo*. New York: Salsoul Records, SAL-4110 Stereo, 1976, jacket notes.

Hernández, Norma Iris. *Precious Moments*. New York: Parnaso, 1981.

Laviera, Tato. *Enclave*. Houston, Tex.: Arte Público, 1981.

———. *La Carreta Made a U-Turn*. Gary, Ind.: Arte Público, 1981.

Matilla, Alfredo, and Iván Silén (eds.). *The Puerto Rican Poets/Los Poetas Puertorriqueños*. New York: Bantam, 1972.

Pietri, Pedro. *Puerto Rican Obituary*. New York: Monthly Review Press, 1973.

Puerto Rican Forum on Poetry, The. The Political, Cultural and Social Implications of the Term Nuyorican. New York: Hunter College, May 16, 1979. Panel discussion.

Rivera, Louis Reyes. *Who Pays the Cost*. New York: Shamal, 1977.

Sutton, Lorraine. *SAYcred LAYdy*. New York: Sunbury, 1975.

Voices from the Belly: Spring 1980 Poetry Series. New York: El Grupo Moriviví, May 2, 1980.

20

The Feminist Viewpoint in the Poetry of Puerto Rican Women in the United States

Sandra María Estéves

Throughout the world today women are demanding the right to determine the major issues concerning their lives on their own terms. The late 1960s witnessed the advent of a new phase in women's liberation struggles. This movement was aided by social, economic, and political ideologies such as Marxism, the Socialist Workers Party, the Young Socialist Alliance, the Young Lords Party, the Puerto Rican Socialist Party, and numerous other politically active organizations which sprang up nationally in universities and urban communities.[1]

The impact of these times left a definite mark on the consciousness of young Puerto Rican women growing up on the mainland. In her poetic essay "I became the one that translated . . . the go-between,"[2] (sic) Iris Morales describes the political evolution of young Puerto Rican women in New York as a sharp awareness of culture, self, and committed activism toward social change.

This change in consciousness of Puerto Rican women in the United States is most profoundly symbolized and directly connected to the influences of two major women in Puerto Rican history and culture, as well as literature: Julia de Burgos and Lolita Lebrón. In an elegy dedicated to Julia de Burgos, Juan Avilés states:

> Julia de Burgos has sung of a hope for an insensitive world that does not heed her prayer. She moved through her world of strange fantasies with irresistible rapidity, as if she was fleeing from the world of men, trapped in its conventions, grim with intolerances, impersonal, severe. She wanted her world molded to her whim, expanded, distant, without norms nor boundaries.[3]

Julia de Burgos[4] symbolizes the hopes and aspirations of emigrating Puerto Ricans. She is a symbol of both failure and success. She failed because she was unable to conquer her environment, the streets of New York, which ultimately destroyed her. Her success was the triumph of her spirit to surmount the drudgery of her existence. Through her writings she became an immortal voice on behalf of the Puerto Rican nation, a voice in tune with the social consciousness of her culture. In her poem "Río Grande de Loiza"[5] her poetic skill lies in her ability to describe simultaneously the love for the river she knew as a child, the passion for the man of her desires who becomes as the river, supporting her in a lover's dialogue, and the patriotic love of her Puerto Rican country, whose strength and independence, like the man and the river, symbolize the fulfillment of her womanhood. It is the powerful national image she conveys which causes Julia de Burgos to be considered among the greatest of the nationalist poets.

Besides being a potent nationalist in defense of Puerto Rican independence, we find in Lolita Lebrón a poet who also echoes the social conscience of the Puerto Rican people. Lolita is the warrior, the martyr, the woman who takes on the challenge for the sake of liberation and who refuses to acknowledge defeat. In "Alabanza de Lares"[6] we read of the existential woman who lives in a world beyond bars. She demands democracy for Lares and becomes a powerful symbol against exploitation, favoring the struggle and survival of the Puerto Rican woman. Throughout Lolita's and Julia's writings we encounter the rude realization of North American intentions toward the Puerto Rican, and in understanding the circumstances of their lives we find a point of focus from which develops the literature of the Puerto Rican woman in the United States.

Lorraine Sutton is perhaps one of the first and most significant poets to emerge writing in the Nuyorican style. Sutton describes her cultural identity in *SAYcred LAYdy*[7] (sic) as a product of North American male chauvinism. In her poems "You Snatched"[8] and "Oh Say Can Ju Lay,"[9] she portrays women as sexual victims, robbed, raped, and demoralized by drugs and alcohol. In "Saycred Laydy"[10] she focuses on Lolita Lebrón and the Puerto Rican nationalists. In this poem Sutton establishes her linkage with the social consciousness of her culture. She compares herself to the island of Puerto Rico, vulnerable at the hands of harsh colonial domination. Her voice is anguished but defiant. In "Dawson St. Blues"[11] and "Temptation"[12] she vows to rid herself of the depression attempting to control her and reaches through the window that leads to the discovery of her particular individuality as a woman within her cultural and social identity. She is not the stereotype of the hot-blooded Latin spitfire dancing in the street in a red dress. She does not smile;[13] she is angry, suicidal,[14] needing, and searching.[15] Finally, in "Your Olive Face,"[16] she identifies the condition she shares with other people of the world as a life of struggle pitted against a military enemy forever present and inescapable. She is certainly not the accepting humble housewife nor the dull-witted peasant often evoked by North American visions of Puerto

Rican women. Instead she is a young street woman, vocal, literate, aggressive, and political, who expresses her reality in critical symbolism, existential and surreal awareness.

Another contemporary Puerto Rican woman writer, Salima Rivera, a Chicago-based poet, describes in "The Crazy Woman from Plaza Mayo"[17] her anger against the military rule imposed by the colonial society which has stolen and murdered her son by sending him off to war. Her attitude is militant, aggressive, and critical.

Luz María Umpierre, another unique contemporary, in "Jaculatoria in Nomine Domine,"[18] offers her own version of a prayer adjusted to current lifestyles in a hostile North American environment. Among her petitions to God she begs for protection of her pocketbook and assistance for her husband so that he does not come home plastered on payday. It is a statement that is both sincere and surreal, its underlying message being an appeal for dignity on behalf of her culture. Symbolically, she breaks away from the traditional images of the devoted Blessed Virgin, good wife and mother, humbly fulfilling her duties. Not only do we discover through this poem the importance which the Christian ethnic has had on the religious-cultural lifestyle of the Puerto Rican community, but also a dramatic invocation to bring about social change. In "Rubbish,"[19] the poet becomes even more defiant when she states that she will no longer support the subservient position assigned to her and her cultural class.

Among the new generation of contemporary Puerto Rican women writers publishing predominantly in English in the United States, we should mention Amina Muñoz,[20] Luz Marina Rodríguez,[21] Denis Ríos,[22] Norma Iris Hernández,[23] Martita Morales,[24] Carmen Rosario,[25] Brunilda Vega,[26] Josie Rolón,[27] Magdalena Gómez,[28] Rota Silverstrini,[29] and Suzanna García. All these voices share a common expression, a declaration of the universal causes of women, and represent a testimony of the *puertorriqueña* in the United States. Their statements are unique and their themes are as varied as the experiences constantly surrounding us.

In the poems of Magdalena Gómez entitled "One of Too Many,"[30] "He Got Me the First Time,"[31] "For My Lover the Artist,"[32] "Dream Medley,"[33] and "Rookie Dyke T.V. Toddler,"[34] we discover themes based in New York poverty. Her themes, unlike those we find in the writings of Lorraine Sutton and Suzanna García, are not necessarily nationalistic. They are highly political, nevertheless. Her statements are clearly on behalf of the cause of womankind, struggling in madness for survival, confronting in her daily routine hunger, imprisonment, rape, alcohol, male chauvinism, and loneliness. She contradicts all those statements about the Puerto Rican people which claim that a poor environment produces an impoverished mentality. On the contrary, Magdalena Gómez is a survivor, she has returned each punch that life has thrown at her, blow by blow. Unlike a punching bag she has developed her expressive skills verbally—she is not only eloquent, but critical, impassioned, compassionate, and sincere. If her focus is not directly on behalf of more patriotic Puerto Rican ideals, it is certainly in support of the struggles of womankind, and is symbolic of the general trends of Puerto Rican literature produced in the United States.

In "Puerto Rican Graffiti"[35] Amina Muñoz is an impressionistic Nuyorican voice who paints pictures of displacement in a series of visual images describing cultural shock in the streets of New York. In "149th St. Winter"[36] she defines her identity as "disposed gods. . . dressed in grey, whose colorful attire is in cold storage," a symbol of mainland experience. In "Welcome to San Juan, Oldest City in the U. S.,"[37] Muñoz sharply dissects the North American presence on the island as it affects the daily lifestyles of the Puerto Rican people, revealing also the nationalism inherent in her work.

While examining the poetry of Suzanna García,[38] a poet equally fluent in English and Spanish, we discover, again, preoccupations with themes of womanhood. In "The Impostor" she deals with various levels and manifestations of motherhood in a deep soul-searching review of her anxieties, sorrows, and triumphs. But she is also committed to the cause of Puerto Rican independence and perpetuates a clearly defined national consciousness in her writings. In her poem to Julia de Burgos[39] she establishes her national identity and commitment to revolutionary ideals. In a detailed account she examines the effects of colonialism in Puerto Rico where there exists "40% unemployment, one-third of the land and 85% of the businesses are owned by foreigners, the destruction of natural resources by offshore petroleum processing plants, and genocidal clinics which are responsible for the sterilization of one-third of all Puerto Rican women of childbearing age." She describes this information as a cancerous illness afflicting the island. Her prognosis is "fatal," but her message is one of hope, struggle, inspiration, and liberation for Puerto Rican people.

In Rota Silverstrini we discover another decidedly nationalistic poet. In "The Boricua Presentation,"[40] we find a direct and fierce confrontation with the national identity, where she reaches into the deepest aspects of her soul and the fragments of her many selves which have fallen victim to the reign of "vampires." In "The Dance,"[41] a poem from the same anthology, she describes a war dance of the gods, and in her dedication to Don Pedro Albizu Campos and Lolita Lebrón, again, reestablishes her connection to the national conciousness. When she speaks of herself as "I, la isla prostituted,"[42] she is speaking on behalf of the entire Puerto Rican culture as a colonial society. Her visions of Puerto Rican life in New York are tragic and critical interpretations. Her strength is the awareness of her cultural identity, the greater part of her soul, from which she finds motivation and direction to inspire her life.

These are but a few voices among the abundance of women writing today; they are fragments of a growing literature. More and more Puerto Rican women are finding expression on the published page at a rapidly accelerating rate in the United States. No longer are women traditional symbols of passive resistance to male domination. No longer are women content to be slave workers or cheap laborers. The modern woman is making a vital and active contribution to participate in the politics of her destiny; and the Puerto Rican woman is a very real part of that movement.

The literature of the Puerto Rican women in the United States today is an aggressive political expression, an affirmation on behalf of the rights of all people. Not only does it favor the autonomy of the nation of Puerto Rico, but also the autonomy of men and women throughout the world.

Notes

1. Mary Alice Walters, *Feminism and the Marxist Movement* (New York: Pathfinder, 1972), p. 7.
2. Iris Morales, "I became the one that translated . . . the go-between." In *The Puerto Ricans: Their History, Culture, and Society*, ed. by Adalberto López (Cambridge, Mass.: Schenkman, 1980), p. 439.
3. Federico Ribes Tovar, *The Puerto Rican Woman* (New York: Plus Ultra Educational, 1972), p. 224.
4. Julia de Burgos published *Poemas exactos a mi misma* (1937), *Poemas en veinte surcos* (1938), and *Canciones de la verdad sencilla* (1939). She was a member of the CEPI (Círculo de Escritores y Poetas Iberoamericanos) and published verses in *Insula*, a magazine of Puerto Rico founded in 1941 to encourage the evolution of a truly indigenous literature.
5. Alfredo Matilla and Iván Silén (eds.), *The Puerto Rican Poets/Los Poetas Puertorriqueños* (New York: Bantam, 1972), p. 62.
6. Federico Ribes Tovar, *Lolita Lebrón la prisionera* (New York: Plus Ultra Educational, 1974), p. 50.
7. Lorraine Sutton, *SAYcred LAYdy* (New York: Sunbury, 1975).
8. Ibid., p. 8.
9. Ibid., p. 9.
10. Ibid., p. 17.
11. Ibid., p. 12.
12. Ibid., p. 14.
13. Ibid., p. 25, "Solid."
14. Ibid., p. 26, "Inside III."
15. Ibid., p. 27, "Inside (Again)."
16. Ibid., p. 31.
17. Norma Alarcón (ed.), *Third Women* 1 (Bloomington, Ind.: Third Woman Press, 1981): 25.

18. Nicolás Kanellos and Luis Dávila (eds.), *La Mujer* (Houston, Tex.: *Revista Chicano-Riqueña* 6 (no. 2, 1978): 18.
19. Efraín Barradas and Rafael Rodríguez (eds.), *Herejes y mitificadores* (Río Piedras, P.R.: Huracán, 1980), p. 108.
20. Miguel Algarín and Miguel Piñero, (eds.), *Nuyorican Poetry* (New York: Morrow, 1975), p. 107.
21. *Voices from the Belly: Spring 1980 Poetry Series* (New York: El Grupo Moriviví, May 2, 1980).
22. Ibid.
23. Norma Iris Hernández, *Precious Moments* (New York: Parnaso, 1981).
24. *Nuyorican Poetry*, pp. 49, 102.
25. *Voices from the Belly: Spring 1980 Poetry Series.*
26. *Voices from the Belly: Spring 1982 Poetry Series* (New York: El Grupo Moriviví, November 28, 1982).
27. *New Rican Village: Summer 1978 Poetry Series* (New York: New Rican Village Cultural Center, August 25, 1978).
28. Sara Miles, Pat Jones, Sandra Estéves, and Fay Chiang (eds.), *Ordinary Women* (New York: Ordinary Women Books, 1978), pp. 61–65.
29. Louis Reyes Rivera (ed.), *Womanrise* (New York: Shamal, 1978), pp. 60–75.
30. *Ordinary Women*, p. 61.
31. Ibid., p. 62.
32. Ibid.
33. Ibid., p. 63.
34. Ibid., p. 65.
35. *Nuyorican Poetry*, p. 107.
36. Ibid., p. 108.
37. Ibid., p. 109.
38. *Voices from the Belly: Spring 1980 Poetry Series.*
39. Ibid.
40. *Womanrise*, p. 60.
41. Ibid., p. 63.
42. Ibid., p. 62, "The Boricua Presentation."

Bibliography

Alarcón, Norma (ed.). *Third Woman* 1, no. 1 Bloomington, Ind.: Third Woman Press, 1981.

Algarín, Miguel, and Miguel Piñero (eds.). *Nuyorican Poetry* New York: Morrow, 1975.

Barradas, Efraín, and Rafael Rodríguez (eds.). *Herejes y mitificadores*. Río Piedras, P.R.: Huracán, 1980.

Hernández, Norma Iris. *Precious Moments*. New York: Parnaso, 1981.

Kanellos, Nicolás, and Luis Dávila (eds.). "La Mujer," *Revista Chicano Riqueña* 6 (no. 2, 1978).

Lopéz, Adalberto (ed.). *The Puerto Ricans: Their History, Culture, and Society*. Cambridge, Mass.: Schenkman, 1980.

Sutton, Lorraine. *SAYcred LAYdy*. New York: Sunbury, 1975.

Matilla, Alfredo, and Iván Silén (eds.). *The Puerto Rican Poets/Los Poetas Puertorriqueños*. New York: Bantam, 1972.

Miles, Sara, Patricia Jones, Sandra Esteves and Fay Chiang (eds.). *Ordinary Women*. New York: Ordinary Women Books, 1978.

New Rican Village: Summer 1978 Poetry Series. New York: New Rican Village Cultural Center, August 25, 1978.

Ribes Tovar, Federico. *The Puerto Rican Woman*. New York: Plus Ultra Educational, 1972.

———. *Lolita Lebrón la prisionera*. New York: Plus Ultra Educational, 1974.

Rivera, Louis Reyes (ed.). *Womanrise*. New York: Shamal, 1978.

Voices from the Belly: Spring Series 1980 Poetry Series, May 2, 1980. New York: El Grupo Moriviví.

Voices from the Belly: Fall 1982 Poetry Series, November, 28, 1982. New York: El Grupo Moriviví.

Walters, Mary Alice. *Feminism and the Marxist Movement*. New York: Pathfinder, 1972.

Part IV
Translations

21

This Uncanny, Tricky Business: Translation and Ideology in Puerto Rican Literature

Orlando José Hernández

In 1532, almost at the height of the Spanish empire, the humanist Juan Luis Vives declared: "Interpretations [referring to translations] are not only beneficial, but they are of prime necessity for all disciplines and all arts, as well as for all circumstances of life."[1] This statement, a product of an imperial, expansionist, multilingual and muticultural—however much denied—sectarian, feudal, repressive, and authoritarian society, is not entirely inadequate or irrelevant to a colonized, underdeveloped, and demoralized society, a society increasingly fragmented in its institutions, increasingly disbelieving and more cynical as to capabilities—and consequently each day more impotent—the society whose literature we will examine. I do not believe that the relevancy of this statement is necessarily the result of a stroke of irony. It responds to a need and to a process which has become controversial, long neglected by a significant part of our intelligentsia, and certainly a traumatic process, but above all, one which is *central to our historical experience*, with deep, though largely ignored, cultural implications. I am referring to the diaspora, the massive uprooting of hundreds of thousands of Puerto Ricans, that bidirectional movement which leaves its mark as much on those who leave as on those who stay behind, and those who now will remain here or on those who return. All this has become intrinsic to our national experience, and curiously enough it validates for the colony the same appreciation given 450 years earlier for the metropolis, although with different causes and purposes.

I am interested in discussing here issues resulting from the transformations which take place in a culture affected by massive emigration, and some of the inferences from employing an ideological approach to the field of translation.

It will not be necessary to elaborate upon the fact that literary translation is an art, as opposed to a science. An "exact art," to put it in Steiner's terms,[2] but definitely an art, and of a re-creative, rather than creative, nature.[3] As such, its essence is not ideological, but may be considered in its purely artistic as well as in its ideological aspects. Furthermore, regardless of its specificity as an artistic product, it is concerned with a type of cultural production which is also socially and historically conditioned. This has not been emphasized enough. Developed countries, for example, tend to have more and better translators. The works which are to be translated (and those which are not), or who will translate them, are not factors which respond exclusively, or on occasion primarily, to commercial considerations. Cultural trends or "likes" of the North American reading public, factors subject to manipulation, also play a role.

The history of the translation of Puerto Rican works into English is incomplete, little known, and fragmentary. A bilingual edition of Cuban and Puerto Rican poets, published by *El Boletín Mercantil* (San Juan, 1903), appears to be the first of the entries, at least in this century. Its title, *Musa bilingüe*, which would now read as contemporary and up to date, actually showed traces of a late romanticism, in tone as well as in the selection of poets.[4] Except for the inclusion of De Diego in the "Panamerican" anthology of Gorham Press, published in 1918,[5] and for two anthologies of poetry in which Puerto Rican texts were included, the main characteristic during the first five decades of this century was omission. It was the manner—a sort of bitter law of ignorance or exclusion—in which almost all our writers were treated. Not even the works of an author such as Palés, whose quality and poetic genius were widely recognized by Spanish American and Spanish critics of the 1940s, and who continually proved himself with each new poem that he published, gained any notable recognition until the 1960s. That lack of information is at times astonishing. In 1949, Langston Hughes and Arna Bontemps edited an important anthology of Black poetry for Doubleday in which poems by Nicolás Guillén, Claude Mckay, Jacques Roumain, Plácido y Regino Pedroso, and Aimé Césaire appear, yet Palés's poems are not included.[6]

The other anthologies previously mentioned close the desolate panorama of the unavailability of Puerto Rican works in English during the first half of this century. In 1920 the *Hispanic Anthology: Poems Translated from the Spanish by English and North American Poets*[7] was published. Its editor, Thomas Walsh, included poems by Muñoz Marín, Antonio Pérez-Pierret, Lola Rodríguez de Tío and, curiously, also by Muna Lee. In 1942, in the bilingual anthology edited by Dudley Fitts for New Directions, *An Anthology of Contemporary Latin American Poetry*,[8] Palés's name finally appears, next to that of Carmen Cadilla and of one still considered "a promising poet": Muñoz Marín. As far as poetry is concerned, that was the outlook, meager and discouraging, of translations of works by Puerto Rican authors into English. In the prose genres, we were completely left out of the picture. But in that we were not alone.

The decade of the 1960s and even more that of the 1970s mark significant changes which lessen the gap for our authors, at least in matters of translation. Anthologies of narrative or editions of Puerto Rican letters including prose and important cultural texts begin to appear in translation. Even so, the opening which has taken place in the last two decades is very partial. Omission still continues, though not as blatantly. A very recent, ambitious, and widely distributed anthology published by Knopf and compiled by the Uruguayan critic E. Rodríguez Monegal[9]—as Professor Gerald Guiness pointed out to me—does not include a single Puerto Rican author. So one could hardly call the current interest a breakthrough, for it has barely uncovered the tip of the iceberg; it is simply a beginning. This becomes immediately apparent: Where is the anthology of the poetic works of Luis Palés Matos or Julia de Burgos translated into English? Where is the selection of texts from the essayists of the 1930s, whose coherence and importance are undeniable, even for those of us who do not share their viewpoints and who in fact rejected their conclusions? Where is the bilingual anthology of short stories by José Luis González or René Marqués, who have until now been our most successful exponents in this genre? Why have the works of one of our most fundamental novelists (the headstone of our novel, one might say) had to wait for so long? For so it is with Manuel Zeno Gandía, whose case dramatizes perhaps more than any other the arbitrariness and shortcomings of this uncanny, tricky business. And what of the selection of Puerto Rican drama, theater being one of our most vital genres? These questions are not intended to be an inventory, but to suggest the partiality of that opening. There is a similar lag on the other shore.

If translating serves to legitimize and validate, or reflects a desire to know and a willingness to accept, then the publishing houses and magazines from the island have often played a frankly irresponsible and sometimes disrespectful role. And this has not been necessarily due to ill will, nor has it always been a conscious decision on the part of the editors, but sometimes the reflection of a Hispanophile ideology—in the sense that Marx applies to this term: in opposition to science[10]—which is still prominent among our intellectual trends, even if it is formulated or manifested in a different fashion. On other ocassions, it has been due to the continued use of less than professional, outdated practices, which clearly attest to the underdevelopment of the island society. (For example, I know cases in which publishers have made arrangements for translation of material without obtaining rights or even notifying the authors. The result of these "editorial slips" is the infringement of the author's rights; the production of unauthorized versions; the waste of the translator's time and efforts, whose meager wages already constitute an abuse of sorts; the reinforcement of the proverbial climate of friction or inability to see eye to eye between the editor and the writer; and finally, the wronging of everything that was first set out to be righted.)

I do not have exact figures at hand, but I am sure that island publishing houses have published no more than a handful, literally, of books written by English-speaking Puerto Ricans, and to a lesser extent the same thing occurs with the larger category of Puerto Ricans who live and write in the United States, irrespective of the language used. Besides, the supposed poor marketability of these publications is not even remotely convincing in some cases. A book such as *A Puerto Rican in New York and Other Sketches*,[11] the extremely valuable testimony of Jesús Colón, whose first edition appeared more than twenty years ago, as far as I know has not been published in Puerto Rico, and for its testimonial nature as well as human and political interest, its publication in Spanish would not only be important for our culture but would also be perfectly viable from a commercial point of view.

There is, on the other hand, a somewhat chauvinistic tendency which resents the approach of North American intellectuals genuinely interested in understanding an promoting our culture. This seemed to be the reaction of some of our intellectuals to the translation by Gregory Rabassa of *La guaracha del Macho Camacho*, by Luis Rafael Sánchez. This is less cause for concern, and seems understandable in light of the intellectual exchange which has historically taken place with the United States. Time and good will should contribute to change that attitude.

A translator returns to society that which he receives from it, only augmented. Those of us who translate have the responsibility to recognize the social and even pedagogical usefulness of our profession in the context in which our literature is defined and takes shape, as a process of national affirmation and the telling of an experience, on an individual as well as collective level, with a value-oriented and aesthetic function and also a historical one. This cannot respond to subjective whims or decisions, or to any type of arbitrariness. I am now referring to the problem of approach and to the issue of exclusion. No editor or anthology compiler, under the guise of good translator or concerned poet, has the right to impose exclusions based on his or her inability to appreciate or translate a style or on personal or subjective criteria. I know of anthologies—and current ones, such as *Inventing a Word*[12]—where the exclusions are arbitrary and given the exchange function of this type of publication, deny recognition instead of validating the work of authors whose contribution is undeniable. Clearly an anthology is not what one would consider a matter of personal preference. (If this may be somewhat true in the Anglo-Saxon world, it is not the base of what we could learn from its rich store of literary traditions.) Each day I feel less confident about the miracles of individual work and believe that it is healthy to recognize its pitfalls. Even a job as lonely as the translator's often allows a combined effort to help correct the distortions of individual work. This presupposes, though, a different methodology and a theme for a different occasion.

Translation has become an important necessity in our culture. The task which we, Puerto Rican intellectuals, have before us is to insure that the progressive forces in favor of a national project, as defined by the emergence of an independent nation, can transform that necessity into opportunity. May we bear in mind that the culture which we are determined to defend need not be monolingual, when our national experience has been moving precisely in the opposite direction, and especially when in certain contexts a hierarchy shows through with certain class connotations, based on the use of one of the two languages. This does not mean either that we are to bastardize, destroy, or allow the destruction of Spanish, since—must we be reminded of this again?—though it was the language of the colonists, and an imposition, it was later enriched and appropiated by our population. The matter at hand is to try to lay the foundation so that the exchange between sectors of our nationality who have had diverse linguistic experiences can become a true dialogue which will strengthen and not weaken, and which at no time will jeopordize the viability of this national project. As far as everything else is concerned, upon laying such foundation we will not be moving one inch away from the polychromatic Caribbean experience, where multiethnicity and linguistic diversity became long ago, more than exception or dismemberment, a welcome pleasure. We could come out winners in this also.

Notes

1. Juan Luis Vives, *Obras completas*, vol. 2, trans. Lorenzo Riber (Madrid, Spain: Aguilar, 1948), p. 804. The quote is from "Versiones e interpretaciones," ch. 12 of the Third Book of *El arte de hablar*.
2. Steiner discusses fully the problem of how to conceptualize translation, criticizing and assessing different approaches. See George Steiner, *After Babel* (New York and London: Oxford University Press, 1975), esp. ch. 1, 4. See also Peter Newmark, *Approaches to Translation* (Oxford: Pergamon, 1981).
3. Gregory Rabassa discusses the re-creative nature of the art of translation in "Translation: The Recreative Art," *Humanities* 3 (December 1982).
4. Francisco Javier Amy (ed.), *Musa bilingüe* (San Juan: Boletín Mercantil, 1903).
5. Agnes Blake Poor (ed.), *Pan American Poems: An Anthology* (Boston: Gorham, 1918).
6. Langston Hughes, and Arna Bontemps (eds.), *The Poetry of the Negro, 1746–1949* (New York: Doubleday, 1949).
7. Thomas Walsh (ed.), *Hispanic Anthology: Poems Translated from the Spanish by English and North American Poets* (New York: Putnam, 1920).
8. Dudley Fitts (ed.), *An Anthology of Contemporary Latin American Poetry* (Norfolk: New Directions, 1942).

9. Emir Rodríguez Monegal (ed.), *The Borzoi Anthology of Latin American Literature*, 2 vols. (New York: Knopf, 1977).
10. For a rigorous discussion of the concept of ideology in Marx, see Ludovico Silva, *Teoría y práctica de la ideología* (México: Nuestro Tiempo, 1979), especially the first essay.
11. Jesús Colón, *A Puerto Rican and Other Sketches* (New York: International, 1982). First ed., 1961, by Masses and Mainstream.
12. Julio Marzán (ed.), *Inventing a Word (An Anthology of Twentieth-Century Puerto Rican Poetry)* (New York: Columbia University Press and Center for Inter-American Relations, 1980).

Bibliography

Cary, E., and Jumplet, R.W. (eds.). *Quality in Translation*. Proceedings from the Third Congress of the International Federation of Translators, Bad Godesberg, Germany, 1959. New York: Macmillan, 1963.

Engber, Marjorie (ed.). *Caribbean Fiction and Poetry*. Bibliographic Manual. New York: Center for Inter-American Relations, 1970.

Newmark, Peter. *Approaches to Translation*. Oxford: Pergamon, 1981.

Rabassa, Gregory. "Translation: The Recreative Art," *Humanities* 2 (Decemeber 1982).

Silva, Lodovico. *Teoría y práctica de la ideología*. Mexico, D.F.: Nuestro Tiempo, 1979.

Steiner, George. *After Babel*. New York and London: Oxford University Press, 1975.

Sur. "Problemas de la traducción." Special issue dedicated to translation (Buenos Aires, January-December 1976).

Tabernig de Pucciarelli, Elsa. *¿Qué es la traducción*? Buenos Aires: Columba, 1970.

22

Is *Macho Camacho's Beat* a Good Translation of *La guaracha del Macho Camacho*?

Gerald Guinness

There are, roughly speaking, three ways in which one work can be considered a good translation of another. The first is what we might call the minimalist way, and it consists of the greatest possible fidelity to the original text, to the point of pedantry; high priest of this method is Vladimir Nabokov and its holy writ Nabokov's delightful, and unreadable, *Eugene Onegin*. A good translation should be a "trot," Nabokov roundly affirms, and it is a principle not without its merits, particularly where poetry is concerned. In other words, let those who want to read Rilke in German *learn* German; otherwise let them stay at home and continue to paddle in their own shallow pools.

A second type of good translation is the maximalist type, whereby a text is lifted wholesale from one cultural context into another. For example, when Samuel Beckett translates Gogo's "Assez. Aide-moi à enlever cette saloperie" as "Ah stop blathering and help me off with this bloody thing," he transforms a Parisian existentialist *clochard* into an Irish drunk at closing time, something that perhaps only the author-as-translator could get away with in our own day. The principle here is a free reconstitution of the text, as much in terms of cultural setting as of language, as though the translator were its prime creator. You will remember that it was in this sense that Pierre Menard wrote (not rewrote) part of the *Quixote*.

And finally, the third good translation is a more or less unsatisfactory compromise between the first two, where minimalist fidelity and maximalist license are combined to the extent that what we get is basically a lie—neither the original nor a fresh and original creation of its own. This definition covers ninety-five percent of the translated works that we buy in our bookshops.

Gregory Rabassa's translation of Luis Rafael Sanchez's *La guaracha del Macho Camacho* is an admirable achievement, but it is very definitely "good" only in the third of these three senses. It is not pedantry, but then neither is it magic; more readable than Nabokov's *Onegin*, it is yet less electrifying in its creative perfection than Menard's *Quixote*. Poor, unsatisfactory hybrid! Like most excellent translations, it fails to move mountains or cleave a passage through the Red Sea; throughout it remains a trans-lation, and readers can never forget they are being carried across the language gap albeit in as efficient a vehicle as it was possible to devise.

But now I must begin to justify these bold assertions, and I shall do so by quoting from Rabassa's *Macho Camacho's Beat* and its original in some detail. Starting first at the minimalist end of the spectrum, we expect a translation to be accurate, and in this respect *Macho Camacho's Beat* is well-nigh impeccable. I say "well-nigh" because in addition to less than a dozen small flaws that any translation may perpetrate on an off-day (for even Rabassa nods), there are a few delightful mistakes of ignorance that anyone who has lived in Puerto Rico for any length of time will doubtless enjoy. For example, "en las Fiestas Patronales de Carolina" becomes "at Carolina's Nameday Party," and "más golpes que un baile de bombas" achieves a delicious transmutation into "more clout than a brace of bombs"—which at least keeps close to the explosive potential of the original. There is no reason why poor Rabassa should have been expected to pick up the reference in "taumaturgo de los soles truncos" to a leading Puerto Rican patriot and one of his most famous plays, with the result that his translation has a decidedly odd ring to it: "wonderworker of close-up suns." And to turn Mari Bras into a woman on pages 103-4 is one of the lighter moments in the career of that doughty warrior for independence.

What I find remarkable about Rabassa's translation is how few such mistakes there are, given the intensely local character of the original text. Few too are Rabassa's omissions, and if I mention these it is only because I am curious about their cause. Was it just boredom at having to find yet another equivalent for the relentless word-play, or an admission of defeat when faced with a particularly obdurate localism? I am thinking of phrases like "de que yo moteleaba," and "y tres cosas son con cuatro," where the specialized functions on the Puerto Rican motel are not easily conveyed to North American readers and where, for readers who do not recognize an allusion to the musical instrument the *cuatro*, there is just no way of conveying the pun. More puzzling is Rabassa's omission of the following passage: "Hoy hoy, hoy: las nalgas gastadas del Viejo trepadas a caballito sobre la barriguita de ella, barriguita de bombín." Usually he is enormously inventive when it comes to vulgarity, and I am surprised that on this occasion he failed to rise to the challenge.

Rising to challenges does perhaps have a faintly erotic ring to it, and this gives me the opportunity to propound a pet theory: that in translations of works with a high level of content, the relation between creative writer and his translator is directly erotic. In run-of-the-mill translations that relation is like a marriage, where both partners must learn to cohabit for better or worse; but in a play context the relation is like a brilliant "affair," where the supplicant partner must pull out all the stops to hold his partner's interest. As in a seduction there is a strong element of performance, with the peacock spreading his tail to dazzle the peahen. Change "peacock" to "translator" and "peahen" to "creative artist" and you will get a good idea of the tense yet joyful complicity that prevails on these occasions.

Let it be said at once that Gregory Rabassa is one of the best of all possible translator-peacocks. His inventive faculty is dazzling and his ability to turn resources of a Spanish rich in innuendo into an English similarly endowed, beyond praise. Here are just a few examples from a rich store:

> Se desmadró la Tiquis-Miquis/Miss Hoity-Toity has flipped.
>
> Yo soy un tipo listo, o sea que en sexto grado me decían Benny Listerine/I'm a cool cat, what I mean is that in the sixth grade they used to call me Benny Kool-Aid.
>
> Como hace el Ace/the way her can can.

(Incidentally, American friends tell me that the provenance of "como hace el Ace" is "Duz does everything," so this is a nice example of a joke-jingle that has crossed the language-gap three times in the course of its wanderings.)

The best of Rabassa's efforts are however obscene—I shall safely give one or two of the less lurid examples. "La jodificación de Benny" is delightfully retooled into "Benny's screwtiny," "Benny quería empezar para acabar" comes over nicely as "Benny wanted to go by coming," and the resounding "carajus, puñetum" acquires a firm Bronx flavor in "shee-eets, fuckitallium." One or two equivalents in this department are a little puzzling—I cannot imagine why Rabassa translated "gente genésica" on page 200 as "peepee people." Probably I am not the only reader of the two versions whose vocabulary of bad language has expanded dramatically in the course of the experience of reading Sánchez-Rabassa, to the extent that quite a lot of what I hear in the streets of Río Piedras is now intelligible to me for the very first time.

At this point we have reached the summit in our praise for Rabassa's translation of *La guaracha* and must now begin to glide down the other slope. But such a descent from praise does not necessarily imply criticism, since what I shall increasingly be concerned with are matters over which a translator, whatever his skill, has little control.

Let us begin with one area where he has no control whatsoever, namely, the "translation" of phrases in the target text that are already in English or in that barbaric mixture of Spanish and English known as "Spanglish." What is the translator to do when he meets phrases such as the following: "footnote sin el foot"; "la disposición full time"; "el primer tineger del país"; "me pongo isi, rilás, redi para el toqueteo"; "la clientela de los siquiatras era high life, jaitona, mainly tiquis miquis"; "lo mas nice"; "el Contri?" To translate "me pongo isi, rilás, redi para el toqueteo" by "I take it easy, relax, ready for the flattering" is neat and necessary, but hardly conveys the mongrel quality of the original.

Perhaps even more difficult to convey across the language gap are syntactic horrors like "El Doctor Severo Severino lo llamará para atrás." José Luis González has pointed out, on the second page of his *Conversación* with Arcadio Díaz Quiñones, that "aquí [en Puerto Rico] la población culta ha sido y sigue siendo la más afectada por la interferencia linguística extranjera" (here [in Puerto Rico] the educated classes have been and continue to be the ones most affected by foreign linguistic interference), a problem of language which ten pages later he calls "fundamentally a political problem." Exactly. And since much of the expressiveness of *La guaracha* comes from its exploration of this linguistic impoverishment, which is ultimately a symptom of—and cause of—colonial dependency, to miss this in translation is to rob the work of what is perhaps the greatest single element of its significance.

But the problem is more than just an inability to convey the horrors of linguistic transculturation; it has even deeper roots. What Rabassa's text fails to do (at least for this reader) is to convey the whole feel of a culture and the manner of being of its people. To make the point I shall group my material under three subheadings: (1) intransigent localisms of social description; (2) intransigent localisms of speech; and (3) the different specific gravity of two languages. The meaning of each of these subheadings will, I hope, become clear in the course of my discussion.

A good example of "intransigent localisms of social description" comes from the description of la China Hereje with which the book opens: "Cara de ausente tiene, cara de víveme y tócame" (She's got a dreamer's face, a wake me up and touch me face). But in fact nothing about la China suggests a dreamer, a type probably more Nordic than Latin. To be "ausente" is to have a short attention span, sharply focused but intermittent, the very opposite of "dreamy." Similarly "cara de víveme y tócame" is sharply evocative of a specific culture, whereas a "wake me up and touch me face" conveys nothing. (Incidentally, a "come hither face" might have been closer to the spirit of the original.) And when later down the same page la China says "ay deja eso," we catch a tone of good-natured badinage that is only imperfectly conveyed by the English "oh cut it out," with its flavor of the New York subway.

A more radical example of this same difficulty comes from the next page of both texts: "Lealtad a todo lo que sea vacilón. Cuerpo y corazón: trampolines de la guasa/faithful to all balling. Body and soul: springboards for a spree." But no Puerto Rican bilingual can accept "balling" and "spree" as exact equivalents of "vacilón" and "guasa," just as it would be preposterous to describe a group of "sanjuaneros" drinking Don Q and playing guitars on Luquillo Beach as having a spree.

It is amusing to watch Rabassa turn slowly on the spit as he casts about for an English equivalent for "vacilón." Here are some of his offerings: "good time" (p. 64), "shindig" (p. 59), "fun" (p. 62), "a ball" (p. 91). A kindred term, *relajo*, lands him similar difficulties. For example, "paraíso cerrado del relajo/closed paradise of depravity," where there is an obvious miscarriage of justice though no more so than on another page where he translates "relajo" as "dissipation." Much closer is his rendering of "industria nacional la guachifita" as "the national industry of poking fun." Comparable to "vacilón/shindig" as not-very-close fits are "friquiterías/freakeries" (why not "baloney," incidentally?). "Bien friquits que es. Bien wilis naiquin que es/Freaky as he is, flaky as he is," and "tipos bien wilson/real clean-cut types." What all these versions have in common is that they ship us off the island and back to the mainland. There is a lot more to be said on this particular subject and I have given some further examples in an article on Rabassa's translation to be published shortly.[1]

Let me move on to my second subheading, "intransigent localisms of speech." Some of these localisms are beyond the skill of any translator, as with "lloré como una huerfanita. Pobre pobrecita exclamado con pena penita por el Doctor Severo Severino," rendered by Rabassa as "I cried like a little orphan. Poor poor thing exclaimed with sorrowful sorrow by Doctor Severo Severino." Here the *ito-ita* phenomenon with its mixture of affection and mocking patronage is not easily caught in English, with the exception perhaps of the Scots' *wee*. Another example is "irme de artista con el nombre de la Langosta, y hacerme famossssa y dar opinionessss y firmar autógrafossss," where the social significance of pronouncing the final "s" just has no clear-cut English equivalent.

More subtle are locutions where *tone* changes in the transference from Spanish into English. An early example from the opening section where la China says "a mí no me resulta que se amañe a venir tarde," and where the English equivalent "I don't dig his trick of coming late" makes her sound like an inhabitant of the lower Bronx. (Incidentally, I have never been to the lower Bronx and so all my references to it are purely mythical, like Atlantis or Xanadu.) Read the following examples and see if you do not agree with me that there is a perceptible cultural switch in moving from the Spanish to the English version: "una vampira, una manganzona, una culisucia que regó, que yo era una quitamachos/a vampire, a lazy bum, a dirty-assed bitch who spread it around that I was a man-stealer"; "tanta monería quién ha visto/ who would have thought of all those niceties"; "piropero, picaflor, enamoriscado andarín/flatterer, flirter, gadabout"; "un balde de ropa sucia entre las dos patas/a basin of dirty clothes between her two legs." And I can hear la China saying "a mí todo plin"—but "everything is plink to me?" Never!

Of course the simple answer to what I have been saying is that there is a comparable loss in raciness and authenticity in *all* translation, and this no one can deny. But the problem becomes serious in novels where dialect or the distinctive patterns of ethnic speech become the medium whereby the meaning of a work is conveyed. Vronsky, Julien Sorel, David Copperfield, Johann Buddenbrooks, don Fabrizio di Salina: these are all characters who travel easily and without a loss of selfhood in the passage. But with characters where a manner of expression is selfhood, more is lost in the translation between languages than we can spare. La China Hereje, the pompous senator conscious of his machismo and his *abolengo* (words expressing concepts that themselves remain shipwrecked on one side of the language gap), the senator's wife who crosses herself after making love, the horrible *piti-yanqui* Benny—these are all irretrievably *Latin* types, and to Anglicize them is to deprive them of their raison d'être and their virtù (two more terms for which no equivalents in an Anglo-Saxon culture are readily available!).

Now I come to my third and last subheading, "the different specific gravity of two languages." Perhaps it is easier to illustrate what I mean by this than to describe it. Racine's "c'était pendant l'horreur d'une profonde nuit" is notoriously untranslatable in its quintessential "Frenchness," as is Shakespeare's "this sensible warm motion to become/A kneaded clod" in its "Englishness," where the effect depends on an Anglo-Saxon density and succinctness ("A knealed clod") that *enacts* the meaning. Spanish by contrast is fluent and graceful, at its best wonderfully elegant and eloquent and at its worst wordy and tending to empty rhetoric. It is these last qualities that Luis Rafael Sánchez exploits with such relentless glee throughout *La guaracha*:

> La estudiante no se está tranquila, la estudiante no se queda tranquila, la estudiante no se deja quedar tranquila, la estudiante no es epiléptica, la estudiante no es sanvitera. Tampoco la posee un hongo alucinante ni la ha picado una serpiente amazónica ni la ha marcado la aranã Black Widow que asienta su ponsoña en Ponce, ni la habita el espíritu malgenioso de la Virgen de Medianoche, Virgen Eso Eres Tú. . . . La estudiante masca guaracha como una vil chicletómana, hasta convertir las quijadas en castañuelas roncas. Pausa para que den audiencia a las roncas castañuelas de sus quijadas, pausa, pausa, pausa.

Rabassa's version of this is gallant but unavailing:

> The schoolgirl isn't calm, the schoolgirl won't be calm, the schoolgirl won't let herself be calm, the schoolgirl isn't epileptic, the schoolgirl isn't autistic, the schoolgirl hasn't got Saint Vitus. Nor does she have a hallucinating mushroom nor has she been bitten by an Amazon snake nor by the black widow spider that has its poison in Ponce, nor is she inhabited by the evil-genius spirit of the Virgin of Midnight, the Virgin That's What You Are. . . . The schoolgirl chews guaracha like a vile chiclemaniac until her jaws become low-keyed castanets. A pause to give the low-keyed castanets of her jaws an audience, pause, pause, pause.

The maddening clatter of the original becomes altogether too crisp and Anglo-Saxon in translation and even the rate of chewing speeds up, from bovine *pau-sa* to monosyllabic *pause*.

Many of the rhetorical *rodeos* that characterize *La guaracha del Macho Camacho* seem thin or forced in *Macho Camacho's Beat*:

> Ella, mal educada, habla que te habla con la boca llena: pero usted. El interrumpiéndola: ¿cuándo me vas a decir tú, tutéame, tuteémonos, el tuteo es el atrecho, el ustedeo no va con el cameo, pideo y exigeo el tuteo que para eso pagueo, bieneo?/She, ill-mannered, talking away with her mouth full: but you. He interrupting her: when are you going to use the familiar form, the *tú*, with me, let's be familiar, the familiar form is the shortcut, the formal doesn't rhyme with to bed, to ask, or to demand the familiar because that's what I want to pay for, you *too*?

> Espejito, espejito, le da un bomboncito al espejito para que se haga su amiguito/ Mirror mirror on the wall, she gives a little piece of candy to the little mirror so that it will be her little friend.

> La Universidad de Puerto Rico está controlada por los fupistas, los marxistas, los comunistas, los fidelistas, los maoístas, tantos istas que perdona que yo insista en la pista/the University of Puerto Rico is controlled by FUPI independentists, marxists, castroits, maoists, so many that I've lost track of them, which is why I have to backtrack to the track.

In these examples, what I have called the "difficult specific gravities" of Spanish and English have deflected Rabassa's efforts to keep in step with the original. Sánchez's strategies of incremental repetition and redundancy are in themselves expressive of language habits, and so of states of mind; his exploitation of assonance is a kind of verbal *relajo* which mirrors at the level of language the sexual, social, and political deformations that constitute the subject matter of the novel. But Rabassa is forced to imitate an uncongenial rhythm and alien music, suggesting in the process not so much *relajo* as its opposite, strain. No wonder the reader has often the sense of peering through a glass darkly at Sánchez's brilliant Caribbean landscape, which at times seems tantalizingly near, but for the most part remains puzzlingly just out of reach.

I began by asking whether *Macho Camacho's Beat* is a good translation of *La guaracha del Macho Camacho*. My answer to this question should by now be obvious: "Yes, it is. No, it is not." As an example of a happy compromise between minimalist fidelity and maximalist license it could not perhaps be bettered, and probably when Juan Mari Bras is given his rightful sex in the second edition it will not be bettered. But as a miraculous entry into the psychic and social realities of a nation beset on all sides by consumerism, self-righteous politicians, an eroded national culture, and a shaky sense of its own identity, it is only a partial success. Nor can I see how it could very well have been any different.

Miracles do sometimes occur in the world of translation when we have the uncanny feeling that we have been trasported on a magic carpet into the world of the original. But for this reader there is no such magic carpet effect in Rabassa's traslation of *La guaracha*. La China Hereje, Doña Chon, the senator, his snobby wife, the unspeakable Benny—they all stubbornly remain Puerto Rican types, even though mysteriously they address the reader in accents ranging from Brooklyn to Palm Beach. The rattle of verbal *relajo* is recreated as a verbal tour de force, but, robbed of its primacy function, it comes across as a performance in its own right. Ironically, we are often more aware of the translator as performer than of the performance that constitutes the original text. In short, a jolly *vacilón* at Luquillo is transformed into a North American "spree" on Long Island—and we all know where we would rather spend the afternoon.

A formula I would suggest by way of conclusion runs as follows: The more insistently a novel insists upon its own "writerliness," the more it is, to use Roland Barthes's expression, "scriptible," then the harder the work of transference to an equivalent writerliness becomes. A novel which is all surface is a novel which can be nothing else but what it is; to substitute another surface for the first is less to translate than to traduce. The truth is that the great play-novels—*Pantagruel, Petersburg, Tristram Shandy, Tres tristes tigres*—are all locked stubbornly within the cupboards of their national literatures, and if we want to fully enjoy them we have to pick the lock and move right in.

Perhaps in literature we should more often be prepared to accept the wisdom that certain works are inherently untranslatable, thereby remaining out of bounds to anyone not willing to learn the language. And in fact this is not as great a handicap as it sounds. Why after all *should* everything be translated? And why can we not leave a little room for a total incomprehension between cultures, instead of the dangerous semicomprehension that, as a result of the world boom in translation, prevails today? *Macho Camacho's Beat* is as good a translation as one is likely to see, but a "dangerous semicomprehension" is just what it gives. Better, in my opinion, buy a good dictionary of Puerto Rican slang and work one's way through the original text, page by page and line by line. That way in which we "trans-late" ourselves into Luis Rafael Sánchez's world is the only really "good" sort of translation there is.

Note

1. For a detailed analysis of Rabassa's translation see my article "*La guaracha* in English: Traduttore Traditore?" *Revista de Estudios Hispánicos* (Universidad de Puerto Rico, 1981): 107–22.

Part V

Puerto Rican Literature in the Public School Curriculum

23

Image and Identity: Puerto Rican Literature in the School Curriculum

Angel G. Quintero Alfaro

From the documents that I have received from the organizers of this meeting, I gather that their principal concern is the image and identity of the Puerto Rican as it is reflected in literature. I also note that the agenda of the conference could be divided into two parts. The first and most important one is the clarification of the topic. The second refers to more practical matters, which although they can help shed light on the major theme, depend greatly for their analysis on the previous clarification of the topic. Such is the case with the theme of our panel: Puerto Rican literature in the school curriculum.

The theme we are concerned with is very interesting, but also complex and difficult. I wonder whether the central concern of the organizers of this meeting is the image and identity of the Puerto Rican living in the United States. This presents immediately one of the complexities of the theme. Identity has been and is still discussed in Puerto Rico in a context in which there are important differences. It could be argued that it is the same discussion. In a very general way it is, but I fear that the differences between the two situations, as well as their interrelations—the situation of the identity of Puerto Ricans living in the United States and that of those living in Puerto Rico—could make communication difficult.

The two matters of image and identity are understood by many as if they were the result of a single relationship: colonialism, capitalism, or imperialism. Without denying that colonialism, capitalism, and imperialism must be taken into account in the explanation of questions about identity, one must also ask whether these historical currents confront in the same manner and affect in the same way the Puerto Ricans who live in Puerto Rico and those who live in the United States.

Consideration of this issue leads to one of the most difficult questions facing this meeting: Where are those cultural trends taking us? Are they leading us in the same or different directions? Do they tend to unify our attitudes, values, and customs or, on the contrary, do they separate and make us different? Do they clarify the process of identity or do they cloud the issue?

The migratory process of Puerto Ricans to the United States, especially as it has developed during the last half of this century, is one of the most critical forces affecting the contemporary development of Puerto Rico and the Puerto Rican. More than one-third of all Puerto Ricans live in the United States, many of them having been born and raised here. A little more than half live in Puerto Rico. Others, in increasing numbers, flow between one society and another. All of them are called Puerto Ricans as a result of a long historical experience. Those living in Puerto Rico are not "islanders." It is not the island that is important in our identification, but the historical experience leading to a society that is the basis of our identity, which started and developed over centuries in the geographic setting of the island.

We have already referred to one major problem about "identity": the identity of each of the groups that has resulted from the migratory process and the image that each one has of the other. Families are very often intermingled, so are friends, and even dreams and life projects. But at the same time, separations begin to take place and identifications are made of those from "here" and "there." To the separation of place we could add separation of classes and cultural perspective. The situation resulting from the migratory process is a determining factor not only for our image but for our social reality, and as such for the character of our identity. It is the basis for much of our drama, and therefere a source for literary expression and scholarly analysis and reflection.[1]

The Puerto Rican identity of today is the result of a long historical process. This process has been widely studied and discussed. The discussion, as this meeting illustrates, is still alive. Recently, in a very provocative essay, José Luis González suggested that Puerto Rican history consists of varying stages, which he calls *pisos*, in which an identity has been forming; but before an identity is fully developed and adequately integrated it is superseded by another.[2] So, for example, in the three centuries following the first Spanish settlement, out of a relatively small number of Spanish settlers, Indians, and Blacks, a first nucleus identifying itself as Puerto Rican began to emerge. Originally it was a small group which grew to about 150,000 inhabitants at the end of the eighteenth century. The people were for the most part dispersed, living in relative isolation, with a simple culture and an economy characterized by self-sufficiency. In the twentieth century, to a large extent because of the revision of Spanish policies which liberalized commerce and made immigration easier, Puerto Rico became a real melting pot. There was a rapid increase in population, surpassing 900,000 by 1898. The nature of the agricultural system changed, a new economy emerged, organized around the hacienda,[3] more land became productive, commerce increased, and there was a greater use of technical skills. The new social groups which controlled agriculture and commerce began to see themselves as the ideal Puerto Ricans. The great majority of the original scattered farmers were practically recolonized and became *agregados* (dependent peasants). The question arises: To what extent was the new situation integrated to the former? Was there progress and development or a set of new conflicts based on a superimposed structure? It seems to me that by 1898 Puerto Rico was a hierarchical society in which there were profound social differences. A small section of the population (about 15 percent) spoke for the rest of the country. This small dominant group aspired to transform the society so that the remanining group (about 85 percent) would come to accept its values, attitudes, and lifestyles. As this process moved toward its final solidifying stage with the autonomy granted by Spain in 1898, the Spanish-American War broke out and Puerto Rico became a U.S. possession.

There is no doubt about the abruptness of the ensuing change and the profound transformation it caused in the economy, culture, and social organization of Puerto Rico. In our limited space we can only sketch this development, subdividing the period into three stages: the initial stage, from 1900 to 1930; the following stage, from 1930 to 1968, characterized by Operation Bootstraps and the Free Associated State; and the contemporary situation, from 1968 to the present.

The first period is characterized by the transformation of the hacienda social system into one dominated by the sugar corporation. It is characterized by a more intense use of technology and by a greater political and cultural conflict. The discussion about identity is of paramount importance during this period. There is an intense debate about the significance of our history and the meaning of our identity. Antonio S. Pedreira's *Insularismo* and Tomas Blanco's *El Prontuario Histórico* are the most significant expressions of that debate in which the most well-known Puerto Rican intellectuals participated. This debate about identity was very different, in content as well as context. There was a great fear of losing what was thought to be a characteristic way of life. But there was also a great deal of vigor in the debate. It can be seen as the expression of a social class that felt threatened but at the same time sensed the potential for self-development.

Around the middle of the 1930s it was already clear that the phase of social and economic development based on the sugar economy had reached a standstill. Dissatisfaction with the prevailing social and political situation was also increasing. The critical situation of those years lead to the formation of a new political movement which gained control of the country between 1940 and 1968. The program of action that was developed was aimed at the great problems created by colonial development: the concentration and poor distribution of wealth, lack of job opportunities, and inadequate health, education, and recreation services. The solution to these problems was to be governed by a pragmatic ideology in which knowledge and imagination were to be applied to concrete social problems.

This program accelerated and substantially modified the process of social change which had taken place in the first part of the century. It altered the economy, significantly changing the nature of employment, increasing salaries, and improving their distribution. Through the limitation of landholdings by corporations and the creation of proportional benefit farms and new agricultural communitites, the *agregados* were practically abolished. Urbanization was accelerated and a middle class, principally dedicated to commerce, professions, and other public service-related jobs, increased considerably. Education was broadened and health, recreation, and transportation services were greatly improved. The statistical indexes on average income, life expectancy, illiteracy, and other education, health, and work indexes are relatively impressive.

The developments between 1940 and 1968 aimed toward a healthier democracy promoting individual effort and a more just distribution of power and wealth. But from the start there were important defects in the development process which led to increasingly unbalanced social development. The basic principle on which the program of development was based was that the new industries would continue to absorb the existing excess of manual labor. But the effects were different. Instead of producing an integrated transformation of the previous economic structure, that structure was upset; the lack of coordination between the industrial program and agricultural development increased unemployment instead of reducing it. A new type of unemployment was produced, characterized by a higher degree of uprootedness leading to an enormous population movement to urban centers and a constantly increasing flow of people between Puerto Rico and the United States. For internal and external reasons industrial development gradually decreased, thereby increasing population mobility, while the problem of marginality became serious.

This situation lead to the third, contemporary stage. This stage is characterized by the relative stagnation of economic development and increased dependency on programs of federal aid. These forms of aid maintain an economy without a real basis. Much more is consumed than is produced. Unemployment is maintained at extremely high levels and the uneven balance in the distribution of wealth increases. Gradually a situation is created where integrated programs and a social project for the future hardly count. *La guaracha del Macho Camacho*, a caricatured characterization of the present situation, is perhaps the best example of this in literature.

To summarize: The development of the Puerto Rican identity has been a long, dynamic, and complex historical process. It has resulted from abrupt changes, not integrated development. The most crucial of these changes was the invasion by the United States in 1898 and the social, economic, and cultural developments that followed. The most recent and one of the most critical changes in the present results from the migratory process to the United States. The net result has been a diverse, confusing identity, often with very conflicting images.

Using the perspective outlined above, let us now examine more directly the questions before our panel: (1) How does the school curriculum contribute to the development of the image of the Puerto Rican and to the process of his identity? (2) What is the role of Puerto Rican literature in that task?

The formation of the Puerto Rican, his education in the widest sense, takes place within the historical experience previously outlined. Our school system as we know it today is a recent development. It originated in a colonial context and in many ways is alien to and in conflict with the realities of the environment. It has developed in a context of profound change in which grave social inequality has prevailed.

The colonial origins of the school system have been studied quite extensively. The system was established around 1900 and until 1948 was directed by a commissioner appointed by the president of the United States. The first of these commissioners were North Americans. Aida Negrón de Montilla establishes clearly in her important study that the academic policy of the first commissioners was directed toward making North Americans out of the Puerto Ricans.[4] Although after the first ten years the commissioners appointed were Puerto Ricans (of the latter Aida Montilla deals only with Juan B. Huyke's period), and although some of them, such as José Padín, tried to modify this policy, the situation remains the same. Even a president with a more open vision like Franklin D. Roosevelt, after appointing Gallardo commissioner, wrote him a letter indicating that the academic system of Puerto Rico should teach Puerto Ricans to speak English and to behave like other citizens of the United States.[5]

This policy has created protest, conflict, and resistance in Puerto Rico. I have some doubt as to its success in practice. The vast majority of Puerto Rican educators and also the studies carried out by U.S. educators are agreed on its negative effect on the education of the Puerto Rican and academic education in Puerto Rico. It has made the teaching of languages into a matter of party policy. This has caused the study and research of matters concerning language and academic policy based on arguments and pedagogical evidence, rather than ideological preferences, more difficult. The policy has also made deliberate attempts to mold an ideal type of person in terms of ideological preferences. This tendency is questionable. We will return to this matter later for further examination.

The Puerto Rican academic system is of recent development and exists in an environment of profound social inequality. When the system was established in 1900, only 15 percent of the children attended school. Illiteracy surpassed 85 percent. Of those who did attend school, the majority abandoned the classroom before reaching the third grade. Those attending came for the most part from urban areas and were the children of people belonging to social groups with greater economic means and with more academic preparation. Even in 1940, when academic opportunities had increased considerably, only half of the school-aged children attended school. Even then the number of children not attending school was still at the same level as in 1900, about 285,000 children, although naturally the percentage of school-aged children had decreased proportionally from 85 to 50 percent. It was not until the 1950s that universal registration in the first grade was attained, and in the mid-1960s there was universal elementary school. I mention these facts in detail to present clearly the limited effect of the academic curriculum.

The academic curriculum includes programs of study, materials, and methods for teaching them, and ways of evaluating results in elementary, secondary, and university-level schools in the country. It has been widely studied, though the majority of these studies do not refer directly to matters which concern this conference. But there are some factors about the teaching in general and especially about the use and teaching of Spanish which may be useful to us. It is pointed out, for example, that texts and teaching materials are thought of in terms of an average student, without the diversity of students or the very special situation in which they developed being taken into account. It is found that there is a great distance between the goals and objectives formulated and the practical experience acquired in the classroom. While the importance of the learning process is emphasized as an objective, in practice the emphasis is on information. This information tends to be out of date and offered in an irrelevant manner, without taking into consideration the interests and ways of learning of the students or the different contexts in which their life has developed. The objectives point toward the importance of basic skills and the diagnosis and evaluation of the students' progress in achieving them. Very often it is presumed that the repetition of a task leads to the acquisition of the skills involved, without taking into consideration what is happening with the students—whether they are involved, know what they are learning, and are exercising their intelligence. In many classrooms students copy, repeat, and memorize matters which are of no interest to them and often of no interest to the teacher either. The learning process is to a large extent absent from the classrooms.[6]

Puerto Rican literature is more integrated with historical reality than the curriculum. The writer is formed within the historical experience which we have already outlined. He lives, in part, the drama of that experience. He reacts to it within his own special perspective; his work is both a reflection of his experience and an effort to recreate and affect it. Until about 1930 there was almost no Puerto Rican literature in the school program. It was then that one of the first attempts to offer a course on Puerto Rican literature at the university level was made by Antonio S. Pedreira. In public school, under the direction of Carmen Gómez Tejera, the formulation of a new program for the teaching of Spanish in elementary and secondary schools was initiated. Included in this program are a greater number of works by Puerto Rican authors, although Spanish and Spanish American literature dominate the selection. Since 1960, the tendency to increase significantly the number of Puerto Rican authors in the school curriculum has continued. At present the most important consideration for improving the program is not so much the quantity of works but the selection and ways of teaching them.[7] It is noted that there are important gaps in selections; generally there is a tendency to overemphasize the traditional and avoid the controversial. Of course, there are exceptional cases in which good teachers partially fill in these gaps. But the most recent studies indicate a lack of agility and creativity in the teaching of literature and the absence of an adequate presentation of the most contemporary matters.

There are few studies which specifically touch on the problem of the image of the Puerto Rican which is to be inferred from the curriculum and, more specifically, from the use of Puerto Rican literature in the curriculum. Most important among those which focus more closely on the matter are some of the theoretical and practical studies by Luis Nieves Falcón;[8] the study by Isabel Picó, *Machismo y educación en Puerto Rico*;[9] and the study by Isabelo Zenón Cruz, *Narciso descubre su trasero: el negro en la cultura puertorriqueña*.[10]

Luis Nieves Falcón has indicated in many studies the inadequacy of the image transmitted by the school curriculum for children of the poorest classes. He also indicated that the image transmitted in text illustrations and in reading materials is that of the middle-class Puerto Rican. He has developed materials more related to children who live in the poorest areas and promotes methods of teaching which cater to what he calls low self esteem, which is found in these children and which these materials and methods of teaching tend to promote rather than attack.

Isabel Picó shows the extent and ramifications of machismo Puerto Rican education, which presents men as superior to women. She analyses basic reading books for elementary school and social studies books from the first to the sixth grade. In the readings from the basic Spanish series, she finds that girls and women are presented as inferior to men, both in quantity and character. Men surpass women in bravery, creativity, perseverance, and spirit of adventure. Girls and women surpass men in weakness, passivity, dependency, and fear. Picó finds that the image of women in these books is conceived in a narrower fashion than it is in our contemporary cultural reality.

The ideology of the sexes in the social studies books excludes women as an active and integral part of society. They are, for the most part, assigned domestic roles. They are excluded from history. Women rarely appear building or creating the communities or countries being studied. Picó also examines teachers' expectations in the classroom and proposes strategies of change.

Isabelo Zenón, in his study of the Black, dedicates a section to matters of instruction and another to the aspects of literature studied; in both cases he points out there is racial prejudice against the Black and his cultural contribution.

There is no doubt that the academic curriculum in Puerto Rican schools has important defects, gaps, prejudiced viewpoints, and inadequate focuses. But perhaps its major problem is the perspective from which it is formulated. Those who have studied the curriculum and those who have contributed to its formulation have tried to formulate in advance an image of the Puerto Rican, the ideal Puerto Rican, which it is hoped will result from the programs constituting the curriculum.

If what has been said so far in this paper is true, if Puerto Rican history is one of conflicting images, confusing at times, disperse, and fragmented, this is going to manifest itself in the school and the curriculum. If the teachers' experience is such that they have differing ideas about the meaning of the country, and if the same is true of parents, the elderly, and even students, we can hardly expect to find a solution to the problem of cultural ambiguity through the school curriculum.

The ambiguity experienced in Puerto Rican society and therefore in the school curriculum and in literature cannot be resolved by a logical-theoretical type of definition. Perhaps many of our failures have been the result of our denying this reality instead of using it as a ponit of departure. This ambiguity and diversity could be a great virtue within our contemporary situation. Our effort would not then be aimed at achieving security within the diversity and ambiguity which characterize our situation.

The problem for the school and the school curriculum should not be so much the search for the ideal Puerto Rican nor the building of a Puerto Rican utopia, but rather to work adequately with every child and every person day by day, promoting their improvement as well as that of the community. School should be a more lively place, much more creative, a place where pupils and students enroll to study situations, materials, and books which they can get involved with and which are at the same time genuine efforts to understand and transform their reality.

Literature is usually lively and expresses according to its quality the concerns of skillful and creative minds. It reflects the conflicts of reality and tries to affect them at the same time. But like all materials used in the academic program, it can become dead when taught, something which is studied to fulfill a requirement without involving the student. The amount of Puerto Rican literature in the curriculum should be increased, and the list of books included should be reviewed continually, and students should have a greater opportunity to select what they read. The school should give them the stimulus to read through the example set by teachers and by creating the right environment for study and analysis; but students should not be told what to read. School should be a more open, more lively place. It should be open to the trends of the community, constantly trying to develop students by using their interests as an incentive and by continually exercising their capacity to see, hear, think, imagine, and judge the matters of vital interest to them.

Some years ago, about 1968, I completed a study analyzing the Puerto Rican school which may still be of use:

> The recommendations which we have made go in that direction. In order to prevent it, we propose prompt attention to, and a modification of the way in which the school is organized and in dealing with socialization. We consider that basic security is derived from the fundamental acceptance of what one is, from self-respect, and this has its basis in what happens in the first years. Given this early healthy development, it is easier to face up to social change with integrity.
>
> We have proposed, in addition, a more active academic process in which intelligence is constantly developed in close relation to the outside and inside environment of the student. Not to teach from outside, but rather to facilitate the continual expression of feelings, emotion, and thought, within conditions which lead to the development of the abilities of expression and reflection.
>
> We also propose a closer relationship between practice, action, and teaching. We have said that the school delays too much the confrontation with reality. It lessens the value of and deforms this relationship. In every academic process there must be a closer and more authentic relationship with reality. It is that which the best educators have meant when they affirmed that education should be "life," not preparation for life. The only preparation for life is to live with satisfaction, integrity, and intelligence. And the satisfaction is produced, not by inaction or isolation, but by confronting the problem of existence and utilizing the capabilities at one's disposal for the encounter. The body, character, and intelligence are developed in the same process. That is a process which, because it is more natural, should prove to be easier; however, our present-day conceptions make this impossible at times.
>
> School should not only be preparation for life, but it should also allow one to constantly live. While it must have and promote a critical attitude toward everyday living, it must be an attitude full of understanding, compassion, and humility, not pride and arrogance. So, one must allow the pupil to live and to

express himself in the living and about his living in his own terms, the only ones which are accessible to him. To help them to grow in that process of reflective perception of their existence is the essence of the basic task of the teacher.

The good teacher, it has been said, is he who makes himself unneeded as soon as possible. Today we would say more: in a situation of social change and relative confusion, the good teacher is he who shares generously his effort to learn with the students that help him and who at the same time teach him. The academic process, according to the way it is received today in most schools, winds up being excessively long and pretentious. We have suggested shortening it, simplifying it, integrating it to the vital process. To understand that the family, community, factory, political party, and civic action teach; to help all these institutions fulfill their educational function, without trying to do it all—should be the function of the new school. A school that can do much more, by doing well much less.[11]

Notes

1. There are now a great number of literary works and essays which try to describe and analyze this situation.
2. José Luis González, *El país de cuatro pisos y otros ensayos* (Río Piedras, P.R.: Huracán, 1980).
3. Sociological concept used both in English- and Spanish-language documents. It refers to a semifeudal type of organization based on medium-sized and large landholdings.
4. Aida Negrón de Montilla, *Americanization in Puerto Rico and the Public School System, 1900–1930* (Río Piedras: Editorial Universitaria, 1975).
5. Thomas Mathews, *Puerto Rican Politics and the New Deal* (Gainesville: University of Florida Press, 1960), 317–18.
6. I have based this summary on studies of the school system until 1972. The recent study by Eduardo Rivera Medina (*An Analysis of In-Service Training Needs of English Teachers and Spanish Teachers to Returned Migrants*, NIE, 1982) confirms in 1982 the summary we have gathered. This is a valuable study, in addition, because it introduces the situation of the teaching of students who have returned to Puerto Rico from the United States.
7. Study of the Education System, 1960, Spanish Programs from the Department of Public Instruction, and personal testimony of Gladys Pagán Soto, former supervisor and director of this program.
8. Luis Nieves Falcón, *Diagnóstico de Puerto Rico* (Río Piedras, P.R.: Edil, 1972); idem, *Acción comunal y educación pre-escolar* (Río Piedras, P.R.: Acción Social, 1970); idem, *Fabián* (Río Piedras, P.R.: Edil., n.d.).
9. Isabel Picó, *Machismo y educación en Puerto Rico* (Comisión de los Derechos de la Mujer, 1979).
10. Isabelo Zenón Cruz, *Narciso descubre su trasero: el negro en la cultura puertorriqueña* (Carolina: Furide, 1973).
11. Angel G. Quintero Alfaro, *Educación y cambio social en Puerto Rico: una epoca crítica* (Río Piedras: Editorial Universitaria, 1972), pp. 191–92.

Bibliography

Abbad y Lasierra, Iñigo. *Historia Geográfica, Civil y Natural de la Isla de San Juan Bautista de Puerto Rico*. (New annotated edition on the historical part and follow-up on statistics and the economy by José Julián Acosta y Calvo.) Puerto Rico: Imprenta y Librería de Acosta, 1866.

Babín, María Teresa. ''A Gap in Puerto Rican Education.'' *San Juan Review* (June 1965): 27–28.

Blanco, Tomás. *Prontuario Histórico de Puerto Rico*. Madrid: Imprenta Juan Pueyo, 1935.

Cámara de Representantes de Puerto Rico, Comisión de Instrucción. *Estudio del sistema educativo* (under the direction of Ismael Rodríguez Bou). Río Piedras, P.R.: Universidad de Puerto Rico, 1961.

Campos Ricardo, José Luis González, Juan Flores and Angel G. Quintero Rivera. *Puerto Rico: identidad nacional y clases sociales*. Río Piedras: Huracán, 1979.

Caselmann, Christian, Lamberto Borghi, and Morten Bredsdorff. *El sistema educativo de Puerto Rico* (recommendations). San Juan, P.R., May 1959.

Columbia University, Teacher's College, International Institute, *Survey of the Public School System of Puerto Rico*. New York, Bureau of Publications, 1926.

Conferencias (21) Literatura Puertorriqueña. San Juan: Instituto de Cultura Puertorriqueña, 1960.

Díaz Quiñones, Arcadio. *El almuerzo en la hierba* (Llorens Torres, Palés Matos, René Marqués). Río Piedras: Huracán, 1982.

Fernández Méndez, Eugenio. *La identidad y la cultura: crítica y valoraciones en torno a Puerto Rico*. San Juan: Cemí, 1959.

González, José Luis. *El país de cuatro pisos y otros ensayos*. Río Piedras: Huracán, 1980.

Información final de la comisión de Reforma Educativa. Hato Rey: Talleres de Artes Gráficas, Departamento de Instrucción Pública del Estado Libre Asociado de Puerto Rico, 1977.

Laguerre, Enrique. ''If I had it all to do over . . .'' *San Juan Review* (June 1965): 41-42.

Levine, Barry B. *Benjy Lopez: A Picaresque Tale of Emigration and Return*. New York: Basic Books, 1980.

Mathews, Thomas. *Puerto Rican Politics and the New Deal*. Gainesville: University of Florida Press, 1960.

Mellado, Ramón. *Culture and Education in Puerto Rico*. New York: Columbia University, 1947.

Nieves Falcón, Luis. *Diagnóstico de Puerto Rico*. Río Piedras: Edil, 1972.

——. *Acción comunal y educación pre-escolar*. Río Piedras: Acción Social, 1970.

——. *Fabian*. Río Piedras: Edil, n.d.

Osuna, Juan José. *A History of Education in Puerto Rico*. Río Piedras: Editorial de la Universidad de Puerto Rico, 1949.

Pagán de Soto, Gladys. ''Reflexiones sobre los objetivos y el contenido del programa de español en las escuelas publicas de Puerto Rico.'' Personal report, 1983.

Pedreira, Antonio S. *Insularismo: ensayos de interpretación puertorriqueña*. Madrid: Tipografía Artística, 1934.

Picó, Isabel. *Machismo y educación en Puerto Rico*. Comisión para el Mejoramiento de los derechos de la Mujer, 1979.

Programa de Español. Hato Rey: Departamento de Instrucción Pública de Puerto Rico, 1970.

Quintero Alfaro, Angel G. *Educación y cambio social en Puerto Rico: una época crítica*. Río Piedras: Editorial Universitaria, 1972.

Rivera Medina, Eduardo. *An Analysis of In-Service Training Needs of English Teachers to Returned Migrants in Puerto Rico* (Summary Report). NIE, 1982.

San Juan Review (June 1965). Special Education Issue.

Seda Bonilla, Eduardo. *Interacción social y personalidad en una comunidad en Puerto Rico*. San Juan: Juan Ponce de León, 1964.

Steward, Julian H., et al. *The People of Puerto Rico: A Study in Social Anthropology*. Urbana: University of Illinois, 1956.

Toward a Language Policy for Puerto Ricans in the United States: An Agenda for a Community in Movement. National Puerto Rican Task Force on Educational Policy (bilingual edition). New York: Research Foundation of the City of New York, 1982.

Zenón Cruz, Isabelo. *Narciso descubre su trasero: el negro en la cultura puertorriqueña*. Carolina: Furide, 1973.

24

Self-Affirmation or Self-Destruction: The Image of Puerto Ricans in Children's Literature Written in English

Sonia Nieto

In setting the stage for the discussion of Puerto Rican children's literature, one is immediately faced with two central questions. What is the image of the Puerto Rican in children's literature? And, how can we define Puerto Rican literature for children? Each of these issues will be analyzed within the larger questions of self-affirmation and self-destruction vis-à-vis children's literature.

As of the 1980 Census, there were 2,013,945 Puerto Ricans living in the United States. Of these, over 1,107,000 were living outside of New York City.[1] Every major city, particularly those in the Northeast, has a sizable Puerto Rican community. The Puerto Rican presence is making itself felt in these communities, whether it be through *bodegas* or bilingual education, *botánicas* or *salsa*. Another important statistic concerns the age of the Puerto Rican community. The median age of the Puerto Rican living in the United States, according to a 1979 study, was 19.9 years, compared to 31.9 years for the overall population.[2]

Taken together, these two facts describe a community which is very young, growing in numbers, and geographically dispersed. Given this reality, one might assume that the Puerto Rican experience has by now significantly permeated American culture and that this is reflected in the media, including books. Additionally, one might assume that a growing number of books for children reflect the Puerto Rican reality in U.S. society.

Both these assumptions are wrong. There is widespread ignorance in this country about Puerto Rico and Puerto Ricans, even in areas where there is a significant Puerto Rican community. The media has, of course, created images of the Puerto Rican over the past thirty or so years. Some images, for the most part negative and destructive, come at us larger than life. *West Side Story* and *Fort Apache*, to name only two of the worst offenders, have become imbedded in the popular mentality as truly reflective of the Puerto Rican community. Other subtle and not so subtle images have likewise become generalized: the passive, all-suffering woman or the sultry, fiery prostitute; the supermacho or the welfare-cheating, good-for-nothing hustler hanging out on street corners; and, of course, the knife-wielding gang member. Yet most non-Puerto Ricans know little of our community, our roots, our values, and our everyday lives.

We must thus turn to the popular media to understand how the image of Puerto Ricans in children's literature is created and perpetuated. As we shall see below, the images in children's literature borrow heavily from the stereotypes created in other media, particularly the visual media.

Although some images of the Puerto Rican are obviously present in media, children's books hardly seem to have kept pace, at least in terms of numbers. In 1972 the Council on Interracial Books for Children reviewed 100 children's books with Puerto Rican themes printed in English. Most had been written in the 1960s and 1970s; some went back as far as the 1940s. In 1982 the council asked me to update this earlier issue with two basic goals in mind: to determine if the numbers of books published since 1972 had kept pace with the growing population; and to evaluate whether the newer books had changed in perspective from those published prior to 1972, which had been characterized by the council as overwhelmingly racist, assimilationist, sexist, and colonialist.[3]

In terms of numbers, the results were distressing. In 1978, according to statistics compiled by UNESCO, a total of 2,911 children's books were published in the United States by the principal publishing companies.[4] We can conservatively estimate that in the 1972–82 decade there were approximately 20,000 children's books published in the United States. Of these, only 57 can be classified as books with Puerto Rican themes.[5] These represent about three hundredths of 1 percent. Both statistically speaking and in real terms, this is an insult. To represent this geographically, let us assume that each book is 1 inch thick. If we were to lay them on top of each other, we would have a stack over 139 stories high, taller than any building in the world. (The World Trade Center in New York, in comparison, is 110 stories high.) The children's books with Puerto Rican themes would be less than 5 feet high, or shorter than most adults. If we add to this the fact that of the 57 books, 29 are nonfiction, we are left with an even more minuscule number to consider in this study. We can only conclude that the Puerto Rican presence is almost nonexistent in the field of children's literature.

Another interesting fact concerns the years in which the majority of books were published. Diagram 1 represents the number of books with Puerto Rican themes written each year since 1972. The peak year was 1973 in which 21 titles were published; the worst year was 1980, with no titles. Probably because of the demands of the 1960s and 1970s, the publishing companies responded by marketing a larger number of books concerned with Puerto Ricans. Ironically, as the number of Puerto Ricans, particularly young people, increased, the number of children's books decreased dramatically. Diagram 2 shows the number of works of fiction published during these years as compared to the number of all books. Again, the peak year was 1973, but instead of slight peaks and valleys, the number of works of fiction decreased almost steadily each year.

Numbers alone, of course, do not tell the whole story. We are now left with the second question posed at the beginning of this paper. What is Puerto Rican literature for young people? In the context of the present study, any book of fiction in which at least one of the central characters is Puerto Rican will be considered. This is not to suggest, however, that they are "Puerto Rican children's literature," that they are written by Puerto Rican authors, that they are authentic, nor that they are of high quality. It is a problematic choice for several reasons, not the least of which is that most of the books were authored by non-Puerto Ricans. These authors by and large characterize the Puerto Rican with what tends to be a limited and ethnocentric perspective. The books are included here not because they were necessarily written by

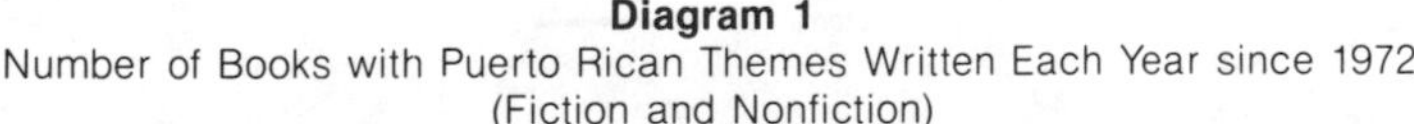

Diagram 1

Number of Books with Puerto Rican Themes Written Each Year since 1972
(Fiction and Nonfiction)

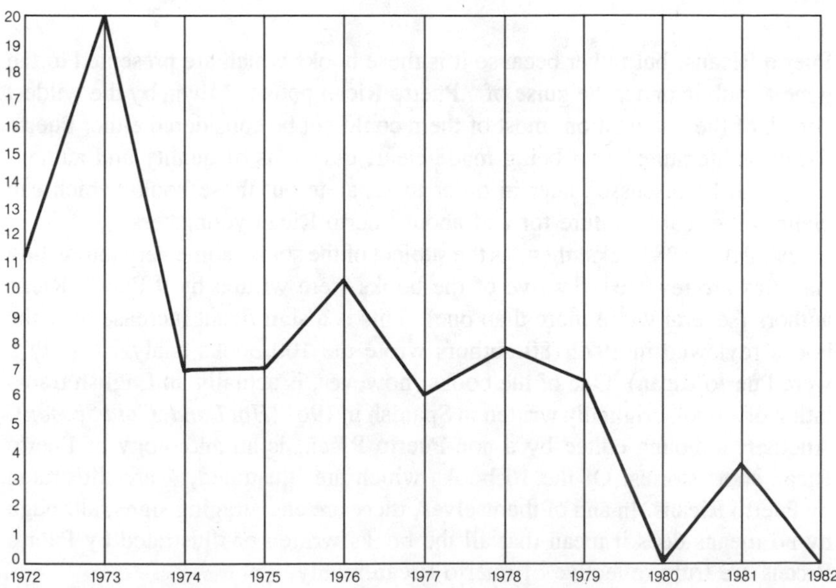

Diagram 2
Number of Books with Puerto Rican Themes Written each Year since 1972

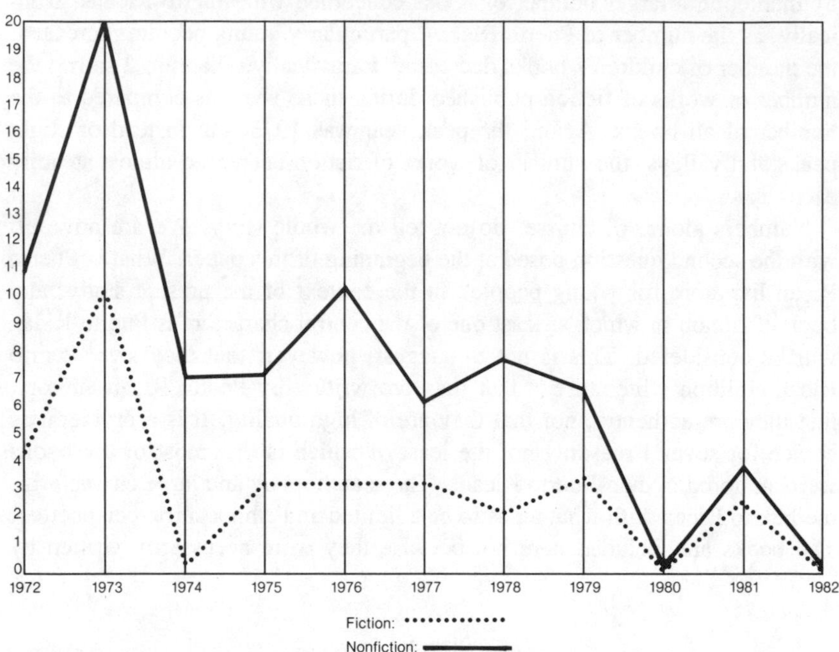

Puerto Ricans, but rather because it is these books which are presented to the general public under the guise of "Puerto Rican books." Even by the wildest stretch of the imagination, most of them could not be considered either Puerto Rican or literature. That being made clear, questions of quality and authenticity will be discussed later in order to separate out those books which can claim to be real literature for and about Puerto Rican youngsters.

Using these 28 books, then, as the subject of the study, some very interesting statistics are revealed. Twelve of the books were written by 9 Puerto Rican authors (several wrote more than one). This is a significant increase over the books reviewed in 1972 (80 authors wrote the 100 books analyzed; only 5 were Puerto Rican). One of the books, however, is actually an English translation of a book originally written in Spanish in 1961 (*Hot Land, Cold Season*). Another, although edited by a non-Puerto Rican, is an anthology of Puerto Rican short stories. Of the 16 books which are illustrated, 4 are illustrated by Puerto Ricans. In and of themselves, these are encouraging signs, although by no means does it mean that all the books written or illustrated by Puerto Ricans are truly reflective of Puerto Rican reality.

Interestingly enough, fantasies are absent from the books except for a small number of legends. Most of the stories tend to focus on problems of adjustment, the gloom and doom of the ghetto, and the so-called culture of poverty as interpreted by these authors. The result is that only a handful of the books are appropriate for young children. Furthermore, the rich oral tradition of the Puerto Rican experience is almost totally missing. Another genre missing from the books is poetry. This flies in the face of Puerto Rican tradition where poetry is so central, whether it be written, memorized, or spontaneous, whether it be traditional poetry or that of the newer poetry focusing on the Puerto Rican New York experience. The dearth of this kind of literature is a serious issue; it contradicts the true history of Puerto Rican literature. Most of these stories have been written from a perspective which is decidedly non-Puerto Rican. That is, our issues and our style have been interpreted primarily by those outside our culture.

As was the case in the 1972 study, boys are much more popular than girls as central characters. In titles alone, boys outnumber girls two to one. In terms of the sex of the principal characters of the remaining books, all are boys or, where there are a number of characters, primarily boys. More will be said later about the characterization of boys and girls and men and women in the books.

Returning to the question of quality and authenticity, the remainder of this paper will focus on important trends and directions signaled by the books. What should be said at the outset is that, although the situation is better in some respects than it was ten years ago, very little has changed in terms of the perspective of the books. That is, they are still decidedly racist and sexist, reflecting a colonialist mentality. A look at some of the most common and blatant stereotypes found in the stories will confirm this. First, though, it would be instructive for us to imagine that we are youngsters coming across these books for the first time. Whether we are Puerto Rican or not, girls or boys, light- or dark-skinned, certain images are likely to make an imprint in our souls which will be difficult, if not impossible, to erase later in our lives. We can then reflect on some important and basic issues. Who speaks for Puerto Ricans? Who defines our lives? Who are the guardians of the self-identity of our youth? And ultimately, who is responsible for determining to a large extent how others perceive us?

Let us begin with the perspective. Several dominant features characterize the stories: assimilation, dependence, elitism, racism, sexism, and stereotypical physical features, settings, and language. Examples will be given of each.

In many of the worst stories assimilation is not only a primary goal, but a positive one as well. In these books, everything associated with U.S. history, language, and culture is valued, while everything Puerto Rican is disparaged.

All the books written by Peggy Mann echo this theme. In one (*The Secret Dog of Little Luis*), the object of the Puerto Rican boy's affection is a little North American girl who is constantly referred to as "the blond-haired girl" with "eyes so blue that he had to notice." Not once are the physical attributes of Puerto Ricans mentioned in the story. In another of her books (*How Juan Got Home*), the protagonist's mother is convinced that he must go to the United States, saying, "A boy educated on the mainland may dream of becoming a doctor. A lawyer. A Senator of the United States." She goes on to say that if he stays in their hometown, his highest aspiration will be to become a público driver. Ironically, their hometown is Barranquitas, the home of Luis Muñoz Rivera and Luis Muñoz Marín. Another example of this assimilationist thrust can be found in *Gaucho*, by González (not a Puerto Rican). The main character, a Puerto Rican adolescent, hates *plátanos* and Spanish music, at one point saying "he couldn't understand how anybody could listen to that junk . . . . He'd take the 'Top Ten' anytime." He goes as far as to say, "If a Spanish [sic] person ever lost his hands, he wouldn't be able to dance." The only truly positive character in the entire book is a White police officer. Puerto Ricans, on the other hand, are primarily drug addicts, number runners, pimps, welfare cheats, and other sundry criminals. In Thomas's *Pablito's New Feet*, all the Puerto Ricans come across as slightly superstitious and somewhat ignorant, save for Miriam, the most Americanized of all the characters. She is presented as the standard for success by which the others should be measured.

The dependence, helplessness, and passivity of Puerto Ricans are constant themes in many of the books. One is left wondering whether Puerto Ricans are capable of doing anything at all on their own without the help of the benevolent Whites who populate the books. These take the shapes of kindly cops, friendly store owners, helpful teachers, and understanding welfare workers. Passivity is perceived as almost a national characteristic, so that Whites are compelled to step in and help: the "White man's burden" updated. In Hall's *Danza!* the most positive character is a man from the United States; not only is he strong, affectionate, and understanding, but he is also half a head taller than all the Puerto Ricans! The grandfather, in contrast, is depicted as illogical, traditional (a negative characteristic, to be sure), superstitious, impassive, and bereft of affection. At the end of the story, the grandfather shows some humanity while the North American loses some of his shine, but the damage is already done; first impressions, even in children's books, die hard.

Many of the books are elitist as well. That is, the values and lifestyles of the rich are the primary standards for success, while the day-to-day struggles and jobs of the poor are neglected or minimized. The dignity of working-class folks is rarely depicted. In *Gaucho* the central character is emphatic on this point: "When he grew up he never wanted anyone to look at his hands and mark him as a poor person or a laborer." His uncle reaffirms the message by saying, "Here you get an education and then you get a good job, a clean job inside an office, and you save your money and go home whenever you want for a vacation." What is the message for Puerto Rican youngsters, the majority of whose parents are working in factories, small businesses, offices, or farms? Certainly self-confidence and pride are not likely to be developed as a result of exposure to this book. Further on in the story, Gaucho's uncle earnestly tells him that in Puerto Rico, "Young men can't go to college." Yet, according to the latest figures available, 119,083 students were enrolled in colleges and universities in Puerto Rico in 1978.[6] The problem with statements such as these is that they are presented as fact and are often internalized by both Puerto Rican and non-Puerto Rican youngsters. The result can be self-alienation.

This does not mean, of course, that the reality in which Puerto Ricans live is absent from the stories. Nevertheless, it is generally filtered through the authors' perception of the so-called culture of poverty—the conception of what Puerto Rican reality is. There is a real confusion between what happens to immigrants struggling to survive in a new environment and the social cost of being a member of the oppressed group. Crime, drug addiction, and prostitution are not intrinsic to any particular culture, but are rather symptoms of alienation and racism. What happens is that we are repeatedly treated to blaring music, "shrill" women, drunks, garbage, and gangs. While these may exist in Latin communities, they are often presented as the only features of our neighborhoods. In some instances, the results are ludicrous. In *Gaucho*, for example, the author says, "On really hot, humid, stifling nights, everyone slept on the roof. As many as fifteen families[!]." And in *Tomas and the Talking Birds* Puerto Ricans are depicted as being unfamiliar with the blessings of modern U.S. conveniences. When Tomas's mother sees a refrigerator for the very first time, she exclaims, "I have heard about these refrigerators . . . they are truly remarkable." In real life, we would be hard-pressed to find a Puerto Rican home, even in the most remote countryside, without a refrigerator.

Related to this is the fact that many books "blame the victim." Although never stated directly, the reader is left with the distinct impression that the characters in these books are the cause of their own oppression. This is particularly convenient because it fosters the image of the guiltless society. And although most of the main Puerto Rican characters, particularly the children, are presented as sweet and affable, it is somehow their own people who are responsible for the ghetto, the filth, the poverty, the crime, the drugs, and even for the hard life they lead. Once they learn English, or move out of the ghetto, or become assimilated, or "work hard" (a catch phrase often used in books of this kind to imply that most Puerto Ricans do not in fact work hard), their problems disappear. Time and again the blame is placed on the community, but the solutions are generally individual ones. The fact that human oppression is caused by institutions which are by their very nature racist, sexist, and exclusive is not addressed. When the viewpoint is reinforced daily by the media (i.e., individual success in the face of adversity), children are left with no alternative but to look to the characters themselves as the cause of their lot in life. In a sense, however, books do not create these images, but rather reinforce them. The media is not wholly to blame, for these same messages are heard daily by Puerto Rican youngsters, especially in the schools. A particularly devastating example of this is found in an article published in 1965 (but just as meaningful today) in a sociological analysis of education for Puerto Rican youngsters. In this study, the researcher simply sat in a classroom and recorded the interaction between teachers and students. At one point the teacher is discussing different kinds of homes. She tells the children that many families in her neighborhood have "houses all to themselves, with sometimes two bathrooms upstairs—one for each bedroom and one for the first floor too." When Juan, one of her students, tells her that only rich people live in those places, she responds, "Not exactly rich, Juan. But they do work hard, and every day."[7] What is the message for Juan, whose father does indeed work hard every day, and even, as Juan says, on Sundays? Clearly, he is left with little choice but to blame his own father.

Stereotypes of what Puerto Ricans look like, where they live, and how they speak are also popular in many of the books. The boys in *Little League Hotshots* are all thin, wiry, and small, somewhat undernourished and ideal candidates for charity cases. In Peggy Mann's novels it is often difficult to tell one boy from another in the illustrations. Puerto Rican children are generally described as quite small for their age with olive skin and straight or wavy black hair. They are usually appealing waifs, to be sure, but the racial and physical diversity so characteristic of Puerto Ricans is missing. Dark-skinned Puerto Ricans are almost absent from the books, as are tall, blond, freckled, and curly-haired ones. It becomes apparent that the majority of the authors of these books have had little contact with real live Puerto Ricans. Rather, their perceptions are based on common stereotypes propagated by the media.

Behavior is likewise presented in grossly stereotypical fashion. In some of the worst books, the exotic is emphasized. The main character is *Tomas and the Talking Birds*, for example, provides a vivid example of what the author apparently believes is exotica Puerto Rican style. When Tomas listens to drumbeats, he reacts in an almost genetic way: "Tomas felt his whole body begin to quiver. He began to shuffle his feet to the rhythm of the drum as he had seen dancers do at the fiesta. . . . His dance was a kind of ritual, a kind of joyous prayer."

The treatment of the behavior of Puerto Ricans is typical of children's books in general. In fact, what tends to be true of most children's books is their sentimentality and soppiness, their tired story lines, and their overall drivel. The overwhelming unfamiliarity of the authors with real children's lives is more than evident. This becomes even more apparent in the case of children's books about Puerto Ricans, because the authors' lack of familiarity with the language and culture of their subjects is obvious as well. Instead of the traditional Dick and Jane, we are faced with Dick and Jane with brown faces.

The depiction of the role of women in the stories is full of misconceptions, half-truths, and omissions. In most of the books, women play an insignificant or supporting role. Bethancourt's *New York City Too Far from Tampa Blues*, for example, depicts a mother and her three daughters as having no "personality" and crying a great deal. Another book by the same author (*Where the Deer and the Cantaloupe Play*) reiterates the simple-mindedness of women: "The womenfolk in the back of the wagon were chattering and laughing. . . . It was just as well they were unaware of the dangers facing them." Women, if depicted at all, are generally soft-spoken, passive, long-suffering, and clinging vines. Passivity, moreover, is described as a lack of initiative and intelligence. In the Puerto Rican experience, passivity does of course exist, but it is often a sign of respect and inner strength. This dimension is missing from the books. In the few cases where females reach for other goals, the message is often confusing. In *Josefina Finds the Prince* the main character discovers that she can indeed strive to try out for the part of the princess in the class play. She discovers this when she befriends a frog and finds, "A prince can be as green as grass. A prince can have yellow eyes. A prince can be cold and bumpy." The moral? Even if she *is* Puerto Rican and not as attractive as blond, blue-eyed girls, she can still try out for the play! In *The Dark Side of Nowhere* Eloise wants to be a nurse, but is discouraged from doing so presumably because "in the Díaz family, girls weren't supposed to be nurses—or secretaries or sales clerks or hairdressers. Earning a living was for the men. Women stayed home and raised kids." This is highly unlikely, for the reality of Puerto Rican women is quite diferrent. A significant percentage of Puerto Rican families in the United States (41 percent as compared to 11 percent for White families) are headed by women, many of whom have no alternative but to join the work force.[8] Even in 2-parent families, the economy is making it almost impossible for women not to work. The woman who has the option of staying home to raise children and take care of the house is quickly becoming the exception rather than the rule. While it is true that Puerto Rican women participate in the labor force to a lesser degree than other women,[9] the fact is that many are eager to work but are denied the opportunity. A study undertaken by the Puerto Rican Legal and Defense Fund found that training opportunities for Puerto Rican women are almost non-existent.[10] Yet this is scarcely reflected in the stories, where women are usually homemakers, pregnant, or on welfare. In fact, this is true for every single book in the sample, except for some of those written by Puerto Ricans. Nowhere are professional women to be found. While it is true that only a small percentage of Puerto Rican women are in professional positions, it would seem important to include at least a couple in these books. They seem to have gotten lost between the cracks. The message is clear: Puerto Rican females have nothing to strive for and nothing to offer; they are defeated victims of a sexist society. Strong women who struggle against an oppressive system, who have a vision of a better world, and who demand change, are missing from these stories, stories which will inevitably form images in the minds of young people about what Puerto Rican women are really like.

Men do not fare much better in many of the books. They are strong, stoical, sexist, and in control; or down and out alcoholic hustlers. They are supposedly macho, but machismo is reinterpreted with an Anglo-Saxon slant. For example, maleness is shown to mean lack of affection, aloofness, and complete suppression of emotion. The old grandmother in *Pablito's New Feet*, for example, "will not be moved by the tears and words of a woman." In *Miguel Robles: So Far*, the protagonist says such things as, "I hate crying because crying is for girls and creeps." *Danza!* extends its sexism to the animal kingdom. Describing the joy of horseback riding, the book notes, "But for the mares this joy was rare. They were female. A man was less than a man if his mount was less than a stallion, and a mare's value lay in the fame of her sire, or her sons."

The foregoing is not to deny the existence of machismo within the culture. But to present it as the primary way that Puerto Ricans have of relating to one another is to tell only part of the story. And to present women as meekly accepting its dictates is to be unaware of our history. What about women in our history, women such as Mariana Bracetti, Juana Colón, or Lolita Lebrón? What about all those other role models that our own mothers, sisters, and gradmothers have provided? They are not to be found in these books.

The setting of the books is also unbalanced. Of the twenty-one stories that take place in an urban setting, sixteen are set in New York City. The geographic diversity so typical of the present-day Puerto Rican community would never be guessed from these books. More than half of all Puerto Ricans living in the United States, for example, live outside of New York City, most in urban areas to be sure, but many also in small towns and rural areas.

The use of Spanish is another issue raised by these books. When all is said and done, one significant indication of the respect a language and culture command is the accuracy with which the language is depicted. This being the case, we can safely conclude that Spanish as presented in many of the books is at the very least treated with scorn. The mistakes found in the books range from misspelling to inappropriate use of idioms and inaccurate use of the accent mark. These kinds of mistakes would never be tolerated in English, yet they occur with exasperating frequency in Spanish. The problem would diminish considerably if non-Spanish-speaking or non-Puerto Rican authors did not feel the need to make their books more ''authentic'' by adding a sprinkling of Spanish words and phrases to them. We could do with less autheticity and more respect.

Some of the mistakes are laughable: ''Uncle Pacheko'' (with this spelling, he could very well be East European), as well as ''dozena'' and ''novella'' in *Gaucho*; ''pastillas'' to mean *pasteles* (one can almost visualize a Puerto Rican family cooking a big pot of pills for dinner!) in *Pablito's New Feet*.

Some books, of course, make more mistakes than others. In *Luis: A Bilingual Story* (in English and Spanish) the author seems to have done a Spanish traslation himself. The result is a book with so many serious errors that it cannot be used with Spanish speakers. The mistakes in this book are particularly distressing because without them this would be a fine book. The worst offender is Heuman, author of *Little League Hotshots*. Not only does he have a Puerto Rican frying frijoles (not what one would call a typical Puerto Rican dish) and throughout punctuates dialogue with ''sí, amigo,'' but he also seems to have invented all the names of the principal characters himself: Luis Santo, Jiménez Rivera, Pedro Leone, José Hernán. Obviously he is sufficiently familiar with Spanish to make the names sound believable; they are nevertheless probably fabricated. In *Danza!* too, the names are unusual to say the least: Paulo, Res, Fidelina, Mira, and Rameriz. These are good examples of the dictum, ''A little knowledge is a dangerous thing.''

Also particularly irritating is the fact that the central characters in many of the books use stilted English. While their speech is punctuated with a handful of Spanish words, their English is also completely unnatural. The use of both Spanish and English in these cases is insulting. In *A Shadow Like a Leopard* the main character constantly refers to his mother as ''my mama,'' even when speaking with others. This phrase in the mouth of a street wise Puerto Rican adolescent is less than credible. Tomas, in *Tomas and the Talking Birds*, is in the improbable position of teaching a parrot English as he himself learns the language. For both Tomas and the parrot, the main obstacle to acceptance is not knowing the language. Typical of the silly speech used by Tomas is the following: ''I will be back *pronto* and talk to you again, *amigo mío*. But now I must go back to school to learn the americano words I am to teach you.'' At the end of the story, Tomas writes a letter in which he describes his friend the parrot by saying, ''He is truly a most remarkable parrot,'' implausible English usage at best, particularly for a child just learning the language. Finally in *Miguel Robles: So Far*, Miguel, the narrator, has become so assimilated that he says his friend Lenny ''talks English funny—with an accent.''

What are the results of these images created by children's books focusing on Puerto Ricans? When Puerto Ricans are presented as helpless, passive, one-dimensional characters eager to assimilate and largely responsible for their own oppression, young people are left with few alternatives. Puerto Rican children can either accept the images or question their validity based on their own experiences. Because of the immense power of the written word, they generally do the former. For non-Puerto Rican youngsters the choice is more restricted still, for many have little or no contact with Puerto Ricans to either confirm or reject these images. The result is damaging for both: for Puerto Rican youngsters, the image provides fuel for self-alienation; White youngsters are left with an impression of Puerto Ricans which helps reinforce the negative stereotypes found in the media, while at the same time perpetuating White superiority. Needless to say, Puerto Rican children are the ones who lose the most.

This analysis of children's books, nevertheless, should not end on a gloomy note for now, in contrast to ten years ago, there are a number of books which accurately portray the diversity and complexity of Puerto Rican reality. Not surprisingly, most of them have been written by Puerto Ricans. Instead of simply providing superficial characteristics which are supposedly Puerto Rican, some books provide much more authentic and in-depth portrayals of relationships within the family and with the outside world. Examples of these are the books written by Nicholasa Mohr, especialy *Felita* and *Nilda*, Piri Thomas, Cruz Martel, and the anthology of Puerto Rican short stories edited by Kal Wagenheim.

Piri Thomas's *Stories from El Barrio*, for example, is a treasure. Although they convey a diversity of experiences both painful and joyful, the overriding virtue of these eight stories is the humanity of the characters. In spite of the often oppressive weight of living in El Barrio, these people enjoy one another, struggle through adversity, and make mistakes. Throughout there is a sense of warmth and affection, of family ties and friendship being one's real strength in this life. Add to this the humor, irony, and plain good writing skills of Thomas, and we have a book which can truly claim to be ''Puerto Rican literature for young people.''

Most of the books written by Puerto Ricans tend to be appropriate for older readers. They are generally open-ended, reflecting a characteristic of Puerto Rican literature which often deliberately poses problems but does not solve them. This technique can provoke readers into becoming involved in fighting the oppression depicted, but also opens the way for youngsters to become overwhelmed and apathetic about the possibility of change. This is especially likely because these books tend to portray the realities of oppression—drug abuse, alcoholism, crime, and physical abuse—but not the diversity of the responses of the Puerto Rican community to these situations. What is missing from some of these books is the strength and spirit of a people in combatting oppression. Nevertheless, these books for older readers are in a sense dialectical, for they point out the contradictions of colonialism, oppression, racism, and sexism, and make young people think about these issues. Such stories should be read, for they will certainly help young people become aware of the conditions under which the majority of Puerto Ricans live. Their open-ended nature makes them ideal discussion starters with young adults. A note of caution, however, should be sounded: not all young people, and particularly those who are not Puerto Rican, can respond in an analytical way to the situations presented in these books. Even these books can perpetuate stereotypes and negative images about Puerto Ricans if not used in appropriate ways.

That some of these books have shortcomings, however, should not be denied. For example, in *Nilda* there are several references to "Japs," and in *El Bronx Remembered* there is an extremely negative portrayal of Romany people (gypsies), a disappointing stance given the unfavorable images of Puerto Ricans which books of this kind seek to counter. Likewise, both Soto's *Hot Land, Cold Season* and Mohr's *Nilda* characterize women in less than complimentary ways. Women are either simply victims or they look to marriage, having babies, or escape to the suburbs as a solution to their problems.

The short stories by Puerto Rican authors edited by Kal Wagenheim provide a sorely needed element to literature for young adults. Organized with English and Spanish on facing pages, it is an excellent introduction to this genre for high-school students, for it includes some of the most notable Puerto Rican short story writers. Many of the stories—some set in New York—focus on political/cultural tensions and provide a historical dimension missing in other works.

Returning to books geared to younger readers, *Yagua Days* by Cruz Martel is a gem. Here, a young Puerto Rican boy living in New York gets to find out what "*yagua* days" are when he visits Puerto Rico. Unlike other stories in which the role models for Puerto Rican youngsters are invariably White people, the significant people in his world are other Puerto Ricans who are depicted with dignity and respect. Belpré's *Once in Puerto Rico* also offers a mostly positive collection of folk tales primarily set in Taíno times.

However, we should not jump to the conclusion that all children's books by Puerto Ricans are good literature. Geraldo Rivera's *Miguel Robles: So Far* is a case in point. It is neither good literature nor self-affirming of Puerto Ricanness. In what amounts to a disjointed narrative, Miguel talks about his family and friends and his life on the Lower East Side. The message that comes across is not much different from that found in books by most non-Puerto Ricans: Assimilation is the first prerequisite to "making it" in this society. Unfortunately, assimilation in this case means aspiring to go to college (certainly a laudable aim in itself) "so I can buy a new car when I'm old enough" or to be "a rich and famous lawyer." No mention is made of Miguel's responsibility to his community or of his awareness of himself as part of a collective process.

Some books by non-Puerto Ricans offer more positive and powerful alternatives to the majority of books focusing on Puerto Ricans. For example, *Luis: A Bilingual Story* centers on the life of a young Puerto Rican boy living in Lowell, Massachusetts, who returns to Comerío for a visit. While not romanticizing either the United States or Puerto Rico, the book achieves an underlying sense of honesty, family strength, and hope. Luis comes across as a spunky and spirited kid, one who is straightforward and unafraid, taking both joy in and responsibility for his family. (Unfortunately, as stated before, the book's Spanish translation leaves much to be desired.) *Fat Sam, Cool Clyde and Stuff* by Walter Dean Myers depicts the friendship of Puerto Rican and Black youngsters, both boys and girls, who interact in caring and nonsexist ways. *Juan Bobo and the Pig*, as retold by Bernice Chardiet, is faithful to the much loved folktale, and is especially appropiate for younger readers. Levoy's *A Shadow Like a Leopard* is also a book worth mentioning. Not only is it well written, but it portrays Ramón, a 14-year-old, in a realistic and sympathetic, yet unsentimental manner. While all the characters in the story are presented as struggling with some very difficult issues, all of them emerge with some degree of dignity and self-respect. These latter books cannot be called "Puerto Rican children's literature," of course, because they were not written by Puerto Ricans. They are nevertheless both creative and sensitive to Puerto Rican realities and should be recommended for this reason.

Some progress has been made in giving children a more complete and accurate picture of Puerto Rican reality. Likewise, progress has been made in the publication of a few examples of quality literature for young people written in English. And certainly the fact that some good books are being written by, about, and for Puerto Ricans is an encouraging development. Nevertheless, this progress should not be overemphasized, for the majority of children's books about Puerto Ricans still perpetuate negative, racist, and simplistic portrayals of our people. Consequently, we as people must take a stand against the perpetuation of such images. Children's literature is no less important than literature for adults; it can be reasonably argued that it is even more important in the sense that it helps create images and perceptions which sometimes last a lifetime. Puerto Rican authors must take the leadership in making children's literature a high priority on the Puerto Rican agenda. As

Toni Cade Bambara has said, "The responsibility of a writer representing an oppresed people is to make revolution irresistible." Let us propose a revolution in children's books, a revolution which results in Puerto Rican literature which is self-affirming, realistic, and liberating. Nothing less than our children's self-determination and pride are at stake.

Notes

1. U.S. Bureau of the Census, *1980 Census* (Washington, D.C.)
2. National Puerto Rican Forum, *The Next Step toward Equality: A Comprehensive Study of Puerto Ricans in the United States Mainland* (New York: National Puerto Rican Forum, 1980).
3. Council on Interracial Books for Children, *Special Double Issue on Puerto Rican Materials* 4, nos. 1, 2 (Spring 1972).
4. *Bowker Annual of Library and Book Trade Information*, 27th. ed. (New York: R.R. Bowker, 1982), p. 444. Quoted from the *UNESCO Statistical Yearbook, 1980*.
5. The following sources of information were consulted in locating the books: *Subject Guide to Children's Books in Print* (1972–82) (New York: Bowker); Library of Congress catalogs; Paquita Vivó, *The Puerto Ricans: An Annotated Bibliography* (New York: Bowker, 1976); UNICEF Information Center on Children's Cultures, New York City; Puerto Rican Research and Resources Center, Washington, D.C.
6. Data from the Office of the Commonwealth of Puerto Rico, New York City.
7. Eugene Buccioni, "The Daily Round of Life in the School." In Francesco Cordasco and Eugene Buccioni, *The Puerto Rican Community and Its Children on the Mainland: A Source Book for Teachers, Social Workers, and Other Professionals*, 3rd. rev. ed. (Metuchen, N.J.: Scarecrow, 1982), p. 210.
8. National Puerto Rican Forum, 1980.
9. In 1978, only 32.5 percent of Puerto Rican women aged twenty and above were in the labor force, lower than for any other group in the United States. National Puerto Rican Forum, 1980.
10. Lynn Angel Morgan, *Access to Training Programs: Barriers Encountered by Hispanic Female Heads-Of-Household in New York City* (New York: Puerto Rican Legal Defense and Education Fund, 1981).

Bibliography

Belpré, Pura. *Once in Puerto Rico*. Illus. Christine Price. New York: Frederick Warne, 1973.

——. *The Rainbow-Colored Horse*. Illus. Martorell. New York: Frederick Warne, 1978.

Bethancourt, T. Ernesto. *New York City Too Far from Tampa Blues*. New York: Holiday House, 1975.

——. *Where the Deer and the Cantaloupe Play*. San Diego, Calif.: Oak Tree, 1981.

Bunting, Eve. *Josefina Finds the Prince*. Illus. Jan Palmer. Champaign, Ill.: Garrard, 1976.

Chardiet, Bernice. *Juan Bobo and the Pig: A Puerto Rican Folktale Retold*. Illus. Hope Merryman. New York: Walker, 1973.

García, Richard. *My Aunt Otilia's Spirits*. Illus. Robin Cherin and Roger I. Reyes. San Francisco, Calif.: Children's Books, 1973.

González, Gloria. *Gaucho*. New York: Knopf, 1977.

Gray, Genevieve. *The Dark Side of Nowhere*. Illus. Nancy Inderieden. St. Paul, Min.: EMC, 1977.

Hall, Lynn. *Danza!* New York: Scribner's, 1981.

Heuman, William. *Little League Hotshots*. Illus. Harvey Kidder. New York: Dodd, Mead, 1972.

Levoy, Myron. *A Shadow Like a Leopard*. New York: Harper & Row, 1981.

Mann, Peggy. *How Juan Got Home*. Illus. Richard Lebenson. New York: Coward, McCann, & Geoghegan, 1972.

——. *The Secret Dog of Little Luis*. Illus. Richard Lebenson. New York: Coward, McCann, & Geoghegan, 1973.

Martel, Cruz. *Yagua Days*. Illus. Jerry Pinkney, New York: Dial, 1976.

Mohr, Nicholasa. *El Bronx Remembered: A Novella and Stories*. New York: Harper & Row, 1975.

——. *Felita*. New York: Dial 1979.

——. *In Nueva York*. New York: Dell, 1977.

——. *Nilda*. New York: Harper & Row, 1973.

Moore, Ruth Nulton. *Tomas and the Talking Birds*. Illus. Esther Rose Graber. Scottsdale, Pa.: Herald, 1979.

Myers, Walter Dean. *Fast Sam, Cool Clyde, and Stuff*. New York: Viking, 1975.

Ordóñez, Eduardo. *Yukiyu: El Espíritu de Boriquen*. Illus. Manuel Otero. New York: Plus Ultra Educational, 1973.

Rivera, Geraldo, and Edith Rivera. *Miguel Robles: So Far*. Illus. Edith Rivera. New York: Harcourt Brace Jovanovich, 1973.

Rohmer, Harriet, and Jesús Guerrero Rea (eds.), *Atariba and Niguayona*. Illus. Consuelo Méndez Castillo. San Francisco, Calif: Children's Books, 1976.

Soto, Pedro Juan. *Hot Land, Cold Season*. New York: Dell, 1973. Originally written in Spanish in 1961.

Thomas, Dawn C. *Pablito's New Feet*. Illus. Paul Frame. Philadelphia: Lippincott, 1973.

Thomas, Piri. *Stories from El Barrio*. New York: Knopf, 1978.

Wagenheim, Kal (ed.). *Cuentos: An Anthology of Short Stories from Puerto Rico*. New York: Schocken, 1978.

Part VI

Interrelations between Puerto Rican Literature and Other Hispanic Literatures in the United States

25

A Question of Identity: What's in a Name? Chicanos and Riqueños

Juan Bruce Novoa

Nations hardly ever have the luxury to develop their identity in strict introspection; extraneous factors intervene. The process usually includes some degree of contrasting with neighbors or ideal models. Nations develop in the context of other nations. Mexico and Puerto Rico are no exceptions. Their modern history has never ceased to be played out on a field on which the United States has occupied a significant, often monopolizing, percentage of space. And since the United States has long since abandoned any pretense of being a peer in an American fraternity, preferring to blatantly fulfill its arrogated role of overseer of forced hegemony, Mexico and Puerto Rico naturally adopted a defensive stance of radical binary opposition: *we* against *them*.

While binary oppositions suit the needs of scientific and pseudoscientific thinking, they have the deleterious effect of characterizing the space between the two terms as a sliding scale of plus and minus values. As a result, any point between the poles assumes the value of less than completely whole, of no longer one but not yet the other. From the perspective of the poles, the in-between stage is no longer, or not yet, fully acceptable. Linguistic science and structuralism have influenced our cultural thought, and both are examples of the inherent negativity of binary constructs. Terms are defined by what they are not. Languages are opposed in pairs, and to be bilingual is to switch codes from one to another, not to mix them. Anything less than a complete jump from one pole to the other is termed interference, with the negative connotations the word carries. The space between the languages is a forbidden zone of neither this nor that.

The implications vis-à-vis the immigrant's situation are clear. Immigrants are judged from the extremes in opposition, and upon them are projected the demands of the structure. They become less than authentic natives of either side marginals; their mere existence is considered an interference into both poles, a threat to their identity. Attempts to develop customs or a language in an ad hoc manner, ones truly reflective of the material and ideal experiential base of the immigrants, are rejected by the purists at the extremes. Mexican and Puerto Rican immigrants to mainland U.S. and their descendents exemplify well this dilemma, and always have. We are all too familiar with U.S. society's negative attitude toward Mexican and Puerto Rican immigrants, but less attention has been dedicated to the attitudes of the source societies. Here I will concentrate on the latter.

Earlier in this century, during the Mexican Revolution, Mexican intellectuals were forced to spend time in the United States in communities of their compatriots who had settled in this country. Their attitude was sympathetic, though often patronizing, but less than accepting. And as we might expect, they almost always offered examples of language usage to illustrate their point.

Martín Luis Guzmán, while in San Antonio, Texas, was hosted by a lawyer named Samuel Belden. Guzmán calls him a "half Mexican and half North American," who spoke to him "in a rare and difficult Spanish—at times impossible to understand—a Spanish without the third fictitious person and with Anglo-Saxon syntax."[1] Belden, according to Guzmán, had slid to the center of the binary scale and spoke a hybrid speech. The absence of the *usted* (polite) form signified a cultural evolution away from the formalities of Hispanic customs. Belden no longer respected the subtleties of intimacy and familiarity implicit in the use of the *usted*; his more egalitarian environment made them irrelevant. This must have shocked Guzmán and his Mexican comrades who always addressed each other in *usted* despite years of close relationships. Belden's manner strikes Guzmán as "direct and rude," but he goes on to add, one suspects with heavy irony, that his manner made him "friendly at first sight and induced us to treat him from the beginning with certain amicable familiarity" (p. 227). Guzmán was not partial to quick familiarity, so we can read this as a commentary on how Mexican customs had degenerated in Texas, just as the language had reached a point between Spanish and English at which it teetered dangerously at the brink of incomprehension.

José Vasconcelos was less generous. Belden is called "uncivilized as all those who grew up in those territories."[2] With one sentence he condemns everyone raised in Texas, or perhaps the United States itself. Belden is termed a "Mexican-Yankee," with the disparaging connotations of the latter. In Los Angeles, California, Vasconcelos praises the perfect Castillian of some Spanish dancers, contrasting the women's speech with "the corrupted language to which one gets accustomed in these places" (p. 105). Again, the context is significant: these women are not educated, nor even particularly respectable; yet they are culturally preferable to the Hispanics of California. San Antonio, however, epitomizes for Vasconcelos the Mexican-Yankee synthesis: "Not only the North American, but also the Mexican becomes absurd and suffers in the hybrid city a deterioration in category" (p. 786). Vasconcelos's arrogance is that of the supposedly bilingual man whose beliefs can be situated in one or another pole of the binary opposition and from which he can despise those in the middle.

It is also Vasconcelos who popularizes the names for these hybrid beings: *pochos*, "a word used in California to designate the ungrateful who abhors the Mexican, although carries it in his blood, and tries to adjust all his acts to the mimetism of the present masters of the region." To him this synthesis represented "the destruction of the Spanish-American culture of our parents to be replaced by the North American primitivism filtered in the *pochos* since their childhood" (p. 782). Vasconcelos did not tolerate anything less than pure binary terms, but did not hide his preference for his as the right one, although once again he refers to the Spanish and not the Mexican. Beneath this vision is the "ideologeme"[3] of good and evil, and any mixture combines the worst of the two nationalities.

Among Puerto Rican writers we find similar texts, with the difference that these men do not have to travel outside their borders to observe the same phenomena. The U.S. invasion and the subsequent bilingualism and biculturalism provided targets for their pens right at home. Epifanio Fernández Vanga, a contemporary of Vasconcelos and Guzmán, includes an essay entitled "Hablando en gringo" in *El idioma de Puerto Rico*.[4] The author complains about equivocal translations from English into Spanish which appear in newspapers, about the usage of English syntax in the speech of university students, and of the unnecessary proliferation of English words in Spanish. Just as with the Mexicans, the context of the examples is important. Fernández Vanga focuses on a note about baseball. A trivial subject, perhaps, but in truth he laments not only the degeneration of language in Puerto Rico, but, as well, the concentration of popular culture around a foreign ritual. If baseball is the new ritual of the youth, where has the *axis mundi* been displaced? It was not merely by chance that this author chose a game between Washington and the New York Giants as an illustration. The United States looms as a bicephalous monster, whose business head controls its governmental counterpart. Fernández Vanga ends his essay by recommending that his reader turn for relief to an article copied from *El Imparcial* of Madrid. Like Vasconcelos, Fernández Vanga prefers Castillian Spanish to the corrupt speech of the natives. He does not even consider the possibility that this juxtaposition of English and Spanish texts in the environment may be held responsible for provoking in a natural way the synthesis he rejects. His trend of thought is strictly binary.

Ten years later, in 1941, José M. Toro Nazario attacked bilingualism as the cause for the inferiority of Puerto Rican intellectuals. He stated that "bilingualism alerts us about Castillian when we speak English; alerts us about English when we speak Castillian," which accounts for the Puerto Rican's "slow-passed speech" and that Puerto Rico has become "a country of stammering intellectuals."[5] He is unable to see that the unnatural situation of these intellectuals of having to speak one language produces that stammering. Yet he undermines his own tenets when he narrates an incident in Central Park in New York in which he heard children speak both languages in "waterfalls," an image connoting velocity, volume, and beauty. The natural question, which the author does not ask, is why, if children use the two languages equally well and together, do intellectuals stammer and falter. Could it not be due to the repression inherent in Toro Nazario's binary prejudice? So blinding is this prejudice that although Toro Nazario perceives clearly the falsity of bilingualism, he cannot bring himself to welcome the truth of interlingualism; instead, for him it is a tragedy: "The tragedy of bilingualism lies in that its projection . . . generates a new language. Call it a dialect if you wish, but bilingual countries only exist in the imagination of bad politicians and good educators" (p. 1070). And that is so because in such cases the people are interlingual and not bilingual.

A decade later, Jaime Benítez coined a Puerto Rican equivalent for *pocho*: "homo portorricensis imprecisus."[6] Admittedly it is not as convenient as *pocho*, but it summarizes the Puerto Rican preoccupation with faltering speech, as well as the elitist stance of those who condemned the new hybrid culture. Once again the stress falls on the ill effects of bilingualism, the interference of English with Spanish: "Hence this frequent stammer or mumbling. . . . For this, it has been said that he is illiterate in two languages at once" (p. 1193). Neither one nor the other—an imprecise being.

Underlying both the Mexican and the Puerto Rican texts is the assumption of the correctness of the binary system. None of the writers questions the system nor their right to use it to name and judge those supposed unfortunates caught between the poles. They were offended, horrified by what they saw and heard. Yet one can imagine their reaction had they lived to see the new phenomenon apparent in at least a segment—perhaps small but highly visible—of the immigrants and their descendents from those two nations who challenge and reject the binary system. These groups claim legitimate residence in the space between the poles, and from there they demand and excercise the right to self-determination. They have pondered their situation, decided that it is their real state, based an identity on that state, and chose a name for themselves to signify that identity. Chicanos and Nuyoricans or Riqueños blatantly assert a new hybrid identity, which in turn redefines the nationalistic binary opposition into a preliminary dialectic form which has begun to spring the logical, irrepressible international synthesis. And whereas before the apologists of the Latin American source societies could disparagingly characterize these hybrid peoples—simply because they controlled the means of cultural production, the printed word—now the hybrids express themselves as the producers/product of their identity.

When viewed from the point of synthesis, the dialectical poles assume the character of Others, of not-we-though-related, of less-than-fully-us. This is difficult to accept for those still situated at the poles—or those who would pretend to be there despite the reality of their residence in the U.S. mainland. It threatens their world image, displaces centrality, supersedes their strategy. They do what they can to deny the dialectical process and infuse doubt into their synthesis. Mexicans have satirized and attacked Chicanos in ways closely resembling the Guzmán and Vasconcelos texts. Octavio Paz's Pachuco essay, while couched in benevolent comprehension, is actually a reactionary condemnation of hybridness.[7] Three decades later, the marxist David Ojeda rejects the Chicano concept of Aztlán, declaring it to be a false dream and inviting the Chicanos to go back to Mexico to help in the class struggle.[8] Others have been less agressive but, nonetheless, they still insist in appropriating Chicanos to Mexico, encase us within a Mexican scale of values and priorities. Chicano literature and speech are inevitably compared to Mexican literature and language with the resulting rejection of the Chicano. At best the reaction has been patronizing.

Similar results can be found among Puerto Ricans. Pedro Juan Soto, whose *Spiks* could be said to prefigure Nuyorican literature, disclaims the hybrid language of his own text. "I despise . . . the influence of English: from anglicized words which are not yet linguistic loans, to the repetitive use of the gerund. I have chosen to leave alone such errors and use what I have learned for forthcoming works."[9] These mistakes are facets of Chicano and Riqueño native speech. Soto has gone on to ally himself with, to embrace, the Spanish purist pole of the binary prejudice. María Teresa Babín, while including a section of Nuyorican writers in her anthology *Borinquen*, insists on subsuming them to the island tradition. The forced union elicits a comparison in which the island's literature is said to be superior in richness, antiquity, complexity, and refinement. Nuyorican writing is granted, however, the virtue of being recent.[10] Even Ricardo Campos and Juan Flores, who criticize Babín for not realizing how different the Nuyorican writers are from the *Muñocista* ideals she exults, point out these writers' ignorance with respect to what Campos and Flores posit as their true tradition: that of the Puerto Rican working class.[11] Once again the new synthesis is subsumed into one of the binary poles.

Yet to name oneself is an act of conscious self-creation, a right some cultures still grant their offspring. And Chicanos and Riqueños have chosen names to fit a reality—or an ideology. Their literatures are different from that of either national literature or their Latin American relatives. There are ties, similarities, concordances with the mother country and language, certainly, but there are just as many with the United States. That is exactly the point of the names, to emphasize difference in sameness, to affirm a faith in our power to synthesize a language and a new culture, ours.

The names are signs of new identity, perhaps still in the making, but nonetheless real. The literature is both a product and producer of the sign. One can welcome it, decry it, denounce it, belittle it, or revel in it, but one cannot make it go away. Maybe it will disappear, proving itself one more fleeting expression of migration writing; but it could become a manifestation, all the clearer on account of its extremeness, of a new cultural synthesis in full swing in Latin America and the United States. To insist on this national and cultural opposition whether it be beyond or above history, to think that we can avoid the evolution of language, are illusions perhaps harbored by the last Romans in Spain or by the Creoles in Latin America. It is difficult for parents to let go of their children; sometimes the latter must insist on their rights, for the good of all concerned. Names change; new identities are forged. And it is an old literary motif that bastard children are the most loyal, even if they appear to be the less welcomed heirs.

Notes

1. Martín Luis Guzmán, *El águila y la serpiente*, in *La novela de la revolución mexicana* (México: Aguilar, 1964), p. 227.
2. José Vasconcelos, *Obras completas*, vol. 1 (Mexico City: Libreros Mexicanos Unidos, 1957), p. 785. Citation will be from the volume and page numbers given in the text.
3. "The ideologeme is an amphibious formation, whose essential structural characteristic may be described as its possibility to manifest itself either as a pseudoidea—a conceptual or belief system, an abstract value, an opinion or prejudice—or as a protonarrative, a kind of ultimate class fantasy about the 'collective characters' which are the classes in opposition." Frederic Jameson, *The Political Unconscious: Narrative as a Socially Symbolic Act* (Ithaca: Cornell University Press, 198l), p. 87.
4. Epifanio Fernández Vanga, "Hablando en gringo," in *Antología del pensamiento puertorriqueño*, (1900–1970), vol. 2, ed. Eugenio Fernández Méndez (Barcelona: Editorial Universitaria, 1975), pp. 1056–60.
5. José M. Toro Nazario, "Paradoja, ironía y tragedia del bilinguismo," in *Antología del pensamiento puertorriqueño*, pp. 1065–66.
6. Jaime Benítez, "El homo portorricensis imprecisus," in *Antología del pensamiento puertorriqueño*, p. 1089.
7. Octavio Paz, "Pachucos y otros extremos," in *El laberinto de la soledad* (México: Fondo de Cultura Económica, 1967), pp. 9–25.
8. David Ojeda, *Las condiciones de la guerra* (Havana: Casa de las Américas, 1978), p. 41.

9. Pedro Juan Soto, *Spiks* (Río Piedras: Cultural, 1973), p. 10.
10. María Teresa Babín and Stan Steiner, *Borinquen: An Anthology of Puerto Rican Literature* (New York: Random House, 1974), p. xxv.
11. Ricardo Campos and Juan Flores, "Migración y cultura nacional puertorriqueñas: perspectivas proletarias," in *Puerto Rico: identidad nacional y clases sociales* (Río Piedras: Huracán, 1979), p. 136.

26

Toward a History of Hispanic Literature in the United States

Nicolás Kanellos

The roots of Hispanic literature were planted north of the Río Grande quite some time before the landing of the Mayflower at Plymouth Rock. In 1598 Juan de Onate's colonizing expectation up from central Mexico into what is today New Mexico is doubly important as the beginning of a literary and oral tradition. The first is represented by the landmark epic poem *La Conquista de la Nueva México*, by one of the soldiers on the expedition, Gaspar Pérez de Villagrá.[1] The oral Spanish literary tradition was introduced with the improvised dramas, directed by Captain Farfán[2] during the expedition and, we must assume, by the introduction into these northern territories of romances (historical ballads) and other songs, some of which have survived to this date.[3]

The Northeast of what is today the United States, on the one hand, can point to its earliest written and oral expression in Spanish with the founding of the colony of Sephardic Jews in New Amsterdam in 1654.[4] Both the Northeast and Southwest can boast an unbroken literary tradition in Spanish that predates the American Revolutionary War. That few historians and literary critics of the English and Spanish languages have attempted to document, salvage, and/or study this cultural patrimony is indicative of the political and social conflicts that have always surrounded Hispanic peoples in North America, a continent whose very identity has emerged from a protracted, 300-year struggle between the Anglo empire builders and first the Spanish empire builders, later the mestizo Spanish speakers and American Indians.

U.S. expansion westward and southward has most of the time ocurred at the expense of Hispanic Americans, who to this date, if we consider Cuba, Nicaragua, and El Salvador, are cast as amoral, uncivilized enemies threatening the very existence of the empire. Spanish speakers in sizable numbers have always resided within the political boundaries of the United States and have always been in the process of being conquered, dispossessed of land

and property, and swallowed into "the belly of the beast." This is one of the reasons why today the continental United States is home to the fourth largest Spanish-speaking population in the hemispere.

The period from the origins to 1821, the date of Mexican independence from Spain, has been called the Hispanic Period by Luis Leal.[5] During this time, these northern territories were the subject of prose writing of a historical and semihistorical nature, as well as Villagrá's epic. During the 27-year period before the Mexican-American War, called the Mexican Period by Leal, historical accounts, missionary literature, and oral tradition are further developed (Leal, pp. 37–38). But it is in the Transitional Periods (1848 to 1910) that the foundation is really laid for a true Mexican-American literature with the resident population of the Southwest adapting to the new U.S. political framework (Leal, p. 38). It is the period when many Spanish-language newspapers begin publishing throughout the Southwest and when they become an alternative to Anglo-American information and cultural flow. During this period the important commercial centers of San Francisco and Los Angeles support numerous newspapers which cover all types of business, political, and cultural activities of the Mexican community; they also published short stories, poetry, and essays by community residents. Among those are various newspapers that are held on microfilm at the University of California's Bancroft and Chicano Studies Collections: Los Angeles's *La Estrella de Los Angeles* (1851–55) and *La Crónica* (1872–92), and San Francisco's *La Voz del Nuevo Mundo* (1871–55), *La Voz de Méjico* (1862–66), *La Voz de Chile* (1864–68), *La Sociedad* (1869–95), *La Cronista* (1884–85), and *La República* (1879–97).[6]

One of the most interesting literary pieces to come out of the newspapers of the period was an anonymous fictionalized account of the legendary social bandit Joaquín Murieta, published in serialized form in Santa Barbara's *La Gaceta* from June 4 to July 23, 1881.[7]

During the latter part of the nineteenth century various literary authors were published in book form. For a review of the prose works of Manuel M. Zalazar, Eusebio Chacón, Felipe Maximiliano Chacón (a newspaper editor himself), and Miguel Antonio Otero see Charles Tatum's publications.[8]

During the same period, the New York area sustained various Hispanic literary activities and cultural institutions. Again the newspapers are cultural institutions for the community that here is made up principally of Spaniards, Cubans, and Mexicans. Such newspapers as *El Mensajero Semanal*, whose remaining copies date from August 19, 1828 until 1831,[9] and the weekly *El Mercurio de Nueva York*, whose preserved issues date from September 20, 1828 to March 23, 1833, published news of the homeland and political commentary and literature, including poetry, short stories, essays, and excerpts of plays.[10] Two other early newspapers were *La Crónica*, publishing in the 1850s, and *La Voz de América*, issued in the 1860s.[11] An example of early Spanish-language literary publishing in book form is Anastacio Ochoa y Acuna's *Poesías de un mexicano* published "en Casa de Lanuza, Medina y Compañía, 1828."[12] José Luis Perrier in his Bibliografía Dramática Cubana,[13] notes the publication of a comedy by Orman Tu-Caes, *El hermano hermoso* at the Imprenta de J. de la Granja in 1840, and Justo Eleboro's *El rico y el pobre* in 1864. He also provides us with a very interesting note on the poet Miguel Teurbe Tolón (1820–58), who he states was born in the United States, was educated in Cuba, and became a "revolutionary conspirator": he also informs us that Teurbe Tolón published poems in New York.

But it was not until the late nineteenth century that newspaper, magazine, and book publishing really began to expand, doubtless because of increased immigration and the political and cultural ferment caused by the Cuban wars of independence and the Spanish-American War. In this regard, the most noteworthy institution was the Cuban newspaper *La Patria*, whose pages from 1892 to 1898 have been salvaged. In the pages of *La Patria* can be found many of the essays of leading Cuban and Puerto Rican patriots. Also of great importance as the most widely circulated weekly was *Las Novedades*, published from 1893 until at least 1918. After the turn of the century its theater, music, and literary critic was Pedro Henríquez Ureña. An early Puerto Rican contribution was *La Gaceta Ilustrada*, edited in the 1890s by Francisco Amy and designated by *La Patria* as "a competent Puerto Rican literary."[14] Other publications of the time were *El Porvenir* and *Revista Popular*.[15]

Many of the literary books published were also related to the Cuban independence struggle, such as Luis García Pérez's *El Grito de Yara*, published by Hallet and Breen in 1879.[16] Other published plays noted by Perrier are José María Herredia's *Abufar o la familia árabe* (Lockwood, 1854); Diego V. Tejera's *La muerte de Plácido* (Imprenta Ponce de León, 1875); Francisco Sellen's *Hatuey* (A. Da Costa Gómez, 1891); M.M. Hernández's *La apuesta de Zoleika* (1901); G. Gómez y Arroyo's *Polilla regional* (Conner, 1892); and Desiderio Fajardo Ortiz's *La fuga de Evangelina* (Howes, 1898).

The turn of the century brings record immigration from Mexico to the Southwest and Midwest because of the Mexican Revolution of 1910. Luis Leal calls this period from 1910 to World War II the Interaction Period. During this time immigrant workers and elites with an updated version of Mexican culture interact with the resident Mexican populations of the Southwest.[17] It is also a period when elites from throughout the Spanish-speaking world interact with Mexicans and Mexican Americans involved in the cultural life, from publishing to theater, especially in the Los Angeles area where the stage and silver screen enticed writers, performers, and technicians from as far away as Spain and Argentina. This period was also a heyday of Spanish newspaper and book publishing in the Southwest. Both San Antonio and Los Angeles supported competing Spanish-language dailies that served a diverse readership, made up of regional groups from the Southwest, immigrant laborers, and political refugees from the revolution. The latter played a key role in publishing and other businesses and, from an elite class perspective, foment an ideology of a Mexican community in exile, "el México de afuera."

In the offices of San Antonio's *La Prensa*, Los Angeles's *La Opinión*, and *El Heraldo de México* some of the most talented writers from Mexico, Spain, and Latin America earned their living as reporters, columnists,[18] and critics. They also provided the Los Angeles stage with the greatest, consistent supply of plays and vaudeville librettes based on Mexican Life on both sides of the border in the history of the United States.[19] The same newspapermen also authored hundreds of books of poetry, essays, and novels, many of which were published in book form and marketed by the newspapers themselves and by smaller houses like the Laredo Publishing Company, Los Angeles's Spanish American Printing, San Diego's Imprenta Bolaños Cacho Hnos., and many others.

By far the largest and most prolific publishers, however, were located in San Antonio. Ignacio Lozano, owner of *La Prensa* and *La Opinión*, was also the largest Spanish-language book publisher in the United States, active from 1915 until at least 1928. Both newspapers, with the largest circulation even up into the Midwest, regularly printed and advertised Editorial Lozano's books. The other San Antonio publishers were the Viola Novelty Company, probably a subsidiary of P. Viola, publisher of the satiric newspapers *El Fandango* and *El Vacilón* and active from 1916 until at least 1927; the Whitt Company; and the Librería Española which still exists today only as a bookstore, however. Most of the novels produced by these houses were of the Mexican Revolution genre; others were of a romantic or sentimental nature.[20] But hidden among the profusion of these works there are titles that can be considered true forerunners of the Chicano novel of the 1960s in their identification with the working-class Mexican residing in the Southwest, their use of popular dialects, and their political stance vis-à-vis the U.S. government and society. The prime example of this new sensibility is newspaperman Daniel Venegas's *Las aventuras de Don Chipote o Cuando los pericos mamen*, published by Los Angeles's *El heraldo de México* in 1928.[21]

Most of the publishing and literary endeavors in the Mexican American Southwest came to an abrupt halt with the Great Depression and the repatriation, forced and voluntary, of a large segment of that society back to Mexico. Not until the postwar period and the advent of the Chicano movement did the literary and artistic output begin to reestablish itself, but to this date not with the intensity and commercial success of the 1920s.

The period from the turn of the century up into the Depression was also of increased immigration and interaction of various Hispanic groups in New York. It was also a period of increased Puerto Rican migration, facilitated by the Jones Act, and later immigration of Spanish elites and workers as a result of the Civil War in Spain. Many of the cultural events in the Hispanic community came about to support the Puerto Rican Nationalist movement and the Spanish Republic.

At the turn of the century, Cuban and Spanish writers and newspapers still dominated the scene. The first decade of the century witnessed the founding of the daily *La Prensa*, whose heritage continues today in *El Diario-La Prensa*, born of the merger in 1963 with *El Diario de New York*. Also publishing during that decade were *Sangre Latina*, out of Columbia University, *Revista Pan-Americana*, and *La Paz y El Trabajo: Revista Mensual de Comercio, Literatura, Ciencias, Artes*, etc.[22] Even places as far away as Buffalo began to support their own publications like *La Hacienda* in 1906.[23]

The vestiges of documentation that have survived show that Spanish-language literary publishing did not really begin to expand until the late teens and early twenties. By far the most interesting volume that has come down to us from the teens is an early example of the immigrant novel. Somewhat similar in theme to *Don Chipote*, *Lucas Guevara* by Venezuelan author Alirio Díaz Guerra, probably self-published at the New York Printing Company in 1917, is the story of a young man who comes to the city seeking his fortune, but is ultimately disillusioned. At this time, it seems, one of the most important and long-lived publishing houses began issuing literary titles: Spanish American Publishing Company. It was still publishing literature in the 1950s, if we can judge from its *Los padres* by Puerto Rican Violeta Riomar, published in 1954.[24] It too was an early publisher of books on the theme of Hispanics in New York, such as Puerto Rican playwright Javier Lara's *En la metropoli del dólar*, circa 1919. During the same period Las Novedades was also publishing books, including Pedro Henríquez Ureña's *El nacimiento de Dionisos* in 1916.[25]

Although during the early twenties Carlos López Press, The Phos Press, and others were issuing occasional literary titles, it was not until the late twenties and early thirties that there was an intensification of activity. To begin with, various specialized newspapers began to appear. Probably as an outgrowth of the very active theatrical movement which was taking place all over Manhattan and in Brooklyn, *Gráfico* began publishing in 1927 as a theater and entertainment newspaper under the editorship of Alberto O'Farrill, writer and leading comic actor of the *teatro bufo cubano* (Cuban farcical theater). Besides covering general and community news, *Gráfico* was also a veritable *Variety* in covering the Spanish *zarzuela*, drama, *teatro frívolo cubano* (Cuban frivolous theater), and all the offerings of the Teatro Hispano, the haven of the working-class Hispanic community. *Gráfico* also published hundreds of short stories and literary essays, and thousands of poems by the leading Cuban, Puerto Rican, Spanish, and other Hispanic writers of the city.

Most impressive of these were the stories and commentaries of O'Farrill himself.[26]

With the advent of the Depression, workers' and socialist organizations in the Hispanic Community intensified their productions. The newspaper *Vida Obrera* began publishing in 1930.[27] Other New York newspapers of the time in the Bancroft Collection were: *La Diana* (1923), *El Nuevo Mundo* (1929–32), *El Curioso* (1934), *España Libre* (1943), and *Cultura Proletaria* (1943). Also publishing in the thirties was *Alma Boricua* (1934–35).

At this juncture in New York's literary history the Puerto Rican contribution began to gain a greater profile and within a decidedly political context. It also seems that the literature with most impact for the Puerto Rican community of the time was the dramatic literature, if published books are a measure. Poet Gonzalo O'Neill (1867–1942) was a successful businessman who during the twenties and thirties was at the hub of Puerto Rican and Hispanic cultural life, protecting writers, authoring three highly nationalistic books, and serving on the board of directors of the Teatro Hispano. During his youth in Puerto Rico he was associated with the magazine *El Paleque de la Juventud*, which featured the works of Luis Muñoz Rivera, Lola Rodríguez de Tió, Vicente Palés, and many other notables. As Manuel Quevedo Baez states in the prologue to O'Neill's book of poems *Sonoras bagatelas o Sicibanas*, published in 1924: "Gonzalo is a spontaneous and ingenuous poet. . . . He is a poet of Creole stock, passionate, tender, and as melancholic as Gautier Benitez."[28] And, indeed his lyre was patriotic, for his plays, *Moncho Reyes*, published by the Spanish American Printing Company circa 1923 and *Bajo una sola bandera o Pabellón de Borinquen*, are direct appeals for the independence of Puerto Rico. *Bajo una sola bandera* was produced by Puerto Rican leading man Juan Nadal de Santa Colonia and his Compañía de Dramas y Comedias. Nadal, a writer himself and a pioneer in creating a Puerto Rican national theater, also produced his own *zarzuela*, *Día de Reyes*, with music composed by Rafael Hernández and Luis Llorens Torres's *El grito de Lares*, with a prologue by Luis Muñoz Rivera, also orchestrated by Rafael Hernández.[29] The latter was often used to raise funds for such organizations as Club Borinquen Atlético.[30] In 1937 *El grito de Lares* was staged at the Teatro Hispano, along with speeches in defense of Albizu Campos, to raise funds for the Puerto Rican political prisoners.[31]

Despite this being the epoch of Rafael Hernández's patently nationalistic songs, his venture into theatrical publication, composing the zarzuela music for Alberto M. Gonzalez's *Colegiales* published in 1928, was totally apolitical, even frivolous.

This was not the case for Franca de Armino's *Los hipócritas: comedia dramática social en cuatro actos y ocho cuadros*, self-published at the Modernistic Editorial Publishing Company in 1937 and dedicated to "to the oppressed and to all those who work for ideas of social renovation.'' Its premiere was on April 15 and 16, 1933, at the Park Place Theatre by the company's Spanish leading man Manuel Santigosa.[32] The work, set in Spain during the time of the Republic, is pointedly anti-Fascist and revolutionary. In the dedication the author states that publication of the play was delayed four years because of the difficulty of raising funds to print during the economic crisis. Her other works are: *Tragedia puertorriqueña*, ''an intense comedy of social criticism''; *Aspectos de la vida*, ''philosophical essays about life and the nature of things, beings, and the universe''; and *Luz de tinieblas*, ''book of poems on different themes.''[33]

Another Puerto Rican playwright who published a work in support of the Spanish Republic during the Civil War was José Enamorado Cuesta (1892–1976). His *El pueblo en marcha* was published in New York in 1937.[34]

All the above represents only an initial inventory of writers that were published in book form before World War II. It is not a list of the considerable number of works published in newspapers and magazines, nor of works published in English like Jesús Colón's column for *The Worker*,[35] nor of works of talented writers like sailor Alfonso Dieppa who according to Bernardo Vega never made it into print.[36]

The conclusions that we may draw are the following:

1. Dating from before the founding of the United States up until the outbreak of World War II, there is an unbroken tradition of literary publishing and consumption by Hispanic Americans north of the Río Grande.
2. At least until World War II, there seems to have been an Hispanic consciousness and solidarity in the elite world of literary publishing. Writers of diverse Hispanic origins wrote for the newspapers, theaters, and book publishers. Southwestern culture, while still under the cultural domination of Spain in the nineteenth century, was dominated by national authors and cultural entrepreneurs in the twentieth century. New York, however, Spanish- and Cuban-dominated up until the 1920s, at all times maintained a cosmopolitan flavor, with Puerto Rican culture beginning to exercise its influence in the late 1930s.
3. Many of the dominant themes and much of the inspiration for works published in the United States were related to the political and social movements of the homeland, i.e., the Cuban Independence Movement in the nineteenth century, the Mexican Revolution of 1910, the Puerto Rican Nationalist movement, the Spanish Civil War. Except in the case of books published by the Mexican cultural elites fleeing the revolution, the dominant attitudes of Cubans, Spaniards, and Puerto Rican were liberal, if not socialist.
4. While the Depression, along with the repatriation of Mexicans, was catastrophic for literary efforts in the Southwest, such was not the case in New York, where although the Depression interrupted and delayed a great

deal of cultural ferment, it did not result in depopulating the Hispanic community. And even such houses as the Spanish American Printing Company sustained their efforts well into the 1950s. The Lozano, Whitt, Quiroga, Viola Novelty, and Librería Española efforts in San Antonio did not survive past the late 1930s, nor did the majority of the newspapers. *La Opinión*, still operated by the Lorenzo family, and *El Diario-La Prensa*, are two of the three (along with the *Miami Herald*) major Spanish-language dailies publishing today. San Antonio's *La Prensa* succumbed in the 1960s.

Just a few words about literature and publishing in the past two decades. For the most part, the inheritors of the tradition are small, noncommercial presses that issue works in Spanish, English, and in bilingual format. The novelty here is the transition to English and the use of Spanish and English in the same work, plus a definite democratization of the publishing effort, with writers from working-class origins and even what some would call *lumpen*, making their way into the world of publishing. The major English-language commerical publishers ignore the tradition outlined above and publish books that highlight the Hispanic community's illiteracy, criminality, and poverty.

As for publishers and writers in Mexico and Puerto Rico, again writers like Octavio Paz highlight marginality, and Puerto Rican writers like González and Soto further elaborate the literary theme of the misfortune of Puerto Rican life in New York, often ignoring the resouces, cross-fertilization from other cultures, and general dynamism of living and creating in one of the great cosmopolitan centers of the world. What is also ignored is the tradition of Hispanic New York serving as a place for fermenting political and cultural revolutions, and where a nationalistic art could at times be more freely expressed than in nineteenth-century Cuba or precommonwealth Puerto Rico.

While the mainstream press condemns us to the patterns established by *Stranger in a Strange Land, Down These Mean Streets*, and *Hunger of Memory*, Mexican and Puerto Rican presses continue to repeat the cliché of the victimized *campesino/jíbaro*. Some Puerto Rican intellectuals treat the use of English as treachery and some even to the extent of applying the term *nolingues* to bilingual Puerto Rican New Yorkers. The fact is that now, even more than in the past, the pressure of conflict with the Anglo-American mainstream, on the one hand, and the home culture, on the other, have given rise to an exciting, dynamic culture and literature that promises to revolutionize the very concept of literature.

Notes

1. See Ernesto Mejía Sánchez, *Gaspar Pérez de Villagrá en la Nueva España* (México: Cuadernos del Centro de Estudios Literarios, 1970).

2. See Winifred Johnson, ''Early Theatre in the Spanish Borderlands,'' *Mid-America* 13 (October 1930): 121–31.
3. See Aurora Lucero-White Lea, *Literary Folklore of the Hispanic Southwest* (San Antonio: Naylor, 1953), pp. 16–21.
4. ''325 aniversario de la Sinagoga Hispano-Portuguesa de Nueva York,'' *Nuestro Encuentro* 2 (Summer 1981): 3.
5. Luis Leal, ''Mexican American Literature: A Historical Perspective,'' *Revista Chicano-Riqueña* 1 (1973): 35.
6. Here, as in the remainder of this paper, the dates in parentheses refer to the issues of the newspaper which are part of the collections noted; they are not the inclusive dates of publication. See the mimeographed catalog of the Chicano Studies Library, University of California at Berkeley.
7. ''Some Examples of Chicano Prose Fiction of the Nineteenth and Early Twentieth Centuries,'' *Revista Chicano-Riqueña* 9 (Winter 1981): 64–66.
8. See Charles Tatum, *Chicano Literature* (Boston: Twayne, 1982).
9. *El mensajero semanal* was published in Philadelphia from April 25 to March 28, 1829.
10. See *El Mensajero Semanal* (February 7, 1829) for act 2, scene 6 of *Tello de Neira* by Spanish author Dionisio Solís, and May 16, 1829, for a scene from Moratín's *Comedia nueva*.
11. At the University of California at Berkeley's Bancroft Collection of early New York newspapers.
12. In the Bancroft Collection.
13. New York: Phos, 1926.
14. *La Patria* (February 3, 1894).
15. Ibid.
16. See Perrier.
17. Luis Leal, p. 39.
18. Among the columnists, although not of *La Prensa*, whose works were most influential and potentially literary, are Benjamín Padilla and Julio G. Arce. See Arce's *Crónicas diabólicas de ''Jorge Ulica,''* ed. Juan Rodríguez (San Diego: Maize, 1982), and Clara Lómas, ''Resistencia cultural o apropiación ideológica,'' *Revista Chicano-Riqueña* 6 (no 4, 1978): 44–49.
19. See my article ''The Flourishing of Hispanic Theatre in the Southwest,'' *Latin American Theatre Review* 16 (Fall 1982).
20. For an inventory of some of these, see my article ''*Las aventuras de Don Chipote*, obra precursora de la novela chicana,'' accepted for publication in *Hispania*.
21. Ibid.
22. *List of Printed Books in the Library of the Hispanic Society of America* (New York: Hispanic Society, 1910), p. 7174.
23. Ibid.
24. Listed in Nilda González, *Bibliografía de teatro puertorriqueño* (Río Piedras: Editorial Universitaria, 1979), p. 92.
25. Perrier.
26. For a partial list of O'Farill's dramatic compositions see Perrier, p. 71.
27. Bancroft had a run from 1930 to 1932.
28. *Sonoras bagatelas*, pp. 13–14.
29. See *La Prensa* (July 8, August 11, 1933, May 5, 1934).
30. *La Prensa* (November 1, 1933).
31. *La Voz* (October 23, 1937).

32. "Dedicatoria," *Los hipócritas*.
33. *Los hipócritas*, inside front cover.
34. González, p. 44.
35. See Jesús Colón, *A Puerto Rican in New York and Other Sketches* (New York: International, 1982).
36. See César Andreu Iglesias, *Memorias de Bernardo Vega: una contribución a la historia de la comunidad puertorriqueña* (San Juan: Huracán, 1977).

27

Cross-Currents in Hispanic U. S. Contemporary Drama

John C. Miller

Traditionally when scholars have described Hispanic theater in the United States, they conceive a modern phenomenon, generally set in the post-World War II years or perhaps even in the 1960s. However, in recent years, Hispanic U.S. theater has been traced back to its origins, the evangelical missionary theater of the Southwest. On April 30, 1598, near El Paso, Marcos Farfán de los Godos produced a play which described the expected Christianization of the territory. This noteworthy act which preceded by sixty-seven years the first recorded play in English and by eight years the French masque produced in Acadia does not necessarily indicate continuity but primacy. Nevertheless, it awakens traditional American literary historians to a bilingual presence which is being disenterred.

In the second half of the nineteenth century, the Southwest participated in erratic popular expressions of theater. Professional Latino theater companies were established in Los Angeles in 1860. Several decades later other theatrical companies found a permanent home in San Antonio. Between Los Angeles and San Antonio theater remained at a popular level. New Mexico contributed its folk theater. The 1880 plays "Los Comanches" and "Los Tejanos" were popular and drawn from the lives of the people. These plays survived through oral tradition as did the writings of folklorists whose works were performed by small family-owned companies during the late nineteenth century. Mexico, Cuba, and Spain began to provide traveling companies often composed of musicians, dancers, and individuals trained in the *zarzuela*, the Spanish operetta. John Brokaw's "A Mexican American Acting Company, 1849–1924" traces a traditional troupe in the Southwest.[1] By the turn of the nineteenth century Southwestern theater was not limited to roving groups of folk theater. Established groups from Los Angeles and San Antonio were beginning to stop at the smaller towns in the Southwest. From these types of show the *pelado* developed. He was a fellow of crude humor who made audiences laugh at their poverty and the problems associated with Americanization. The Mexican revolutionary period provided an impetus for migration, particularly to the cities of El Paso, Laredo, and San Antonio. Elizabeth Ramírez has traced the Mexican American theater in Texas and has described three types of theater in the Southwestern border territories: (1) touring repertory companies prior to 1910; (2) resident companies (1910–15); and (3) large combinations from Mexico City (1915–35).[2] The *carpas*, another Latino theater, reached their popularity peak during the period betweeen 1910 and the early 1930s. The two world wars and the forced repatriation of many Mexicans slowed theatrical activities but they never died.

The Mexican Revolution, which established significant resident immigrant centers through the Southwest and California, provided an audience for traveling companies from Spain and Mexico which also generally included Cuba and Puerto Rico in their tours and then began to extend themselves to Florida and later New York, the awakening center of a Cuban, Puerto Rican, and peninsular Spanish emigration.

Nicolás Kanellos states that the newspapers of the tens and twenties of this century indicate that Hispanic communities in general hoped to see the latest works from Madrid and Mexico City, all this in a precinematic era. These early manifestations of crossing the Great Divide were destroyed by the vagaries of the cinema, the Great Depression, and changing emigration patterns. The West Coast theater and its Chicano communities and the New York Hispanic community had limited contacts in the thirties, forties, and fifties. However, musical comedy played an important part in maintaining popular tradition in both populations.

> Of the types of musical theater that were produced, the *zarzuela* or Spanish light opera was the most popular during the first two decades of the century. Operas and operettas of German and Italian tradition were also well received, especially when performed by such touring companies as the Compañía Mexicana de Opera. During the 1930s a genre actually called "comedia musical" included works by the famous Mexican composer Agustín Lara. But also during the 1930s the popularity of the *zarzuela* was outstripped by vaudeville with its musical reviews.
>
> Many of the companies would swing along eastern Mexico and tour along the border making extended runs in the major cities of Laredo, San Antonio, El Paso, and Los Angeles.[3]

As a result of the Spanish Civil War, New York developed a Spanish émigré theater centered about the Columbia—Barnard—Middlebury University complexes as well as occasional productions of the two relatively permanent companies of Marita Reid and Alejandro Elliot, which had their beginnings in the twenties. Most of their productions as well as those of the Grupo Futurismo of Rolando Barrera and Gala of Felix Anteló had short runs, often one evening or at the most a weekend. The East Coast with its Caribbean population was as the West being incorporated into a media world of radio, movies, and television. Theater and even musical comedy were soon to be available at home in a small box.

New York's Hispanic theater had an erratic decade in the 1950s and began to flourish in the 1960s. Its base was either traditional European or Puerto Rican. The formation of the three major companies followed traditional lines: INTAR with Elsa Ortiz de Robles, Frank Robles, Antonio González, and Max Ferra; The Puerto Rican Traveling Theater and Miriam Colón's driving energy as well as the aid of Francess Druker, George Edgar, and Stella Holt; Spanish Theater Repertory Company was founded by René Buch, Luz Castaños, Francess Druker, and Gilberto Zaldívar. Cuban refugees, Puerto Rican professional actors, and university professors as well as interested Anglos created this theater.

This renaissance of Hispanic theater in New York also included a number of smaller companies directed by dedicated individuals: Iván Acosta, Mario Peña, Abdón Villamizar, and Manuel Martín. Luis Valdéz was finishing school at San Jose State, working with the San Francisco Mime Troupe and convincing César Chávez that agit-prop theater was more effective than handing out pamphlets. The political activism in California soon spread to other parts of the United States as other Chicano theaters were formed in Chicago, Detroit, Seattle, as well as in the Southwest. Traditional Chicano modes of theater were changing. Political awareness was not restricted to the West as Marvin Félix Camillo began his workshops in the Bedford Hills Correctional Facility developing the framework of the Family, a residential program for former inmates including production of the play *Short Eyes* by Miguel Piñero which was to win an OBIE and the New York Drama Critics Award as the Best American Play of the 1973–74 season.

The New York Shakespeare Theater under Joseph Papp recognized the commitment of theater to the people. Productions in schoolyards, playgrounds, pocket parks; in El Barrio, the Bronx, Queens, and the Lower East Side awakened a new audience. As the Teatro Campesino was taking a leadership role extending its repertory into the general social issues of racism, Vietnam, and bilingual education, on the East Coast the New Rican (Nuyorican) Neoyorquino theater with Miguel Algarín, Lucky Cienfuegos, Miguel Piñero, Tato Laviera, Oscar Siccone, and others was being conceived and born. As TENAZ was founded in 1971 to communicate among West Coast theater groups, East-West barriers were being broken.

This background establishes the history prior to the 1970s and to regularly formulated communication systems which permitted cross-fertilization. The

Nuyorican and Chicano theater of the 1970s was an agit-prop political theater involved in drugs, 42nd Street, prostitutes, and hustlers, as well as labor movements, strike breakers (scabs), discrimination, and *la migra*. It was a naturalistic theater using traditional resources of the Comedia dell' Arte, giant puppets, Brechtian techniques, and elements of encounter therapy—at times reaching the primal scream level. Collective creations often emerged from a single author. This agit-prop theater, now more valuable historically than literaly, includes the *Actos* of Luis Valdéz and *Short Eyes* by Miguel Piñero, *What I Found in New York* of Teatro 4, *América Congo Manía* by Lucky Cienfuegos, and the list could go on.

Theater festivals began to emerge which invited East and West Coast groups. Carlos Morton, a Chicano playrwright, came East and described Nuyorican theater in the early 1970s.[4] Teatro 4 celebrated the first festival of popular theater in Losaida and at the Public Theater. Companies from New York traveled West and South. Popular theater extended its frontiers to international dimensions. Thus, this past summer at the Third Festival of Popular Theater, Teatro de la Esperanza from Santa Barbara was present among the companies from Venezuela, Colombia, Mexico, Nicaragua, and Guatemala. *Once a Family* was a family drama rooted in social issues, no longer agit-prop social issues separate from familiar implications.

While initial Nuyorican-Chicano cross-fertilization was occurring through theater festivals, the Cubans and diverse Hispanic ethnic groups in New York were forging ahead. Under the leadership of Iván Acosta and Omar Torres, the Centro Cultural Cubano established a regular theater series; Luz Castaños founded Nuestro Teatro with a strong focus on children's theater; María Peña and Abdón Villamizar continued their experimental Latinoamerican works. In Queens and Brooklyn, theaters were established by Cuban and Puerto Rican recent arrivals; Manuel Martín and Gloria Celeya established Teatro Dúo. In summary, a core of Hispanic American actors, singers, dancers, and directors, as well as an audience from many countries were established.

Journals began to feature articles about U.S. Hispanic theater. Journals, encounters, theater festivals under the aegis of Middle America—the University of Kansas and George Woodyard; Indiana University Northwest, and Nicolás Kanellos—provided the academic community with important information through the *Latin American Theater Review* and the *Revista Chicano-Riqueña*. Even The *New York Times* in a 1975 article stated that "Hispanic theater discovers strength in ethnic diversity."[5]

The network formed by TENAZ and encouraged by continuous contacts communicated happenings. Academic training was sought by young playrights—Carlos Morton, Rubén Sierra—and stimulated by other academics, poets and writers—Miguel Algarín, Víctor Fernández Fragoso, Jorge Huerta, Rudolfo Anaya.

The Puerto Rican Bilingual Workshop established at the Henry Street Settlement House by Carla Pinza became the Hispanic Playwrights Workshops as staged readings were expanded to include Osvaldo Dragún, Carlos Morton, and Guillermo Gentile.

However, much of this theater was somewhat marginal in general audience awareness until Luis Valdéz's *Zoot Suit* opened in Los Angeles at the Mark Taper Theater and later moved to New York. This production, which was unsuccessful in the New York setting for a variety of reasons, among them a huge theater in which the production was lost, is symbolic of cross-currents which flow sporadically. The Puerto Rican Traveling Theater moved to a new location just next to Broadway, but its previous season was marked by the great success of a naturalistic family drama set in the South Bronx, *Simpson Street* by Eddie Gallardo. The PRTT went totally bilingual as did INTAR. An Anglo audience was agressively sought.

New York actors and actresses were attracted to California by roles in television and in the movies and more communication was established. Ilka Payan produced *Beautiful Señoritas* by Dolores Prida at the Hispanic feminist Literature Conference in San José. National and regional barriers in theater were being broken.

Cross-currents also occurred through publications—the important 1979 collection in *Nuevos Pasos* of Chicano and Puerto Rican drama, the anthologies of *The Bilingual Review*, as well as the variety of textbooks, particularly those edited by Francisco Jiménez. *Nuevos Pasos*, Chicano and Puerto Rican drama published by *Revista Chicano-Riqueña* (1979), merits a detailed study. It includes nine playwrights, eight plays. No Cuban American writer is included. It seems appropriate to mention this fact since Cuban American theater is now emerging in both New York and Miami. Five plays are by Chicano writers; three by Puerto Rican or Nuyorican writers (critics generally consider Jaime Carrero Puerto Rican).

A consideration of the anthology *Nuevos Pasos* shows the contrasts and cross-currents in Hispanic dramatic writing today. Three Puerto Rican works are written by Jaime Carrero, Miguel Piñero, and coauthors Miguel Algarín and Tato Laviera.

Jaime Carrero, traditionally identified with Puerto Rican island literature in the short story genre, in drama reflects the identity quest so often present in first-generation Nuyorican writers. *Pipo Subway no sabe reír* in 1972 and *NooJall* in 1973 are New York-based works. Inner conflicts, linguistic dilemmas, and barrio social conditions are omnipresent. In *The FM Safe*, the crime and violence of the barrio affect not only the storekeeper but all those around him. A fortress mentality penetrates the liquor store as locks, chairs, and alarms fail to protect him from anger and frustrations, theft and murder. Indeed, only the wife of the liquor store owner still protests. Nowhere in the

Chicano works anthologized is there such a negative portrait of urban life portrayed.

In a similar manner, *The Sun Shines for the Cool* reflects a typical Miguel Piñero environment—42nd Street with its pimps, prostitutes, and hustlers. No individual character seems to reflect qualities other than street jive, opportunism, and survival-based intelligence. There is glitter and broad sensuality, a celebration of sexuality and life as the great con game, life on the urban carnival midway.

Chicano drama as represented in this collection approaches the dehumanized New York scene only in the drug-related suffering of the Vietnam vet, *Manolo* by Rubén Sierra. However, as the Chicano population suffered the highest percentage of casualties in Vietnam, this theme naturally appeared first in Luis Valdéz's *actos Vietnam campesino* and *Soldado raso*. Valdés himself later developed the drama further in his *Dark Root of a Scream* as did Raúl Estrada, José Olivera, and Leo Rojas in *A Barrio Tragedy*. The work of Jaime Carrero *Flag Inside* seems more appropriate as a comparison, but Puerto Rican or Nuyorican war experiences tend to identify with Korea and its impact on society. The Chicano works appear to reflect individual destruction in a drug-laden environment.

The Chicano drama represented in the anthology had passed the initial island/mainland identity crisis (or the Mexico/U.S. parallel) and now shows a distinctive capacity to laugh at itself. Three works of varying thematic content entertain the public. In *The Interview* by Ron Arias, the social stratification of the college student/interviewer, i.e., social worker and the astuteness of the barrio dweller, are highlighted humorously. Local "winos" are more astute than the university-trained individual, perhaps a parallel with the streetwise characters of Miguel Piñero, the difference being that few contrasting characters appear in Piñero.

Rodrigo Duarte-Clark in *Brujerías* takes a human failing, jealousy, and converts it into a Chicano comedy. The satire of the *migra* and its use to denounce the neighbor, the church, and the ghosts we create through guilt, all serve to make us smile and laugh. Such humor is rarely presented in the more serious Nuyorican writers.

The religious element presented in *Olú Clemente* comes from African religion, Yoruba culture. As the Afro-Caribbean influences religion, *botánicas*, *espiritismo* is present on the East Coast through its Afro-Antillian roots, so the elegy to Roberto Clemente by Miguel Algarín and Tato Laviera reflects different sources of inspiration.

Both *Rancho Hollywood* by Carlos Morton and *Sun Images* by Estela Portillo-Trambley deal with popular stereotypes. Morton prefers to satirize the media world of television and film, particularly the racism and machismo of early California. In contrast, Estela Portillo-Trambley writes a work which pokes fun at machismo, college life, and male-female relationships. Laughter is light and refreshing. The issue-oriented Eastern drama is not present.

As has been illustrated here, there are cross-currents. Pedro Pietri, a well-known Nuyorican poet and playwright, read his creation with Vietnam veterans at the Public Theater, but his dramatic work does not reflect that experience. Chicano theater does. The Chicano theater anthologized in *Nuevos Pasos* is able to laugh at the foibles of its people; it has passed the identity stage. Humor shows its maturity. Nuyorican theater with the exception of the elegiac *Olú Clemente* is still searching for its identity in a strange African world foreign and yet close to the Puerto Rican.

Recently this past spring, La Tertulia in New York created a series of staged readings, La Nueva Sangre, dedicated to the memory of Víctor Fernández Fragoso. This series typically represents the Hispanic variety present in New York. Three Cuban writers were included: Omar Torres's *Dreamland Melodies*, a family drama set in Cuba and Miami; Mario Peña's *Ammo*, a propagandistic antidrug piece set in the 1960s; and Doris Castellaños's *Yoruba*, reflecting the *santerista* Afro-Antillian tradition. Edit Villareal, Chicana, writes a drama of contemporary family crisis when faced with a rebel daughter who is to join the sandinistas. Guillermo Gentile's (Argentine) *Con las alas encogidas* is a metaphorical exposition of the dreams of the Hunchback (different individuals in society). Three works by young Puerto Rican writers treat emerging sexual conflict themes: Maria Mar's *Y viceversa*—role structure—male/female; Randy Barceló's *Canciones de vellonera*—the gay Hispanic New York world; and Herminio Vargas's *Mucho macho*—role expectations of the Hispanic male society. Bilingual education is represented by Nuyorican teacher Rubén González; Dominican Cándido Tirado's comedy *The Closed Door* describes the writer's bloc and strange encounters; Mila Conway and Jesús Papo Marquéz study the dilemma of the island city transition metaphorically and through comic routines in *La Prenda Brenda* and *La Terapia*.

Stereotypes appear in the early writings of the twentieth century in Chicano literature, particularly *el pelado* who becomes a stock character in the peasant theater of Luis Valdés. Certain stereotypes appear in Nuyorican theater which represent the thematic interests of particular writers—the 42nd Street crowd of Miguel Piñero, the long-suffering mother in *Simpson Street*, and the abused wife with a philandering husband in *Ariano*.

However, in general, in recent works as illustrated by La Nueva Sangre readings of Teatro Dúo, the pattern of stereotyping is breaking down. Six dramatists just mentioned are Puerto Rican or Nuyorican. In the exploration of sexual roles, Marina Man, Randy Barceló, and Hermino Vargas depict the lives of newly defined individuals who do not fit ethnic stereotypes.

Mila Conway and Jesús Papo Marquéz have abandoned the forced rigid types taken from naturalistic theater and using humor, have forged original characters who make the audience laugh and who, in turn, laugh at themselves.

Puerto Ricans, Cuban Americans, and Chicanos in dramatic representations are no longer stereotyped. They have evolved into individuals with all the emotions and crises which the theater presents. In contemporary 1980 writing, individual dilemmas surpass ethnic identity crises and other rites of passage.

Hispanic drama in the United States is recognizing its diversity, communicating with others. No longer can one talk only of Nuyorican, Chicano, or Cuban American drama. Rather it seems appropriate to comment on the cross-currents and mutual assistance which the Hispanic theater today in the United States is enjoying and stimulating.

Notes

1. John W. Brokaw, "A Mexican American Acting Company, 1849–1924," *Educational Theater Journal* 27 (1975): 23–27.
2. Elizabeth C. Ramírez, "A History of Mexican American Professional Theater in Texas: The Resident Companies, 1910–1915." Unpublished paper delivered at the American Theater Association (August 1982).
3. Nicolás Kanellos and Jorge Huerta, "Nuevos Pasos," *Revista Chicano-Riqueña* 7 (Winter 1979): 20–21.
4. Carlos Morton, "Nuyorican Theater," *Drama Review* 20 (1976): 43–50.
5. Nat Hentoff, "Hispanic Theater," *New York Times* (December 6, 1975): 3.

28

Geographic Displacement as Spiritual Desolation in Puerto Rican and Chicano Prose Fiction

Charles A. Tatum

During the last twenty years, Nuyorican and Chicano prose fiction writers have tended to focus on the travails of Latinos, both urban and rural, in their struggle for justice and equality in an often hostile social environment. One of the dominant themes found in many works concerns the disastrous consequences of uprootedness suffered by these two groups when they emigrate from one land to another or when they undergo geographic changes within the United States itself. In this paper I will explore the recurring theme of spiritual desolation resulting from geographic displacement of individuals and groups. As an experience common to both Puerto Ricans and Chicanos, it naturally forms an important link between their literatures. I have limited myself to prose fiction, but the theme can also be found in other genres, especially poetry. My study is not exhaustive, but rather is meant to serve as an introduction and hopefully a stimulus for further research on the subject.

Broadly conceived, spiritual desolation manifests itself in many ways in the novels and short stories under consideration including: (1) a growing attitude of insecurity in a new environment; (2) an attitude of uncertainty and anxiety, an existential impotence, a passivity and disgust; (3) a state of psychological and existencial dependency; (4) a negative self-image; and (5) spiritual frustration and solitude.[1] In short, these works portray an alienated view of the Promised Land, a prevailing attitude that is antithetical to the hopes and dreams of those who left their native land, be it Puerto Rico or Mexico, in search of a better life.

Among Puerto Rican writers, the city of New York is almost always the setting for their protagonists' sense of desolation. For example, José Luis González's well-known story "En Nueva York" is a panoply of an immigrant's negative experiences.[2] Upon his arrival in the metropolis, Marcelino Pérez soon learns that the cousin who generously invited him to visit has been killed by a policeman in a case of mistaken identity. His cousin's widow lives with her aunt and two children in a tiny cold-water flat. Marcelino tries desperately to eke out a living in a factory but he is soon dismissed. After squandering his meager savings on alcohol and women, he becomes desperate, finally resorting to purse-snatching. González poignantly conveys his protagonist's deep anguish in the story's last scene. Realizing that he has resorted to stealing from another Puerto Rican, perhaps as miserable as himself, Marcelino flees like a frightened animal:

> The purse fell next to the body of the woman. She looked at him from the ground, with her eyes wide open still from terror. Marcelino backed away two steps, covered his face with his hands and inadvertently howled like a tortured beast. Then he set out for a desperate run through a dark street, stumbling while loosing one of his shoes, clashing with poles and garbage cans until he disappeared in a corner with a hair-raising scream finally broken by the hoarse sobbing of a tormented animal.[3]

González effectively uses the physical coldness of the season to heighten the inhospitability of the urban environment. It is Marcelino's first impression of the city later reinforced by the bone-chilling temperature of his apartment—both reflect his interior state of feeling lost and alone.

Another of González's memorable short stories, "El pasaje," portrays the alienating experience of New York for a Puerto Rican who is beaten down by the endless hours of mindless activity and physical strain on the factory assembly line.[4] His desolation ends tragically when he is shot robbing a delicatessen in order to obtain money for passage back to the island.

Two novels, *Down These Mean Streets* by Piri Thomas and *Nobody's Hero: A Puerto Rican Story* by Lefty Barreto, highlight the dehumanizing experiences undergone by Puerto Ricans in the city.[5] Both are narrated by youthful protagonists who take us on a labyrinthian journey through the streets of East Harlem's Latino slum district. The dominant image of the city is decidedly negative. Thomas expresses this in his prologue which sets the tune for the rest of the novel:

> I got a feeling of aloneness and bitterness that's growing and growing
>
> Day by day into some kind of hate without *un nombre*.
>
> Yet when I look down at the streets below, I can't help thinking
>
> It's like a great big dirty Christmas tree with lights but no fuckin presents.
>
> And man, my head starts growing bigger than my body as it gets crammed full of hate.
>
> And I begin to listen to the sounds inside me.

> Get angry, get hating angry, and you won't be scared.
>
> What have you got now? Nothing.
>
> What will you ever have? Nothing.
>
> . . . Unless you cop for yourself![6]

He depicts the city, especially East Harlem where he grew up, as harsh and uncompromising. Life there is an unrelenting battle not only with its hostile elements—violence and drugs—but with the growing cynicism within himself. Yet by contrast, the barrio serves as a haven for the author when he leaves to live among Whites on Long Island or travels to the South with a Black friend. These experiences are even more alienating than life at home; consequently, Piri Thomas always chooses to return.

An autobiographical account of growing up in the barrio, *Nobody's Hero* is as vivid as *Down These Mean Streets*. However, unlike Thomas, Barreto does not view the barrio even ambivalently, as a haven. The young protagonist's encounters with drugs and gang violence are simply aspects of a central barrio environment of disillusionment and day-to-day survival. This is highlighted in the contrast that Barreto draws between a preventorium, set in the New Jersey countryside, and East Harlem. While the short time the young narrator spends at the preventorium is not idyllic, he does see it as a kind of refuge, especially when he is forced to return to New York City for breaking school rules. His displacement back to the city is the source of anguish reflected in the following quote:

> While I learned to speak English I fell in love with the New Jersey countryside. Mrs. Johnson was driving the same route we had taken that first day coming to the preventorium. Only I was eight then and now I was almost twelve and had made the trip three times. Butch and Mikie were napping, identifying the makes of passing cars, admiring the big trucks. These two cats were even getting a kick out of being cast from heaven. But not me, man; I knew I was going back to that tenement hallway. I remembered the first time I smelled what a tenement hallway was. Walking through the stale wine of winos, thinking about my *casita* in the woods where there was peace and freedom of mind.[7]

In the case of Chicano writers, the desolation resulting from geographic displacement is not so particularized in the sense that it is not focused on any one city. Rather—and this reflects the nature of immigration patterns since early in the century—they offer a more general view of both young and old Mexican immigrants making the transition from their native country to the United States or changing from rural to urban settings. What is similar, however, is the sense of anguish and alienation that accompanies the sometimes sudden and violent disruption of one's life patterns.

Pocho by José Antonio Villarreal and *Chicano* by Richard Vásquez are the best examples of Chicano prose fiction that focus on the journey north from Mexico to the United States and the subsequent forced adaptation of immigrants to a new environment.[8]

Villarreal captures the immigrants' plight in the following description of their flight from the violence of the Mexican Revolution:

> They came first to Juárez, where the price of the three-minute tram ride would take them into El Paso del Norte—or a short walk through the open door would deposit them in Utopia. The ever-increasing army of people swarned across while the border remained open, fleeing from squalor and oppression. But they could not flee reality, and the Texans, who welcomed them as a blessing because there were miles of cotton to be harvested, had never really forgotten the Alamo. The certain degree of dignity the Mexicans yet retained made some of them turn around and walk back into the hell they had left. Others huddled close to the international bridge and established a colony on the American side of the river, in the city of El Paso, because they could gaze at their homeland a few yards away whenever the impulse struck them. The bewildered people came on—insensitive to the fact that even though they were not stopped, they were not really wanted. It was the ancient quest for El Dorado, and so they moved onward, west to New Mexico and Arizona and California, and as they moved, they planted their new seed.[9]

The immigrants' sense of aloneness in a land where everything is new—language, customs, religion, food—is personalized in Juan Rubio, the once-proud revolutionary officer who has fled northward for political reasons, biding his time until his general—Francisco Villa—rallies his troops for another campaign. This triumphant return to Mexico never occurs and Juan mourns his fate:

> Now this man who had lived by the gun all his adult life would sit on his hauches under the prune trees, rubbing his sore knees, and think, "Next year we will have enough money and we will return to our country." But deep within he knew he was one of the lost ones. And as the years passed him by and his children multiplied and grew, the chant increased in volume and rate until it became a staccato "Next Year! Next Year!"[10]

Like *Pocho*, the first part of the novel *Chicano* traces a Mexican family's flight from revolutionary violence in search of tranquility across the border in California. The Sandoval family's introduction to the United States is filled with despair as they meet with a desolate landscape that shatters their hope of a better life: "A great sense of being alone in unfriendly territory gripped the family. The land was flat. A mile or more away, in opposite directions, were two farmhouses. A dog barked somewhere far off."[11]

Barrio Boy, Ernesto Galarza's autobiographical account of his family's dislocation from their subsequent relocation in Arizona and later California is another example of the consequences of geographic displacement. While Galarza's view of his experiences is considerably milder than either of the fictionalized versions of Villarreal and Vásquez, the reader is struck throughout the book by contrasts between the native setting and the new environment in the United States. Fair in his recollection of life in Jalcocotán, Galarza describes both its negative and positive attributes. Yet what emerges is the young boy's sense of security surrounded by familial and communal ties. Life in Mexico is depicted as traditional and tranquil. Even the barrio in Mazatlán where the family lives for a short time on their way to the United States is filled with the sights, sounds, and smells familiar, and therefore comforting, to the narrator. By contrast, life across the border is raucous and upsetting. Ultimately, it is its differences, manifested in many ways—the layout of American towns; corner grocery stores rather than open *mercados*; the absence of plazas, parks, grandstands, and music; fences between houses, etc.—which disorient the young Galarza. He comments: "Like the city, the . . . *barrio* did not have a place which was the middle of things for everyone."[12]

In Chicano prose fiction, we find not only the contrasting images of life in Mexico and the United States but other expressions of geographic displacement as well. For example, in Miguel Méndez's novel *Peregrinos de Aztlán*, Yaqui Indians and Mexicans who emigrate to the cities of northern Mexico find, rather than opportunity and success, an atmosphere of hostility and exploitation:

> This unique city with airs of having a "doubtful reputation" awakens redeemed by the disturbance of students and the strokes of the bells which announce mass; by the bustle of the workers who earn a handful of pennies, resistant to pay with misery the tribute which honesty collects; and the occasional visit of good willing foreigners who rush to buy inoffensive objects. But as the lights of the day fade away and those of the night go on, the city begins to dress up with adornments of a flirting procurer who seduces the unwary. Like a mythical goddess, cynic and impudent, the city begins to take advantage of human weaknesses to fill its most remote corners.[13]

Another variation of geographic displacement is John Rechy's *City of Night*. This novel constitutes the anguished search for self of an anonymous young male protagonist who, setting out from his native El Paso, travels to five American cities: New York, Los Angeles, San Francisco, Chicago, and New Orleans. Although he refers to El Paso in the later sections of the novel with a combination of fond nostalgia and regret for having left, we come to realize that it contains the seeds of his unhappiness: "Not the great stretching, wide-plained land of the movies, but the crushing city where I had been raised in stiffling love and hatred." While his mother smothered him in tender but carnivorous care and indulgence, his father, an unsuccessful composer, projected his accumulated frustration onto his son, who soon developed an intense and lasting hatred for him. The constant instability and sudden violent eruptions in his home life eventually drive him into a self-imposed isolation from which he will not return. The figure of his dead dog, Winnie, his only souce of affection as a child, recurs throughout the novel as a symbol to him of hopelessness and utter misery. While craving tenderness and attention he is incapable of responding to it. A worsening home life and his inability to form adolescent friendships drive Rechy's protagonist further into himself, deepening his need for affection. Having rebelled against his family and rejected his peers, he plunges headlong into the chaotic and indifferent world of the large American cities. Male prostitution becomes a means of asserting his self-worth in an environment which will eventually deny him all expression of individuality.

The surrealistic images of the Cities of Night visited by Rechy's protagonist graphically reflect his anguish:

> Later I would think of America as one vast City of Night stretching gaudily from Times Square to Hollywood Boulevard—jukebox-winking, rock-n-roll moaning: America at night fusing its dark cities into the unmistakable shape of loneliness. Remember Pershing Square and the apathetic palmtrees. Central Park and the frantic shadows. Movie theaters in the angry morning hours. And wounded Chicago streets. . . . Horrormovie courtyards in the French Quarter—tawdry Mardi Gras floats with clowns tossing out glass beads, passing dumbly like life itself. . . . Remember rock-n-roll sexmusic blasting from jukeboxes leering obscenely, blinking manycolored along the streets of America strung like a cheap necklace from 42nd Street to Market Street, San Francisco.[14]

The second chapter of Piri Thomas's novel *Down These Mean Streets* is titled "Puerto Rican Paradise," and in it Piri's mother nostalgically tells her children about growing up on the island. As she recounts these happy childhood moments, a decidedly paradisiacal image of Puerto Rico begins to emerge. Contrasted are the spirit of generosity that existed among the island people and the cautiousness of mainlanders, the tropical warmth of the island and the cold of the city, the happiness of Puerto Ricans and the sulleness of Nuyoricans. When Piri asks his mother whether everybody loved each other in Puerto Rico, she replies:

> *Bueno hijo*, you have people everywhere who, because they have more, don't remember those who have little. But in Puerto Rico those around you share *la pobreza* with you and they love you, because only poor people can understand poor people. I love *los Estados Unidos*, but it's sometimes a cold place to live—not because of the winter and the landlord not giving heat but because

of the snow in the hearts of the people.[15]

This image of the good life on the island is part of a general trend in both Puerto Rican and Chicano prose fiction to idealize, romanticize, and mythify the place of origin. Efraín Barradas has traced this same tendency in Puerto Rican literature since Colonial times. Commenting on the Nuyorican writer, especially the poet, he says:

> Submerged in an even more antagonistic and oppressive atmosphere—there is no need here to import snow and it is natural to celebrate July 4—and distant from his brothers of the island, the Puerto Rican [who lives in the United States] has to find something to hold on to, a cultural pretext which may give him support in view of the threat of total cultural assimilation which surrounds him in the oppressor's land. He seems to find this support in a myth of his native land, at least in this way he finds it in the first step of his process of self-definition.[16]

This Edenic concept of Puerto Rico as the land of milk and honey is expressed elsewhere in Nuyorican fiction serving, as it does in poetry, as a palliative to the anguish, despair, and alienation of geographic dispacement. In *Nobody's Hero*, Lefty Barreto remembers the role the images of the island he had never visited played in his boyhood:

> Puerto Rico was the Eden of my childhood, my tropical manger. It is a garden where the season is never winter and you cannot help but see the artist's hands in the nature that surrounds you. High above, the branches of the *palmas de coco* fan the ocean breezes down to the land. On either side, hills alternate with green valleys and define the blue horizon where fluffy white clouds are nursed by the golden sun. Green and yellow bundles of bananas hang on low trees. Tiny lizards change color, matching their surroundings as they move from the leaves to the stem of the bamboo tree growing across the creek. Avocado, mango, coconut, and *icaco* trees shade the hillside where spotted cows graze as far as the eye can see.[17]

Pedro Juan Soto evokes this same positive image of the island in his short story "Garabatos" by contrasting the present life of a Puerto Rican couple in New York City with the years of their courtship in Puerto Rico.[18] In a vain attempt to overcome his wife's bitterness for failing to provide an adequate income for their family, Rosendo creates a painting on the wall of their miserable apartment bathroom. A Christmas gift to his wife, he paints a highly sensual scene of a nude man mounted on a horse bending to embrace a nude woman. He never finishes the picture, which he intended to fill with sensuous tropical elements, for his wife, in a fit of rage, erases his work. Symbolically, the paradise of Puerto Rico is irrevocably lost.

In Chicano prose fiction, the clearest example of the Edenic rendering of the homeland is found in Rudolfo Anaya's *Heart of Aztlán*, in which a Hispanic family is forced to abandon its native land in New Mexico to take up residence in an Albuquerque barrio.[19] This tendency in Anaya's novel is closely related to the important role landscape plays in all his work. Landscape is a take-off point for authors' exploration of magic in realism. He says: "It is the place where imagination and the image-laden memory begin their work, and the three forces—place, imagination, and memory—are inextricably wound together in my work."[20] Anaya explores his and his reader's response to land scape, labeling it an epiphany, that is, "a natural response to the raw, majestic, and awe-inspiring landscape in the Southwest, a coming together of man and that landscape."

Anaya's concept of landscape in general and land in particular plays a pivotal role in his second novel *Heart of Aztlán*. Clemente and Adelita Chávez are forced for financial reasons to sell their land in Guadalupe, a rural New Mexican community, and move to the Albuquerque barrio of Barelas. As the family departs, Clemente voices his despair:

> His soul and his life were in the earth, and he knew that when he signed [the contract] he would be cutting the strings of that attachment. It was like setting adrift on an unknown, uncharted ocean. He tried to understand the necessity of selling the land, to understand that the move would provide his children a new future in a new place, but that did not lessen the pain he felt as the roots of his soul pulled away and served themselves from the earth which had nurtured his life.[21]

Once they settle in the city, far away from the land's benevolence, the family, once solid, begins to disintegrate. One daughter drops out of school, another becomes Americanized, a son becomes heavily involved with drugs, and Clemente begins to drink and abuse his wife and children. All the while, another son, Jason, holds the family together. Just as Clemente is about to despair, Crispín, a mythical poet with a magical blue guitar—he is a kind of urban Ultima—shows him the path to his own salvation and urges him to assume a position of leadership among the unemployed Chicanos of his community. Crispín shares with him the sacred legend of Aztlán. The man from Guadalupe, from the land, returns to the barrio to preach the healing power of love.

Related to conceptualization of the homeland as a longed-for but unattainable paradise lost is the search that ends in disillusionment, the realization that, indeed, you cannot go home again, at least to a home that is a collective idealization of Puerto Ricans or Mexicans.

The main characters in works such as Pedro Juan Soto's *Hot Land, Cold Season*, and Oscar Zeta Acosta's *The Autobiography of a Brown Buffalo* ultimately become aware that neither Puerto Rico nor Mexico holds the answers to their questions and that they must return to the United States to struggle with their alienation and marginalization.[22] These two writers share with the first group discussed in the paper a desolate view of America but, unlike the second group, Soto and Acosta deal with the illusory nature of one's land.

In Hot Land, Cold Season Eduardo returns home as a prodigal son or a triumphant athlete initially dazzled by the island's bright colors, the iridescent sea, and the spectacular flora. As in other works, the penetrating tropical warmth is contrasted with the cold he has just left up north. He thinks in disbelief:

> How had this island gotten the reputation of being small and poor and densely populated? Nothing in sight suggested poverty or people crowded together. The immense sky above seemed like a reflection of the vast fields following one after the other as they drove along, with the horizon merely making off other endless stretches of open land. The land, in fact, seemed to him like a big, comfortable house with its doors standing wide open. And he was heir to all this: the boundless fields, the lush vegetation whose green was nothing like the green of dollar bills. He decided that if the thought of a sad, broken old man, a suffering, peevish woman, and a helpless sister there on the other side of this lovely sky became too painful, he would order this blue umbrella moved north so that a kind of beauty would envelop them and a little hope steal back into their hearts. (pp. 25–26)[23]

But as Eduardo reacquaints himself with the island where he had spent part of his childhood, he begins to view his surrounding more objectively. His visit to Camarillo ends in bitter disappointment and his social encounters with young Puerto Ricans show him a negative aspect of his people he did not expect. After surrendering his rose-colored image of the island, Eduardo returns to New York. While he is still filled with uncertainties about what this act will ultimately mean, he at least has a clearer picture of the city's alluring promise of an easy life.

Acosta's protagonist, too, goes back to the homeland in search of self. Although it is cast humorously, the ''Brown Buffalo's'' quest is no less painful nor disheartening than Eduardo's. After an initial period of blessed innocence back home in El Paso-Juárez ''blinded with love'' by the ''brown woman with black hair, graceful asses for strong children; full breasts for sucking life; eyes of black almonds,'' the ''Brown Buffalo's'' bubble bursts. Arrested for indecent language he is thrown in the Juárez jail where he languishes in filth for days. After his release he returns to the United States knowing that his search has been in vain, that he is rootless: ''I stand naked before the mirror. I cry in sobs. My massive chest quivers and my broad shoulders sag. I am a brown buffalo lonely and afraid in a world I never made.''[24]

Geographic displacement as spiritual desolation is then a theme that bonds Puerto Rican—and especially Nuyorican—and Chicano literature. The movement of the masses of people to the United States and within the United States has had and continues to have severe consequences for the Latino population in this country. Novelists and short story writers have sensitively given form to the anguish and alienation resulting from this uprootedness and the inhospitability of new environments. Their artistic rendering of a social phenomenon merits closer scrutiny by other would-be researchers interested in elucidating the commonality of Puerto Rican and Chicano literature.

Notes

1. These dominant attitudes are cited by John C. Miller in his article "The Emigrant and New York City: A Consideration of Four Puerto Rican Writers," *MELUS* 5 (Fall 1978): 82. Miller takes his information from Germán de Granda Gutiérrez, *Transculturación e interferencia lingüística en el Puerto Rico contemporáneo* (Río Piedras, P.R.: Edil, 1972).
2. José Luis González, "En Nueva York," in *En Nueva York y otras desgracias* (Mexico, D.F.: Siglo XXI, 1975), pp. 106–21.
3. "La carterra cayó junto al cuerpo de la mujer. Esta miró al hombre desde el suelo, con ojos agrandados aún por el espanto. Marcelino retrocedió dos pasos, se llevó las manos a la cara y dejó escapar un alarido como una bestia supliciada. Luego emprendió una carrera desesperada por la calle oscura, tropezando al perder un zapato, chocando con los postes y los tachos de basura, hasta desaparecer en una esquina con aquel grito espeluznante quebrado al fin en un ronco sollozo de animal atormentado." González, p. 121.
4. "El pasaje," in *Cuentos puertorriqueños* de hoy, ed. René Marqués (Río Piedras, P.R.: Cultural, 1977), pp. 95–100.
5. Piri Thomas, *Down These Mean Streets* (New York: New American Library, 1967); Lefty Barreto, *Nobody's Hero: A Puerto Rican Study* (New York: New American Library, 1976).
6. Thomas, prologue.
7. Barreto, pp. 19–20.
8. José Antonio Villarreal, *Pocho* (Garden City, N.Y.: Doubleday, 1970).
9. Villarreal, p. 16.
10. Villarreal, p. 31.
11. Richard Vásquez, *Chicano* (New York: Avon, 1972), p. 36.
12. Ernesto Galarza, *Barrio Boy* (Notre Dame: University of Notre Dame Press, 1971), p. 204.
13. "Esta ciudad singular de aires de 'reputación dudosa' amanece redimida con la bullanga de la estudiantada y las campanadas que invitan a misa; el ajetreo de los trabajadores que se ganan un puñito de centavos, tercos en pagar con miseria el tributo que cobra la honradez; y la visita ocasional de los extranjeros de buena voluntad que recalan a comprar objetos inofensivos. Pero a medida que se van apagando las luces del día y prendiéndose las nocturnas, la ciudad va vistiendo sus arreos de alcahueta coquetona con que seduce a los incautos. Como una diosa mitológica, cínica y desvergonzada, se va aprovechando la ciudad de las debi-

lidades humanas para llenar sus últimos rincones.'' Miguel Méndez, *Peregrinos de Aztlán* (Tucson: Peregrinos, 1974), p. 20.
14. John Rechy, *City of Night* (New York: Grove, 1964), p. 9.
15. Thomas, p. 20.
16. ''Sumergido en un ambiente aún más antagónico y opresor—aquí no hay que importar nieve y es natural que se celebre el 4 de julio—y alejado de sus hermanos de la isla, el puertorriqueño de acá tiene que encontrar una tabla de salvación, un asidero cultural que le brinde apoyo ante la amenaza de total asimilación cultural que lo rodea en el país del opresor. Este apoyo lo parece encontrar en un mito de su tierra natal, al menos así lo encuentra en el primer paso de su proceso de auto-definición.'' Efraín Barradas, ''Puerto Rico acá, Puerto Rico allá,'' *Revista Chicano-Riqueña* 8 (Spring 1980): 45.
17. Barreto, p. 21.
18. Pedro Juan Soto, ''Garabatos,'' in *Spiks* (Río Piedras, P.R.: Cultural, 1977), p. 21.
19. Rudolfo Anaya, *Heart of Aztlán* (Berkeley: Justa, 1976).
20. Rudolfo A. Anaya, ''The Writer's Landscape: Epiphany in Landscape,'' *Latin America Literary Review* 5 (Spring-Summer 1977): 98.
21. Anaya, *Heart of Aztlán*, p. 3.
22. Pedro Juan Soto, *Hot Land, Cold Season*, trans. Helen R. Lane (New York: Dell, 1973); Oscar Zeta Acosta, The *Autobiography of a Brown Buffalo* (San Francisco: Straight Arrow, 1972).
23. Soto, pp. 32–33.
24. Acosta, p. 195.

About the Contributors

Miguel Algarín is professor of English and American literature at Rutgers, The State University of New Jersey in New Brunswick. He is also a poet, critic, and translator. His outstanding works include *Mongo Affair* (1978); *Nuyorican Poetry: An Anthology of Puerto Rican Words and Feelings* (1975); *On Call* (1981); and *Body Bee Calling (from the 21st Century)* (1982).

Juan Bruce Novoa is a professor at the University of California at Santa Barbara and a specialist in Chicano and Spanish American literature. He is the author of *Chicano Authors: Inquiry by Interview* (1980) and *Chicano Poetry: A Response to Chaos* (1982).

Norma Carr is originally from New York and is now living and teaching in Hawaii. Her book *Puerto Rican: One Identity from a Multi-Ethnic Heritage* (1980) was published by the Hawaii Department of Education.

Frank Dauster is professor of Spanish at Rutgers, The State University of New Jersey in New Brunswick and a major scholar in Latin American theater and poetry. He is the author of important books of theater criticism, anthologies, and histories. His publications include *Ensayos sobre poesía mexicana* (1963); *Antología de la poesía mexicana* (1970); *Historia del teatro hispanoamericano* (1973); *En un acto* (1974); *Ensayos sobre teatro hispanoamericano* (1975); and *Nueve dramaturgos hispanoamericanos* (1979).

Sandra María Estéves is a poet from New York. She is the author of the books *Yerba Buena: A Collection of Poetical Writings* (1979) and *New Age Poems for One World* (1979), as well as the well-known poem "My Name is Maria Christina." Other poems have been published in *Womanrise*; *Black World*; *The Rican: Journal of Contemporary Puerto Rican Thought*; and in *Revista Chicano-Riqueña*.

Margarite Fernández Olmos is a professor at Brooklyn College. She is a specialist on women authors of Spanish America, about whom she has delivered numerous talks and papers. Her book *La cuentística de Juan Bosch: un análisis crítico-cultural* was published in 1982.

Magali García Ramis is a short-story writer, serigraphist, journalist, and literary critic. Her stories have been published in the journals *Sin Nombre*;

Penélope; and *Les Langues Néo-Latines*. She is the author of a collection of short stories, *La familia de todos nosotros* (1976). She has finished a novel, *Felices días, tío Sergio*. At present she is a teacher at the School of Communications at the University of Puerto Rico and writes a column of literary criticism for the San Juan daily *El Mundo*.

José Luis González is a novelist, essayist, and now professor of sociology and literature at the Universidad Nacional Autónoma de México. Among his works are: *En la sombra* (1943); *Cinco cuentos de sangre* (1945); *El hombre de la calle* (1948); *Paisa* (1950); *En este lado* (1953); *Mambrú se fue a la guerra* (1972); *En Nueva York y otras desgracias* (1973); *Balada de otro tiempo* (best novel published in Mexico in 1978, won the Villaurrutia Award); *La llegada* (1980); *Poesía negra en América* (1976); *Literatura y sociedad en Puerto Rico* (1976); and *El país de cuatro pisos* (1980). In the fifties, he was one of the first to incorporate into Puerto Rican literature the theme of the Puerto Rican moving from the countryside to the big city (San Juan) and to the metropolitan city (New York). His first two novels, *Balada de otro tiempo* and *La llegada* (a chronicle with fiction), have been applauded by Hispanic critics. His polemical long essays, *Literatura y sociedad en Puerto Rico* and *El país de cuatro pisos* explore the literature of Puerto Rico until the end of the nineteenth century and the general subject of Puerto Rican culture within the context of the African experience in the Caribbean. He belongs to the Generation of the 1950s, together with Pedro Juan Soto, René Marqués, and César Andreu Iglesias.

Gerald Guinness is professor of English at the University of Puerto Rico, Río Piedras. He is a contributor to the Sunday magazine section of *The San Juan Star*, where he reports, in English, about Spanish or English books of local interest.

Orlando José Hernández is a poet and translator. He has translated poems by John Ashbery, Elizabeth Bishop, and Wallace Stevens. His poetry has appeared in journals such as *Ventana*; *Zona de Carga y Descarga*; and *Sin Nombre*. He is the author of *Ahora el tiempo Cólera? Canto?* (in press). He is also a professor in the Department of Modern Languages at Hostos Community College, New York.

Bonnie Hildebrand Reynolds is professor of Latin American literature at the University of Louisville. She is editor of the literary journal *Perspectives on Contemporary Literature*. At present she is working on a book, *Space, Time and Crisis: The Theater of René Marqués*. She will coautor (with José M. Lacomba) *Origen y desarrollo del Teatro Experimental del Ateneo Puertorriqueño*.

Nicolás Kanellos is a professor at the University of Houston, Texas. He is the editor of one of the most important literary journals, *Revista Chicano-Riqueña*, and coeditor of *Nuevos Pasos: Chicano and Puerto Rican Drama.*

Barry B. Levine is professor of sociology and anthropology at Florida International University. He is the author of *Benjy Lopez: A Picaresque Tale of Emigration and Return* (1980). He recently edited *The Cuban Presence in the Caribbean* (1983). He is editor of *Caribbean Review*, cofounded in 1969 with Kal Wagenheim. When visiting at the University of Puerto Rico, Dr. Levine coedited *Problemas de desigualdad social en Puerto Rico* (1972).

Carmen Lugo Filippi is coauthor, with Ana Lydia Vega, of *Vírgenes y mártires.* She is also the coauthor of the textbook *Le Francáis vécu.* She is a teacher of French and comparative literature at the University of Puerto Rico.

Marvin A. Lewis is professor of Spanish at the University of Illinois (Urbana), critic, and author of many articles of Chicano and Puerto Rican writers. His book *From Lima to Leticia: The Peruvian Novels of Mario Vargas Llosa* has been accepted for publication, in addition to the monograph *Introduction to the Chicano Novel.*

John C. Miller is chairperson of the Department of Modern Languages at Jersey City State College, and a critic and author of many articles on Puerto Rican and Chicano literature. He is the author of *Los testimonios literarios de la guerra español-marroquí, 1921–1926* (1978).

Nicholasa Mohr is well known as a fine graphic artist and writer. Author of *Nilda* (1974, a Jane Adams Children Book Award); *El Bronx Remembered* (1957, a National Book Award Finalist); *In Nueva York* (1977); and *Felita* (1980).

Sonia Nieto is professor and trainer for the Bilingual Education Service Center (BESC) at the School of Education, University of Massachusetts. She is an authority on many aspects of education of non-English-dominant minority group students. She is the author of educational catalogues, curriculum guides, and workbooks. Dr. Nieto served as a consultant for the book *Bilingual Education Change Agent Manual* (1975).

Angel G. Quintero Alfaro is a professor at the School of Social Sciences and the Graduate School of Education of the University of Puerto Rico and Visiting Professor at Harvard University. He served as secretary of instruction of the Commonwealth of Puerto Rico in 1964–68. His book, *Educación y cambio social en Puerto Rico: una época crítica*, was published in 1972.

Juan Antonio Ramos is considered one of the most promising of the young Puerto Rican writers. Author of *Démosle luz verde a la nostalgia* (1978);

Pactos de silencio y algunas erratas de fe (1981); *Hilando mortajas* (1982); *Hacia el otoño del patriarca: la novela del dictador en Hispanoamérica* (1983); and *Papo Impala está quitao* (1983).

Edgardo Rodríguez Juliá is a professor at the University of Puerto Rico, Río Piedras, and author of important books such as *La renuncia del héroe Baltazar* (1974); *Las tribulaciones de Jonás* (1981); *El entierro de Cortijo* (1983); and *La noche oscura del Niño Avilés* (1984).

Edgardo Sanabria Santaliz received his Ph.D. from Brown Unniversity. He is the author of two collection of short stories, *Delfia cada tarde* (1978), and *El día que el hombre pisó la luna* (1984). He is working on a third book, *Cierta inevitable muerte*.

Luis Rafael Sánchez is a well-known playwright of such plays as *Casi el alma* (1975); *Los ángeles se han fatigado* (1976); *La hiel nuestra de cada día* (1976); *La farsa del amor compradito* (1976); and *La pasión según Antígona Pérez* (1980). He is the author of a collection of short stories, *En cuerpo de camisa* (1976), and of the most important and popular novel in contemporary Puerto Rican fiction, *La guaracha del Macho Camacho*, which has been reprinted eight times since first publication. Besides his numerous critical essays, in 1979 Dr. Sanchéz published his Ph.D. dissertation, *Fabulación e ideología en la cuentística de Emilio S. Belaval*. He is currently working on his second novel, *La importancia de llamarse Daniel Santos*. Dr. Sánchez has lectured extensively in Latin America, Spain, and in the United States at Harvard, Standford, Yale, Brown, Columbia, Princeton, Cornell, and Montclair State College, among other universities.

Pedro Juan Soto is one of the most important writers who has captured in his writings the life of the Puerto Rican migrant in the United States, and the cultural identity crisis produced by the existence of two different cultures. He is the author of such works as *Spiks* (1956); *Usmaíl* (1958); *Ardiente suelo, fría estación* (1961); *El francotirador* (1969); *Temporada de duendes* (1970); *Un decir de violencia* (1976); and *Un oscuro pueblo sonriente* (1982). He has published plays, critical essays, and a doctoral dissertation in France on the life and works of the Puerto Rican poet and novelist José I. de Diego Padró.

Charles A. Tatum is a professor at the University of New Mexico and author of numerous articles and reviews on Puerto Rican and Chicano literature. He is the author of *A Selected and Annotated Bibliography of Chicano Studies* (1976) and *An Anthology of Latin American Women Writers* (1977).

Piri Thomas is a novelist well known for his works, *Down These Mean Streets* (1967), *Savior, Savior, Hold My Hand* (1972), *Stories from El Barrio* (1974), *Seven Long Years* (1974), and a play, *The Golden Streets* (1974). He is the best known Puerto Rican Writer in the United States.

Ana Lydia Vega is coauthor of *Vírgenes y mártires* with Carmen Lugo Filippi. In 1982, she received first prize in the short-story category of the prestigious literary contest Casa de Las Américas for her book *Encancaranublado*. She teaches at the University of Puerto Rico and is the coauthor of the textbook *Le Francáis vécu*.

Name Index